Sylvanus Charles Thorp Hanley

Caliphs and Sultans

Tales Omitted in the Usual Editions of the Arabian Nights Entertainments. Second Edition

Sylvanus Charles Thorp Hanley

Caliphs and Sultans
Tales Omitted in the Usual Editions of the Arabian Nights Entertainments. Second Edition

ISBN/EAN: 9783744752817

Printed in Europe, USA, Canada, Australia, Japan

Cover: Foto ©Thomas Meinert / pixelio.de

More available books at **www.hansebooks.com**

CALIPHS AND SULTANS.

CALIPHS AND SULTANS,

BEING

TALES OMITTED IN THE USUAL EDITIONS

OF THE

ARABIAN NIGHTS ENTERTAINMENTS;

RE-WRITTEN AND RE-ARRANGED BY

SYLVANUS HANLEY, F.L.S., ETC.,

HONORARY MEMBER OF THE ZOOLOGICAL SOCIETY OF VIENNA, OF THE ACADEMY OF NATURAL SCIENCES OF PHILADELPHIA, OF THE LYCEUM OF NEW YORK, ETC.

SECOND EDITION.

LONDON:

L. REEVE AND CO., 5, HENRIETTA STREET, COVENT GARDEN.

1870.

PREFACE.

AS Galland, from whose charmingly free translation of the 'Thousand and One Nights' the common English version of the 'Arabian Nights Entertainments' has been derived, did not himself possess a perfect copy of that Eastern compilation, the pith of what he has omitted is here presented to the public as an Appendix to that popular work. The tales are chiefly gleaned from Scott (1811, 1812), Lambe (1826), Chavis and Cazotte (1793), Von Hammer (through Trébutien, 1828), and from last, not least, that faithful but too literal translator, the Anglo-Egyptian Lane (1841).

Not as a rival to these worthies, but simply from an artistic appreciation of poetical fictions, which he believes to be inadequately known and estimated, does the writer venture to address the public.

He frankly acknowledges he has taken many liberties with the stories, yet almost all the incidents are to be found in one or other of the various manuscripts; only he has so grouped them that their sources cannot always be traced with facility. He has not hesitated to abridge the duller parts, or occasionally to modify customs and sentiments, which rendered his heroes less estimable and more tedious. For it is the imagination displayed in these fine old fictions which is the real and permanent cause of their attractiveness; not the peculiar phraseology and Moslem tone of thought with which they have been imbued by the Arab story-tellers, from whose lips they have been more immediately handed down to us. The habits and feelings depicted by the latter are more frequently those of their own age and class than of the people of the period alluded to. It is actually possible, then, that our tales, denuded of these unessential accessaries, may more nearly resemble the original legends (Indian, Coptic, Persian, Saracenic, and Levantine) than if they had been more literally and fully translated from the Arabic.

Should these pages evoke for his readers even faint images of those bright pictures which have haunted his own mental vision while composing them, the Author will have done well; for he will have increased the sum total of human happiness. To him, at least,

"A thing of beauty is a joy for ever."

CONTENTS.

THE TWO BRIDES;

OR,

THE CALIPH TURNED ROBBER.

IT was the feast of Haraphat. The grand mosque resounded with sonorous chanting; its altar was stained with the blood of the consecrated heifer; incense perfumed the air; a solemn array of holy priests proclaimed the reverence due by man to the Source of all good.

To duly honour the festival, and to display to the assembled multitude, as a meet example for imitation, the piety of the Commander of the Faithful, the devout zeal of the Prince of True-believers, the Caliph himself was present, encircled by a brilliant escort, not alone of his ministers and Emirs, but of those tributary princes who almost vied with their lord in the costliness of their attire and the magnificence of their retinue. All Bagdad had flocked to view the gorgeous spectacle, and at the close of the long and tedious ceremonies, departed, impressed alike with admiration for their sovereign, and envy for his richly clad nobles, whose happiness must, indeed, be great, in forming part of the royal procession. Yet the envied actors were right weary of the pomp; the fervour of the priests had exhausted them; the pious Haroun Alraschid himself was drowsy and tired. Slightly yawning, he thus addressed Giafar, the chief of the Barmecides, at once his friend and his prime minister :—

"The feast of our great Prophet should inspire joy, yet sadness overwhelms my spirit. A strange melancholy, a restlessness, which nought but action can dissipate, urges me to wander unknown among my people, in the hope that I may thus not merely be quit of my own disquietude, but may perchance redress the wrongs which the rapacity or the incompetence of my officers may have occasioned. Let us disguise ourselves, traverse the streets of Bagdad, and by our alms, at least, alleviate the sufferings of the unfortunate. I will see, likewise, whether the police of my city discharges its duty; this sacred day shall be devoted to the interests of my people."

Although conscious that *ennui* and love of adventure, rather than excessive anxiety to protect the interests of his subjects, prompted the Caliph, the minister, whose real goodness of heart, moreover, was at times gratified by the occasional results of his sovereign's peregrinations, was too much a courtier to indicate his surmises by more than a smile. Retiring to a private apartment they doffed their robes of state, and assumed a costume suitable to a more humble station. Sallying from the palace, with well-filled purses, and passing through the more frequented streets, they dispensed their alms promiscuously to all who solicited them. The majority of those relieved exhibited nothing remarkable in either attire or language, and Haroun, scarcely satisfied with his ramble, prepared to retrace his steps.

At this moment he descried an arm, exquisite in shape, well rounded, and of that fairness which indicated a rare exposure to the ardour of the sun, extended to him for charity. More than ordinarily intent upon the excitement of adventure, the Caliph paused to observe that no trace of toil was visible upon the delicate hand; he passed a golden coin to Giafar, who obeyed the tacit injunctions of the giver by dropping it into the outstretched palm.

"Are you aware," said the veiled figure, noticing that the value of the coin strangely exceeded that which was usually bestowed upon her, "that you have given me gold? Do you design this as an alms; or seek you for any recompense from me?"

"It is not to me you are indebted," replied the minister, "but to my companion."

"Ascertain, then, from him, I pray you," rejoined the female, "the motive of his liberality."

"Be not uneasy on that score;" interrupted the Caliph; "charity and the love of God alone influenced me."

"May Heaven then grant thee a long and happy life! if my fervent prayers will avail, such shall be thy lot; most gratefully I accept thy bounteous generosity."

There was a something in the tone, and even in the language of the woman, that impressed him with the conviction that indigence had not always been her portion in life, and that she had succumbed to misfortunes, for which she had been little prepared by previous training in adversity. Though so closely muffled that her features could not be discerned, her full and lustrous eyes, her graceful postures and demeanour, showed that she had not passed the season of youth; her modest bearing and manifest integrity alike interested both the amative monarch and his benevolent comrade.

"Ask her," said the former to the latter, "whether she is wedded or single; tell her, should her heart and hand be still free, I would fain espouse her."

Giafar, not a whit surprised at this new freak of his eccentric master, put the inquiry to the damsel, who replied, "I am as yet a maid, and honoured by the compliment your friend has offered me in proffering his hand, I am willing to be his, if he can only settle upon me an adequate dowry."

"Who can she be," said Giafar, as he repeated her answer, "to doubt whether your highness can make a settlement upon her commensurate with her merits?"

"My disguise pleads her excuse; follow her," for she had departed on her homeward route after having received the money, "and inquire what sum will satisfy her expectations."

Not waiting for the reply, the Caliph turned homewards, and Giafar, having overtaken the fair mendicant, who evinced an impatience to withdraw, little to be expected under her adverse circumstances, delivered his message.

"My dowry should be equal to a year's tribute from Ispahan and Karassin," she sternly replied, as she passed beneath the doorway of her dwelling.

Giafar, repelled by her audacity, shook his head, and

followed his master to the palace. He forthwith informed the Caliph of the conversation, but even he, accustomed as he was to the impulsive fitfulness of the Caliph's mood, was a little startled when, with a hearty laugh at the apparent absurdity of the demand, the latter replied,

"We will astonish her a little; tell her I accept her conditions, and embrace her offer."

The Grand Vizier, wearied as he was with his long ramble, and not overpleased at this sudden alliance, returned, nevertheless, to the spot where he had left the presumptuous mendicant, and abruptly entering her poor apartment, both succeeded in again obtaining an interview with her and viewing for a moment her unveiled countenance. Having acquitted himself of his commission, the haughty beauty—for beautiful, in truth, she was—scornfully asked,

"Who is he that can give such a dowry? Whence is his wealth derived? What is his rank?"

"He of whom we are speaking is called Haroun Alraschid," answered Giafar; "he is our sovereign lord, the Commander of the Faithful."

At the name of the Caliph, her aspect and the sound of her voice altered: the damsel bent, and thanking Heaven for the happy change in her fortunes, modestly and gently continued, "I am the handmaiden of my sovereign; if *he* deigns to be my husband, I am well content; declare to him that I humbly accept him as my bridegroom."

Giafar withdrew, and rejoining the Caliph, reported to him the acceptance of his gracious offer, and the countenance, attitude, and language of the recipient of it.

With characteristic impatience, the Caliph dispatched one of the matrons of the palace, with a large retinue of attendants and a royal litter, to conduct the *incognita* to the baths of his seraglio, from whence she emerged beautiful as a Houri. Clad in the most sumptuous of garments, which glittered with sparkling diamonds, she was then conveyed to a gorgeously-furnished suite of apartments, and reposed for a while upon its silken cushions. Scarcely had the chief of the eunuchs apprised his master of the prompt and thorough fulfilment of his orders, when the Cadi, summoned with like precipitation, presented himself with the hurriedly-written contract of marriage.

The same evening, Haroun entered the apartment of his bride, who, prostrating herself before him, expressed her gratitude with fluent eloquence. Seating her beside him upon a couch, and gazing upon her noble-looking face with repressed ardour,

"Surely you are of noble family," said he, "or your visage misleads me; else, moreover, you would scarcely have ventured to ask for so princely a dowry?"

Glancing her eyes at his smiling countenance, and then rapidly bending them to the ground, "Prince of the Faithful," rejoined she, "in me you behold a lineal descendant of Kassera Abocheroan: cruel fortune and inexorable destiny reduced me to the pitiable condition from which your goodness has raised me."

"Princess," continued the Caliph, "you are, then, the granddaughter of that despot who, valiant as he was, has left a name tarnished by a thousand acts of tyranny."

"And this same tyranny," quickly rejoined the lady,

"has reduced his family to the degrading necessity of begging for their bread. Surely the retribution has sufficed."

"Still, I have been told," continued the enamoured Caliph, "that ere the close of his long reign, repenting his former harshness, he governed his people with moderation, dispensed justice with impartiality, and displayed kindly feelings to both man and beast."

"And for that, O Caliph," returned the Princess, "God has this day requited his descendants: He has taken one of his daughters from the street, to become the proud wife of the Commander of the Faithful."

The cleverness of this reply fascinated still more the royal lover; he clasped his willing bride to his breast, and evinced, by the warmth of his embrace, how precious he held the prize which Fortune or Providence had cast in his way. An abrupt coldness, however, soon succeeded to his raptures. Almost flinging her from him, he cried, with a gloomy countenance and an angry tone of voice,

"Unlucky fool that I have been, to be compelled to tear myself from your charms! Pardon, dear woman, this seeming madness, and commiserate my ill-fortune. Little dreaming this morning of the happiness which now awaits me, I vowed, in the frenzy of my religious feelings, an act of bitter self-denial: to absent myself, for a whole year, from the next bride I might espouse."

And then with a sigh, he added, "Oh, that I had foreseen, imprudent that I was, the joys now forbidden me! Your purer nature, however, will aid me in resisting the warmer impulses of my breast; for imbued, as you have shown yourself to be, with deep religious feeling, the sanctity of my oath will be equally appreciated by yourself."

The modest bride bent her eyes to the ground in token of acquiescence, and the bridegroom sadly withdrew himself from her presence. Conscious of her merits, and enraptured with her loveliness, he promised himself much happiness, hereafter, from his union with her; but, dreading his own weakness under temptation, most scrupulously avoided every chance meeting with her. But the sedulous attentions which were lavished upon her by his orders,—the anticipation of her every wish, the earliest of fruits, the latest of flowers,—all convinced her that she was neither an object of indifference to him, nor forgotten; in fine, that he had not repented of his choice.

The tedious year at length slowly passed away, and again the solemn festival of Haraphat was proclaimed. Again, too, did the disguised Caliph, with his constant companions, Giafar and Mesroor (who officiated both as chief of his eunuchs and the stern executioner of the condemned), explore the main streets of Bagdad, where everything appeared agreeable to his royal notions. Retracing their footsteps, the noble party casually noticed the tastefully displayed delicacies which profusely graced the shop-board of a pastry-cook; the senses of sight and smell were equally gratified as the trio loitered past them. A closer inspection, and eventually the test of the palate, confirmed their opinions of the excellence of the tempting wares.

Arrived at home, the Caliph, having indicated to one of

his attendants the locality of the shop, bade him purchase from its master a hundred tartlets; upon receiving which, Haroun, with his own royal hand, inserted a golden coin in each, covering it with a pistachio nut and finely pounded sugar. Designing to remind his Persian bride that his wearisome year of enforced absence had at length expired, and that she might expect his fond visit on that very evening, he sent the tray of rich pastry to his charming Sultana.

The eunuch who delivered the gift was enjoined to inquire whether the Commander of the Faithful could gratify any unsuspected fancy of her brain. "I want for nothing;" said the amiable descendant of Kassera, "when the inexpressible happiness of again beholding my sovereign lord shall be granted me, my every wish will be accomplished."

Haroun, delighted with her charming message, and more desirous than ever to exhibit the earnestness of his passion, bade Mesroor to insist upon knowing by what possible means he could impart some of his own happiness to her.

"Since my lord is so pressing in his endeavours to please me, tell him I would have a thousand pieces of gold, and the escort of some confidential servant, that I, too, the quondam daughter of distress, may relieve, incognito, the sufferings of the afflicted."

Pleased with a request which evinced the goodness of her heart, the Caliph immediately complied with it. The Princess, with a female domestic in attendance, walked through the streets and alleys of Bagdad distributing alms with lavish hand, until, at length, even the thousand pieces were exhausted.

The heat was intense, and the lips of the charitable lady were parched with thirst. Her attendant would have summoned a passing water-carrier, but there was a something repulsive to the senses in the uncleanly raiment of the man, and the blood of kings revolted against the draught.

"I choose not to drink from the same vessel which has been kissed by the *canaille* of Bagdad," said the not too-fastidious fair one. So they wended onwards, until they arrived at the fragrant sandal-wood porch of a magnificent mansion, within which two white marble seats, or couches, were visible between the richly-embroidered curtains of pale blue that flanked the doorway. A golden chandelier, suspended by chains of the like precious metal, from a ceiling of white-and-gold, completed the picture. There was an inexpressible air of coolness and of purity; and the Princess cast a longing glance at the sparkling fountain which was playing in the background. Intuitively divining her wishes, the confidential domestic rapped at the door, when, instead of the anticipated slave, a comely youth, of light complexion, and apparelled as a gentleman, presented himself. In reply to his courteous inquiries as to what service he could render them, the female replied,—

"My daughter is parched with thirst, yet refuses, with loathing, to quaff from the vessels of a common water-carrier. A single glass of fresh water is all we ask, and for it we proffer our hearty thanks in anticipation."

"Your thirst shall be satisfied without delay," said the young nobleman, for such in truth he was; and quickly filling a golden cup from the plashing fountain, he passed the cooling beverage to the servant, who transferred it to her royal mistress.

The latter, with befitting modesty, turned her face to the wall, that her unveiled features might not be discerned, and drinking the water, passed the golden goblet to her slave, who, humbly bending, returned it to the youthful host. The Princess sedately thanking him for his courtesy, pensively returned to the palace.

Now, when the royal lover had bestowed so much attention upon enriching the dish of tartlets, and sent them to his long-neglected bride, as a pledge of his passionate affection for her, he had omitted, in his message, any special reference to its contents; and the attendant, who, unconscious of the peculiar seasoning (if we may so term it) of the patties, merely regarded the affair as one of common gallantry, scarcely delivered his words with that impressive emphasis in which they had been uttered; the Princess, too, on her part, conceiving the dainties to form part of the Caliph's ordinary attentions, paid little heed to the monotonous repetition of the garbled message.

It happened, on her return from her charitable task, that her eyes lighted upon the tray of tartlets; and the idea was suggested by the sight of them, that her sense of gratitude would be exhibited by giving them to the young noble who had ministered so graciously to her thirst.

"Take the pastry," said she, to the slave who had accompanied her, "and give it, as from yourself, to the gentleman to whom I was indebted for the cup of water."

The slave thus acquitted herself of her message:—

"My daughter and I," said she to the noble, who was then reclining upon his couch in the portico, "pray your acceptance of this pastry, as a slight proof of our estimation of your kindness and gallantry."

Gracefully, yet negligently, thanking her for the dainties, he was still lounging upon his couch, when the watchman of the district in which he lived presented himself with the customary compliments of the season (it was the feast of Haraphat), and concluded, as usual, with a request "to be remembered."

"Take that tray of tartlets, friend, and be off," said the reclining youth; and the watchman, well pleased with his vails, kissed the hand of the giver, and departed with his spoils.

His wife, on seeing him return with so large, rich, and appetizing a dish, loudly exclaimed (she was somewhat of a shrew, as most of her class in all Islam are known to be), "Whence have you stolen this, my man?"

"From none," answered the watchman; "it is the feast-gift of the Grand Chamberlain (long life to him for his freeness!). 'Tis a rare dish. Let us fall to."

"Glutton," cried the enraged wife, "would you gorge yourself with such costly viands? Such extravagancies are not for us; poor folks, like we, must fill our bellies with coarser food. Go, sell them, tray and all, and buy with the proceeds what befits our necessities."

"Wife! Wife!" said the watchman, "Heaven, for once, has sent us tartlets, and tartlets will I eat."

"Not one single morsel, or you shall taste my slipper," shrieked the virago; "your child has neither cap nor shoes, I am in rags, and you in tatters. Go, sell the dish at once, and, mind you, bring back the money."

The watchman yielded to Fate, or rather to Fate's representative, the slipper-wielder, proceeded to the market-place, and resigned the coveted delicacies to the public crier. A merchant purchased them, and carried off his prize. To his dismay he descried certain engraved characters upon the tray, which indicated, too manifestly, that it was the property of his sovereign. Returning hurriedly to the market-place, he forcibly thrust the dish into the reluctant hands of the amazed crier, with a "Do you seek my ruin? Take your tray again, or I shall be charged with robbing the kitchen of our lord the Caliph."

When the crier had read the letters that were engraved on the edge of the tray, he, too, was similarly affected with terror and amazement.

With rapid steps he bore the mischief-bringing dish to the palace, demanded and obtained an immediate interview with the monarch (ever easy of access to his subjects), and exhibited to him the supposed stolen property.

At the first glance, Haroun recognized in the now disarranged and crumbling tartlets, the once tempting dish upon which he had spent so much pains, and which he had mentally intended to have formed part of his evening's collation with the Princess. We are none of us perfect; and he whose fame has descended to us as the greatest monarch of the East, vexed at his pet project of prettily surprising his fascinating bride being thus vexatiously baffled, yielded to a torrent of anger, which distorted circumstances and obscured his judgment. One of his few failings was the attaching an extrinsic importance to any action in which he had been personally concerned; the merest trifle would then become invested, in his eyes, with absorbing interest.

On his whirling brain was stamped the galling conviction that his fond gift to his Sultana was neglected and despised, and that he had degraded himself by an unrequited attention. His wrath was kindled against her whom but a few minutes past he had adored.

"Tell me, at once," said the enraged Caliph to the crier, "from whom you obtained this tray of tartlets?"

The crier, out of breath with his rapid journey, was spared the long and flowery speech he had been painfully concocting. Like a sensible man, he briefly replied, "The watchman of our district brought it me to sell for him." In a trice, that unfortunate individual, whom the rumoured theft had attracted to the palace gates (for he took interest in his vocation), was seized, pinioned, and prostrate before his dread sovereign. Less wise than the crier, he comforted himself by audibly execrating his jade of a wife.

"It was that vile creature who brought this upon me. She forced her silly counsel upon me—turned economist, forsooth, and like her predecessor, Eve, and every one else of her accursed sex, has proved the perdition of her husband. Oh! that I had eaten the tartlets, and thrown away the tray."

"Cease, wretch," cried the Caliph, irritated by his senseless clamour, "and briefly declare, as you would avoid the bastinado, from whom you obtained this dish of tartlets."

"Commander of the Faithful, be not wrathful with the innocent," murmured the trembling official: "your Grand Chamberlain, Yemaleddin, bestowed both tray and tartlets upon me as a feast-gift."

At that name (that of the handsomest man in the city), the anger of the Caliph, whose passion was now tinctured with jealousy, fairly boiled over. He commanded the immediate arrest of that nobleman, the confiscation of his estates, the destruction of his furniture, the razing of his dwelling-place, his instant appearance, as a criminal, before his judgment-seat.

Those who bore the harsh mandates of Haroun, surrounded the doomed house, and rapped furiously at the door. Admitted to his saloon, one of them, without uttering a word, pinioned the master, and untwisting the folds of his turban, coiled it round his neck."

"Is it by the order of my sovereign that I am thus ignominiously treated?" cried the astonished noble. "In what have I offended?"

"My orders are most stringent," replied the principal officer; "the confiscation of your property, the levelling of your home, the leading you bareheaded and barefooted before the royal tribunal, are all included in my instructions."

"The will of Heaven, and of Heaven's vice-regent upon earth, be done," said the loyal subject; "yet, if it be possible, when you destroy the home where I was born, leave, at least, some little nook, as an asylum for my aged mother, for my fatherless and unprotected sister."

Grateful for past benefits, for the hospitality which had

been warmly and frequently offered to them, the officers assured him that their orders should be carried out with the least possible rigour, and conducted him reverently, yet bound hand and foot, to the frowning Caliph.

Prostrating himself before him, Yemaleddin thus addressed the now silent and scowling Prince:—

"O wise and just monarch, whom may Heaven crown with its choicest blessings, wherein have I, the humblest of your slaves, offended you? By what crime merited so severe a dispensation?"

"Know you yon fellow?" growled the Caliph, pointing to an individual who, chained, and now speechless from awe, looked furtively at him.

"He is the watchman of our district, O King!"

"Know you this tray?" again demanded the sullen judge. "Who gave it you? Wherefore insult it and its owner by throwing it away on this coarse clod?"

The answer of Yemaleddin was such as might be expected from an innocent and guileless gentleman. He simply related his interview with the veiled lady and her attendant, and completely exonerated the miserable gift-seeker.

A thousand mortifying reflections flitted through the soul of the monarch whilst he listened to the artless tale. His vanity was wounded to the quick. "The woman," thought he, "whom I have raised from the dunghill repays, in her extravagance, a cup of water with a hundred tartlets, sugared, adorned, and enriched by my own royal hand! Well might she require the revenue of two cities for her dowry! I send her a pledge of my love, a token of my passion, and she would have given it, doubtlessly, to some filthy water-carrier, had not his drinking-vessel disgusted her! So are the gifts of Haroun Alraschid appreciated by the grandchild of Kassera!"

Again directing his discourse to the prisoner—and now jealous imaginations were surging in his darkened brain—the Caliph sharply demanded, whether he had seen the face of the woman *who had drunk the water*. In the confusion of the moment, bewildered by the misfortunes which had so unexpectedly overtaken him, almost stupefied by the terrible voice and aspect of the half-frenzied despot, the unlucky youth, scarcely comprehending the dread import of the question, replied in the affirmative. But the livid look of concentrated rage and jealousy which darkened the face of Haroun, and a silence more awful than speech, which followed this fatal admission, recalled the truth to his recollection. In vain he sought to retract his words: the past was irrevocable. A messenger was dispatched for *her* so recently and rightly a favourite, and the grandchild of Kassera stood before her royal spouse.

"And so," was the greeting which awaited her, "under the pretext of alms-giving, you frequent the mansions of my nobles, to display your charms to the young men. All is known. He has confessed the truth."

The Princess looked fixedly at Yemaleddin. Despite the gloomy surroundings, there was calmness in the tones of her voice (for previous adversity had fortified her soul), when she inquired who was the slanderer that had so falsely asserted her features had been exposed before him.

"Alas! madam," cried the youth—and so distinguished-looking was he in form and bearing (for the coldness of despair had restored to him his wonted dignity of deportment), that a neglected wife might almost have been pardoned for loving him—"I myself am the false accuser. My bewildered lips, and not my heart or mind, have uttered words which may not be recalled. Solemnly do I disavow them. I am ready to expiate my guilt as a false accuser; for *you*, I swear, are innocent."

The words and looks which induced forgiveness and pitying tenderness in the breast of the Princess did not alter the preconceived resolution of the unjust judge. Both the noble and the Princess were condemned to death.

And now the executioner had bound the eyes of the guiltless culprits, and commenced the customary formula of his bloody office.

"Commander of the Faithful, shall I strike the blow?"

"Strike," said the Caliph.

A second time, after taking two or three turns around the doomed victims, did he repeat the dread inquiry.

"Strike," said the Caliph.

A third time did the executioner, after taking his usual rounds, pause, and with uplifted sword, before Yemaleddin.

"Before you die, have you aught to reveal or request of your sovereign? Remember that every chance of life has departed. Avail yourselves, briefly, of the few moments of grace which the leniency of justice awards you."

"Remove the bandage from my eyes, that I may take my last look at my friends and relations."

No sympathizing look from the silent circle around him met his unbound eyes. Dread of the now ruthless tyrant chained both tongues and glances. All were motionless, and, with downcast eyes, seemed changed to stone.

A sudden thought, a latent conviction of the credulity of the Caliph, a certainty that, save under the excitement of passion, his sovereign was habitually just, inspired the words of Yemaleddin.

"Lord of life and death," cried he, "responsible dispenser of rewards and chastisements, delay our punishment for one month only, and marvellous shall be the occurrences of the last three days of my reprieve; marvellous and markworthy, for on them shall depend the future of thine empire."

There was a prophetic tone, a lofty confidence in his own inspiration, which aroused universal belief in his daring assertions. A gentle murmur of admiration arose from the assembled courtiers (for curiosity and kinsmanship had attracted many to this sudden trial), and the Caliph, calmed now that his vengeance was assured, and conscious of the security of his revenge, however protracted it might be, forbore from uttering the word which would have blotted Yemaleddin from the book of the living.

Years roll away, months fly, days evaporate. Such strange things had occurred to Haroun himself in his wanderings, so many wild tales had he listened to as truths, that when three days alone remained of the fatal month, he still confidently expected the realization of the prophecy. Yet, hatred for the man who had deprived him of the company of his now polluted bride still burned within him; and a retribution worse than death would have awaited the arch-deceiver should he have falsely announced the coming marvels.

Nevertheless, the Caliph waxed impatient, and reflecting that strange incidents were less likely to occur to one secluded in his royal abode than when roaming at large in the suburbs of his capital, had again recourse to his usual scheme of solacing his dulness. Now he had conceived the idea, and he ever followed his impulses (a licence permitted to kings alone, and not always safe even for them), that the association of Mesroor and Giafar in his rambles somewhat marred his incognito. This time he would prosecute his adventure-hunting untrammelled and alone.

He disguised himself in the most whimsical manner. A coarse turban encircled his brow; a girdle of dark, untanned leather fastened a tunic, composed of camel's skin, with the hair still unscraped from it; a pale, loose robe, not remarkable for its whiteness, flowed around him; rudely-formed boots, clearly not the trim work of a city mechanic, which reached to his naked knees, completed a costume more correct than prepossessing. The bow and arrows strapped to his back, the long, wooden-hilted sabre of Damascus steel carried in his hand, his face rendered ferocious by artificial shaggy eyebrows of raven black, and stained by walnut-juice to a brownish-yellow hue, his wiry untrimmed beard,—formed an *ensemble* which the cautious traveller would seek to avoid, even by a long détour. In fine, he stalked gloomily from the palace, an Arab of the desert, of the predaceous tribes; but a goodly purse of gold (a thousand pieces) dangled from his belt.

He had not gone far, when the exclamation "Wonderful!" attracted his attention. There was a crowd collected round an old woman, who, in a high and clear voice, with correct emphasis and refined pronunciation, was reading aloud the Koran to her intent listeners. "Wonderful!" repeated the artisan, who condescended to impart his gossip to the uncouth new comer; "the woman has been reading all the morning, and not a soul has bestowed a copper upon her. So much for religion!"

Haroun forced his way towards the dame; she was evidently in extreme poverty, though her faded garments showed, by their cut and material, that the wearer had not always endured her present lot. She was reading the final chapter of the book, having completed which, and made a last and fruitless appeal to the benevolence of her auditors, she arose from the stone bench on which she had been seated, closed the volume, and slowly departed. Before the Caliph, wishful to bestow his alms, could overtake her (he was jostled by a crowd which neither entertained much respect for his dress and appearance nor feared him in so well guarded a city), she had confidently entered the handsome shop of a rich merchant. Curious to discover her business in so luxuriously fitted-up a shop (for the poor wretch could scarcely hope to purchase its costly wares), the inquisitive ruler followed her closely, and perceived her in close conversation with the owner. "You are not married," whispered she to him (the whisper was an audible one); "would you not like a beautiful girl?" "I would, indeed," was the reply. "Then follow *me*, and you shall behold the loveliest of her sex."

When Haroun heard this colloquy, he interpreted it according to the dictates of his own suspicious temperament.

"Accursed hag," thought he, "I took you for a saint, and you are a vile procuress. I'll follow you, now, not to give you the alms I had intended, but to see your mode of trafficking in the virtue of my female subjects." And hastening after the couple, not a little impelled, likewise (for the Caliph was an amorous man), by the desire of gazing upon the asserted miracle of beauty, he just arrived in time to hear the slamming of a solid door, which had been unlatched by the old woman, for the purpose of admitting them.

Haroun Alraschid would have lost his labour had not the oaken planks shrunk from exposure to the ardent sun. As it was, he was enabled to both see and hear. The merchant was standing alone; in a minute the dame led from an adjacent closet a young girl of the most striking beauty. Tall, yet flexible as the palm-tree waving over the waters of Damascus, her bow-like eyebrows discharged the fatal arrows of love from eyes like polished steel; yet at times, though dark as midnight when in repose, they beamed with a soft splendour like the star of the morning. Her mouth was small and round as the mystic ring of Solomon; the lips which enshrined the pearly enamel of her white and even teeth vied with the coral in their vermilion tint; her breath was perfume; her soft voice (few and sparing were her words) sounded like a purling brook. Her bust was that of a maiden in the first dawn of womanhood, her breasts firm and rounded as pomegranates, yet whiter than lilies. Half-clad as she was (and her raiment was poor and ragged), there was an air of virgin modesty about her which enhanced her perfections. The Caliph was in raptures.

When the girl perceived that her mother had exposed her to the eye of the merchant she blushed with shame, and looked, if possible, still more lovely. Shrouding her face with the palms of her hands, she withdrew in haste to the closet-like room from which she had emerged, crying,

"Alas! my mother, what have you done? Shown me to a man! it is forbidden by our Prophet."

"Comfort yourself, my child," rejoined the dame: "where no evil is intended, none can be done. There is no sin in a man looking, for once, upon the damsel he would wed; if fate should unite them, all is well; if not, they meet no more, and where's the harm?"

Haroun began to entertain a better opinion of the old woman. "She has a lovely daughter to marry," thought he, "and this display of her charms is the sole method of obtaining her a husband which her poverty permits." When the girl had retired, the haggard-looking crone thus continued,

"Well! have I deceived you? Is she not incomparable? And as good, too, as she is beautiful."

"I am satisfied—more than satisfied," replied the shrewd merchant. "How much, however, for the dowry, contract included?"

"Four thousand sequins for each," said the mother.

"Would you reduce me to beggary?" cried the man.

"Eight thousand sequins! I do not possess so much; in offering you two, I leave myself but a like sum, for both trade and domestic expenses."

"By the name written on the forehead of the Prophet, not one sequin less will I take. Not a hair of my daughter's head shall you caress, until twice four thousand sequins have been counted out before me."

"You ask impossibilities. Would I had never seen her, then!" were the last words of the baffled suitor, as, with vexation in his countenance, he angrily quitted the apartment. Scarcely had he crossed the road, when the Caliph, temporarily dislodged from his post of espial, opened the door and roughly saluted the old woman.

"What do you want?" said she. Now Haroun had already scanned and counted the perfections of the lovely damsel, and mentally compared them with those of his virgin bride, of her who now languished in prison through the hasty answer of Yemaleddin. He decidedly preferred the fresher beauty.

"I've met the merchant, and know all about it," said the Caliph, affecting a rough voice and a brusque demeanour. "All I've got to say is, give me the girl, and I'll give you the money,—the whole eight thousand, and a bonus for yourself."

The old woman stared at the Caliph from head to foot; he looked like a robber, and a not over-lucky one.

"I suppose you mean to plunder the Mecca caravan," sneered she, "to pay the eight thousand sequins and provide the bride's *trousseau* and the furniture of the house! You! with hardly a rag to cover you! Out rascal, out thief, or I'll call the police."

"And what matters it to you, old lady, if I should be a robber? I'll down with the cash, and do the liberal to you besides."

"Do you mock me, fellow? Because I am poor and helpless, you fancy, perhaps, you can make a fool and laughing-stock of me with impunity. I take you at your word. There's justice still in Bagdad, and woe to you if you should prove a defaulter."

"Well, I'll take the consequences if the money's not paid. I mean to marry your daughter, and you'll find me a man of my word."

He then coolly seated himself, and continued, "Now! I'm ready for the contract-deed, so off to the Cadi; 'tis not a stone's-throw to his residence. You needn't look round so; there's nothing to steal here; there's nothing worth having but your daughter, and you can lock her up if you like."

"So you think the Cadi will come at the bidding of a scarecrow like you!" said the dame; "if you have really money, 'tis ill-got, I'm sure; take care he don't recognize you for a cut-throat; he has a sharp eye and a good memory."

"Don't concern yourself about me, my good woman," said the pretended robber; "only tell him to come, and bring his writing-materials with him. Say *Il Bondocani* wants him."

Somewhat hesitatingly, the shabby dame left her dwelling; in truth, she had nothing much to lose there, but she liked not her errand. "Yet I'll go," she reasoned, "if only to get rid of him; I may thus learn who my would-be son-in-law really is,—some famous brigand, I dare say. More's the pity, if he can really pay me the money."

The sounds of revelry (for the Cadi was feasting with his friends) assailed her ears as she timidly approached the mansion of that official. Shame, the common attendant of poverty, withheld her from knocking. She knew she was ill-dressed, and self-respect, in her sex, is even more dependent upon clothing than in man. Yet there was sufficient of combative self-will in the aged dame to urge her forward, and the alternation of feeling produced a like alternation in her movements. She peeped in at the windows, and then, as if snake-bitten, hurriedly jumped back: again she thrust in half her head, and as instantly withdrew it, in the agony of conscious intrusion.

The guests smiled at the comical bobbing of the queer-looking head, and the good-natured Cadi sent out one of his subordinates to ask her business.

"There is a young man at my house," said the re-assured dame, on entering the saloon, "who desires you to come to him."

"Insolent!" cried the irritated official: "a young man desires *me* to come to him! What next? and at this hour of the day, too. Turn the old fool out," he continued, "or send her to the madhouse."

"Ah! mercy, my lord," exclaimed she, on hearing the wrathful orders; "I am but a poor old woman, and I dared not refuse him. There is a brute, a robber, a villain at my house, who compelled me to come hither. He wants to marry my daughter, says you know him, and calls himself *Il Bondocani.*"

At this name, well known to the higher dignitaries of the city as one usually assumed by the Caliph when disguised, the Cadi started up, donned his official robes, and, with proud humility, apologized for his roughness to the old woman.

"Ten thousand pardons, madam, for my involuntary error," said he. "Do me the favour of guiding me to your house, since it is there I am awaited. Ascribe to my ignorance my hasty language and brief delay."

The spectators, as well as the old woman, were amazed at the sudden effect of that mysterious name. "He is some terrible brigand, I suppose," she whispered to the bystanders, "at least, the chief of some formidable band of Bedouins."

She began to change her preconceived opinion of the ineligibility of her proposed son-in-law. "He must, indeed, be the Emir of some mighty robber-tribe," thought she, "since his mere name strikes terror into the Cadi. Fancy our chief magistrate tumbling on his robes with haste, and running off without his slippers, at the bare mention of his name. He's not such a bad match, after all," and slightly tossing her poor old head, as she observed the respect now shown to her, as she walked by the side of the Cadi. "I'm somebody once more," was the agreeable reflection.

When the Cadi had entered the mean-looking abode of the two females, he immediately recognized in the uncouth and stalwart figure before him, the disguised features of his sovereign. He would at once have prostrated himself, but a sign from the fictitious robber, who was placidly amused at his own clever impersonation of a criminal, deterred him. With a respectful salutation, Haroun thus addressed the magistrate, "I wish, my lord, to have the daughter of this woman for my wife."

Meanwhile, the bustling dame, who in a brief conference had communicated to the caged damsel her own matrimonial notions, led her, pale and trembling, from the closet, and both answered the inquiries of the functionary, as to their assent or dissent from the proposals of *Il Bondocani*, in the affirmative. Then the Cadi demanded what sum should be stated as the amount of the contract and of the dowry.

"Four thousand sequins for one, and four thousand sequins for the other," sharply responded the eager dame.

"And do you, O *Bondocani*, agree to this?"

"Yes, my lord," replied Haroun, "you can draw up the contract to that effect."

The Cadi was embarrassed. In his hurry he had forgotten to bring the needful paper with him; the white lining of his own rich robe was the ready substitute. Having written the first few lines of the document, he inquired of the elder female the names and rank of the father and grandsire of the girl.

"Were they alive," she whiningly answered, "I need not have resigned her to a man whose antecedents I dread to surmise."

"Yet, living or dead, Madam, it is needful to insert their names in the register."

"Her name is Zutulbé, and mine Lelamain," was the snappish reply; "not a syllable more do you get out of me. There's no need of ancestors for a robber's wife."

The Caliph could hardly refrain from laughing outright.

At length the contract was completed, and the Cadi, having cut off the white lining on which it was written, handed the deed, with a profound obeisance, to the fair young bride. Ashamed to walk forth with a robe thus disfigured, he took it off, with a request that it might be disposed of, and its price given to the poor. Again he bowed respectfully and quitted the apartment.

"Poor Cadi!" maundered the old woman. "You are very hard with him. He came slipperless and left robeless. What an awful gang you must lead, that he should be so cowed! Poor fellow, you might have given him something for his services. What a stingy robber you must be!"

"My good mother," answered the Caliph, "all this is no affair of yours. Matters of far more consequence are now to be arranged between us. I am going to fetch the dowry, and when you see my wife's *trousseau* you shall say whether I am stingy or not."

"Ah! I understand; somebody will find his shop empty in the morning, without having seen his customer. 'Tis a cheap way of playing the generous afterwards. Of course you do it on the quiet in a town like this?"

Without vouchsafing a reply, the Caliph quitted the house, returned to his palace, and was himself again. He issued orders to his tradesmen to furnish and decorate the residence of Lelamain, regardless of the cost, to provide every imaginable requisite for the toilet and the table, to finish all by sunset, and, above all, to conceal the real name and station of the donor. "Should the inquisitive lady," he observed, "question you too pertinaciously, say her son-in-law, *Il Bondocani*, gave you his orders."

Before an hour had elapsed, the bare walls of the deserted-looking house of Lelamain (it was part of a large block, which seemed to have been hastily demolished), resounded with the din of workmen. Exquisite Arabesques were beginning to blossom forth; intricate designs in gilded aloe-wood, rich stuffs, and costly tapestry, were mingled, for the moment, in splendid disarray, soon to lie grouped afresh by the magic spirit of order. In vain did the old woman question each new comer. "By orders of *Il Bondocani*," was the invariable formula of the reply.

By sunset the perspiring artisans had completed their hurried task, and transformed the forlorn fragment of a mansion into a palace. Then several porters came, panting beneath the weight of heavy trunks, packed with superb vestments for the bride and her mother. "Who sent them?" said the enchanted old woman, as she opened them, and gazed rapturously upon the finery. "*Il Bondocani*," was the constant reply.

Lastly there arrived a steel coffer, damascened with gold, and guarded by a man of noble presence. "What bring you here?" said the old woman. "Ten thousand sequins: the dowry for the bride, and the surplus for your private purse." And handing her the key, he would have retired.

"Stop, my good Sir," called out Lelamain, "do just tell me who Bondocani is."

"I dare not," was the answer; "but he purposes visiting you an hour before midnight, and you can ask him yourself."

"Ah!" thought Lelamain, "when others sleep, *he* is wide awake. Night is day for him."

"It is no use having a fine house and splendid dresses without displaying them for the envy of one's neighbours." At least, so thought Lelamain, who soon assembled around her every woman in the neighbourhood with whom she could claim the slightest acquaintance. Poverty has few friends, yet ladies of unquestionable rank flocked there, possibly attracted by mere curiosity, possibly to renew an intimacy which had been but lately dropped: Lelamain, though not well born, had for years been wealthy. They busied themselves with admiring the new fashion of the furniture and knick-knacks (there were some European novelties among them, which ambassadors from the West had presented to Haroun from their royal masters), and putting finishing touches to the toilet of Zutulbé, whose dazzling beauty was rather deteriorated than enhanced by her stiff bridal garments. A loud rapping at the door interrupted their pleasant task. All were agreed that the furniture was exquisite, and Zutulbé perfection.

The same remarks were now applied, with like justice, to the banquet, which was ushered in with state ceremony, on dishes of gold and porcelain. The most delicate of meats, the rarest triumphs of the culinary art, were succeeded by a dessert of the choicest fruits, and the most luscious of preserves. Nor was ruby wine forgotten, although unhallowed to the lips of the true believer. It was, of course, designed for the unknown Jewish or Christian friends of the Lady Lelamain: it was thought fitting to provide for every contingency; and, judging from the empty flasks, the orthodoxy of her intimates was somewhat lax. Alas! for the scripture-reader.

Gossiping among themselves, all the while, however, critically discussing the viands, upon whose excellence they experimented (they had the good taste to reserve some of the delicacies for the supper of the feast-giver), the party, before it broke up (and it was a little hurried by the fears of Lelamain), elicited from the latter the whole account of the wooing. A little reticence would have saved her much after-disquietude; but oh! the pleasure and dignity of imparting news! Within ten minutes from the departure of the last lingering guest, the whole city knew for a fact that the beautiful daughter of the once noble Lelamain had been sold, in broad daylight, to an Arab of the desert for the plunder of ten caravans.

The young merchant to whom Lelamain, in the crisis of her fortune, had offered her daughter, had become enamoured of her. Her graceful form, her radiant aspect, would not fade from his memory, however much he might desire it. Hearing the wide-spread rumour, and piqued that a Bedouin should out-bid him, he puzzled his poor wits in devising how he might destroy his rival, regain the object of his passion, and obtain a share of the confiscated wealth of the brigand chief. By a bribe, he obtained access to the head of the police, whom he at once interested by a report of the countless riches which the robber had stored in the abode of Lelamain.

A very covetous man was the head of the police, but he affected to hear the story with indifference, since he had resolved to keep the whole pecuniary fruits of the adventure to himself. With a grave dignity, befitting a station so exalted, so responsible, he bade the young merchant to return at ten o'clock. " It will be his hour for supper and repose," continued he, " and hence the most suitable time for his apprehension. *He* shall be strangled, *you* shall have the girl, and *I* the money. As for the harridan, *she* shall be bastinadoed, for her preference of a robber. Not a word to any one." And raising a precautionary finger, the immaculate functionary dismissed the scarcely satisfied accuser.

Two hours to midnight! Since midday, events which might have occupied months had crowded into that narrow interval. Half the history of a life had been recorded in the book of fate: one month ago, and the career of Lelamain (at first a noble's slave, and then his favourite) promised a like continuance of tranquil prosperity. What further remained for her? A quiet uneventful life of calm animal existence.

But a truce to reflections. It was ten o'clock, when the head of the police, his deputy Hazim (a just and kindhearted man), the accusing merchant, and the rough-and-ready sergeant Chamama (we all need such agents, however much we may loathe them), who, without heart and without conscience, was a fitting tool for one so grasping and corrupt as his principal, with blazing torches brandished by fifty hands, halted before the so lately poor abode of the triumphant widow. It was now brilliantly lit up by clusters of wax candles socketed in candelabra of seeming gold.

A thundering racket on the panels of the door startled the sole inhabitants: the Caliph had neglected, or purposely omitted, to provide them with attendants. Dark as was the night, they plainly recognized, in the glare of the torchlight, the burly form of the truculent Chamama, and the gross, yet fox-like, features of his superior officer. So calm it was when the knocking temporarily ceased, that the remonstrances of Hazim were clearly, though faintly, audible. "This house is of good repute; it has never harboured robbers; the merchant, fatuous with jealousy, may have laid false informations; the asylum of women is held sacred by the law; we may incur the displeasure of the Commander of the Faithful."

Lelamain embraced her daughter in despair. "All is over with us, my child," said she; "the judge has come to arrest our dear brigand, and we shall be poor as ever."

"Keep the door closed, mother," said Zutulbé; "'tis a strong one, and well barred: Providence, perchance, will rescue us, ere long, from our difficulty."

A new actor had appeared upon the scene. The Caliph had resumed his dress of a wild Arab, and came to visit his fair young bride. He was astonished at the flaring torches, and the multitude which surrounded the house. He noticed, especially, the mild arguments of Hazim, and the coarse invectives of the scurrilous Chamama, who, baffled by the want of implements to force open the solid door of oak, threatened fire and sword to the unprotected females, should they refuse to instantaneously unbolt it.

"You scoundrel!" said the Caliph to himself (his equanimity disturbed by this outrage on his wedding-night); "you shall pay dearly for your amusement. I'll make an example of you, you noisy rascal." For Chamama was filling up the intervals of his threatening eloquence by an unmusical solo upon the rapper.

Contiguous to the fragment which formed the house of the widow stood the palatial residence of the Emir Youmis, a nobleman of princely rank, but violent and overbearing; the two gardens were merely separated by a low wall. By this route Haroun proposed to enter, unperceived, the house of Lelamain.

In the porch of the palace lolled a black eunuch, who, on seeing a rough-looking fellow endeavouring to pass, started up, drew his sabre, and without parley, at once assailed him.

"Back, savage!" cried the Caliph, as he in turn became the assailant; "would you murder a visitor without asking his business?" The slave fled to his master, who, seizing a mace of solid brass, sallied from his chamber.

"Is this your palace, Youmis?" quietly said the disguised Caliph, in his natural voice. It was recognized, and instant submission redeemed the furious gestures of the irate prince.

"Your slave is at your feet, and awaits your commands."

"Your neighbour, a poor widow, is harassed by the police. I would fain investigate the case in person. Fetch me two ladders, directly; the gardens are adjacent. And be on the alert to execute my further orders."

Aided by the ladders, Haroun clambered to the terrace

which gave access, by an open window, to the bridal chamber of Zutulbé. It was a pretty sight, which the contrast of light streaming from many lustres and girandoles to the darkness of the exterior set off to advantage. By the skill of his workmen, the scantily furnished room had been transferred into a chamber worthy of a houri; cerulean blue was the prevailing tint of its decoration, and his expectant bride attired in amber satin looked, in the radiance of her beauty, like the golden sun in an unclouded sky of azure. Haroun, as he gazed upon her, was lost in silent ecstasy.

He was roused from this soft dream of delight by the exclamation of Lelamain—"Oh! my darling, they will break the outer door in. Hark! how they are hammering at it. We shall again be stripped of our little all, and devoured by these monsters. Oh! that we had never had doings with that graceless robber."

With streaming eyes (the pearls so long repressed now flowed in an uninterrupted current) the fair young bride replied in gentle tones to her loud-voiced parent:

"You only distress me more, my mother, by terming *him*, to whom you have united me before Heaven as my lord, a robber! I know not what he is, but to us, at least, he has evinced a thoughtful kindness, a boundless generosity. Every reproach cast upon *him* wounds *me* likewise."

It may easily be conceived how pleasing this speech was to the Caliph; it was softest music to his enraptured ear: from that moment real love was substituted in his soul for the coarser passion, which the personal charms of

Zutulbé, and his whimsically romantic wooing, had previously excited.

"Heaven be praised, my child, that you are contented with your lot. There are some points, I own, in your husband which I do not dislike. Would I were a bird, that I might fly and tell him not to come this evening; for if he should venture, his death is certain."

A pebble cleverly aimed at one of the candles by the subject of their theme stopped the conversation. Lelamain would have relighted it, but a second pebble extinguished the taper she was carrying. A little gravel touched her hand, and attracted her attention to the quarter from which it had been propelled. Looking towards the window she perceived the seeming Arab.

"Daughter," said she, "here is your husband: like the rest of his fraternity, he prefers every other mode of entry to the door: and you, my good fellow," continued she, "had better return from whence you came, or the insatiable gang outside will show you no quarter: no good can betide you here."

Meanwhile the Caliph had pulled off his rough boots, his coarse mantle, and uncouth girdle; his bow, quiver, and other disfiguring paraphernalia, had been left behind. The closely-fitting tunic of rich cloth in which he was attired was handsomely adorned with gold, his eyebrows seemed less shaggy, his complexion was changed; his features, naturally handsome, were alone unaltered: he had become another, yet the same. Disregarding the remonstrances of Lelamain, he darted like an arrow into the chamber, saluted the mother with respectful attention, and tenderly kissed his now smiling bride, who rejoiced at the apparent metamorphosis. Then quietly motioning to the tempting repast, he insisted upon the disturbed ladies sitting down to table along with him.

"He is a very devil," whispered the garrulous mother-in-law; "he fears the police no more than I do a flea. And he's not bad-looking, either, now he's dressed. After all, we women *might* fancy a robber; he is active as a goat, and strong as a lion."

Supper was over, and the Caliph amused himself by placidly gazing on the loveliness of Zutulbé, and quietly laughing at the whimsical oddness of his mistaken mother-in-law. The noise from the outsiders, however, had become outrageous: the crashing of one of the thick oaken planks of the doorway was succeeded by a temporary lull, and the harsh voice of Chamama could be heard vociferating, "For the last time, open in the name of the law, or we break in."

"Well, I believe," said Haroun, "it is bed-time, and since this concert is not soothing, we will discharge the performers. Take this ring, Lelamain, and shout through the keyhole that *Il Bondocani* is here, and has forwarded this emblem to the head of the police, who will recognize and obey *its* master, and *his*."

"I go," responded the old woman; "I have already witnessed the magic effect of the mystic name: it subdues all men." Striding to the window, he then bade Younis, who submissively, but impatiently, had been awaiting the *rôle* he might be expected to perform, to take his sabre, descend to the street, and should any one, however exalted his station, dare to resist his mandates, to strike off his head upon the spot. For ruthless determination, Haroun could not have selected a fitter agent through his wide dominions.

It is easier to conceive than express the terror which seized the head of the police when he recognized the seal-ring of his sovereign: as to Chamama, he would have slunk away, had not the fear of his superior officer restrained him, when the name of *Il Bondocani* (so well known to all the officials) sounded in his ears. The crowd rapidly melted away, in the train of the retiring functionaries, and Youmis had no opportunity for exhibiting his stern loyalty until the next morning, when the over-zealous Chamama howling beneath the bastinado, and Hazim substituted for his displaced superior, attested how rightly he had divined the unspoken wishes of his king.

It was with mingled joy and astonishment that Lelamain beheld the effect produced by the name and ring of her son-in-law, and graphically did she describe the scene, in her own fantastic manner, to the laughing Arab.

Haroun now wished to be left alone with his charming Zutulbé. The old woman drew the curtains around them, put out the lights, and left them free to communicate to each other the hitherto unuttered expression of their mutual love.

Day had far advanced when Haroun left the arms of Zutulbé. An appetizing breakfast was prepared by Lelamain, who, as usual, commenced talking:

"Well! I hope our troubles are at last ended. You must know that we were not always so poverty-stricken, and only a month ago had all the luxuries of life at our command. But the injustice of Haroun, who spares not even unoffending females in his inconsiderate wrath, plunged us into ruin. My poor son, Yemaleddin, was actually sentenced to death for giving a glass of water to a fainting woman. Oh! that the Caliph, who punishes so severely the faults of others, would as sternly examine his own conscience." And the old woman, at the request (or rather, I should say, by the passive permission) of the accused, gave a truthful version of those incidents which I have detailed in the earlier part of this narrative.

Even before this the Caliph had at times doubted whether he was justified in his vengeance; but the delusions of anger had then prevailed over the calmer dictates of reason. The new colouring given to the whole transaction by the simple tale of the old woman, and the utter annihilation of jealousy in him who was now in the full tide of ardour for another woman, united to convince him that he had nearly committed an irreparable wrong. In vain he sought to exculpate himself to his mother-in-law: his efforts were futile: his feebly-urged arguments tended rather to confirm his own conviction of the harshness and injustice of his proceedings. He thus concluded the discussion:

"Well! after all, no irremediable harm has been done: your son is still alive, and this very night you shall again embrace him. I shall hasten to his prison, and will effect his release, I promise you, before sunrise."

Lelamain, doubting the ability of the Arab to perform such a feat, yet assured of his determination to achieve it, besought him not to imperil his life by so dangerous a task. Zutulbé would have detained him by her fond arms; but Haroun, forced by the flattering interest shown in his safety to be more candid than he intended, assured them he should not personally encounter the least risk, but had an all-potent influence with the Caliph. And so he departed on his errand of mercy and of justice.

It is the privilege of kings to repair the evils they have done without either the losses or the shame which betide humbler individuals in their repentance. It is very pleasant, too, when we know we have acted badly, to be restored to our own good opinion by redressing the wrong, especially when it costs us nothing to make amends. So the Caliph having inaudibly and mildly censured himself for conduct which would not bear too close a scrutiny, and quite reconciled to himself by the honours and emoluments he had resolved to lavish upon his victim, proceeded, in the best of all possible humours, to his palace.

Clothed in his royal robes, and seated upon his throne, he thus spoke before the viziers and nobles, who were prostrate in meek reverence:

"Let my grand chamberlain be brought hither, apparelled as becomes his station. I have, with much pains, acquired the fullest proofs of his innocence: he has merited honour, and not chastisement."

Mesroor, having apprised the Persian Princess of her restoration to liberty, and reconducted her to her former apartment, announced to her, on the part of his sovereign, who had too grievously offended to venture in her presence, that she was permitted to choose whether she would henceforth reside in the palace as the wife, or as the daughter of its lord; in either case she would enjoy for life the honours and privileges annexed to such exalted rank.

The Princess was much pleased with this offer; for, although she had consented, from her poverty, to become the bride of the Caliph, her affection for him had not been fostered by this cold union. With her usual tact, she sedately replied:

"You behold in me an obedient daughter, full of respect and gratitude for the Commander of the Faithful."

Haroun was gratified by the manner in which his proposal had been received, and immediately conceived the idea of marrying his virgin bride to the wronged Yemaleddin. Upon the appearance of the latter before his throne, the Caliph, in full court, threw around him a rich mantle lined throughout with the richest of furs, appointed him Chief of the Emirs of his empire, and bestowed upon him the hand of his adopted daughter, who, charmed with his former courtesy, his noble bearing at the crisis of his life, and last, not least (in a woman's estimation), by his good looks and handsome shape, gladly received him, but with proud and staid humility, as her husband.

I need scarcely tell you that both affection and duty impelled Yemaleddin to instantly seek his mother and sister, whom he found still installed in the unlevelled nook of his former mansion, how they received him with open arms, scanned his wasted features, condoled with him upon his past sufferings (they thought not of their own now), and gleefully spoke of their prospects in the future.

After the first effusions of joy and sympathy had subsided, his mother related to him the extraordinary adventures which had betided herself and daughter during his month's incarceration. At this recital his indignation blazed forth. "My sister married to a robber, to a wild Arab of the desert! Let him come here, and by the holy stone of Mecca, I will treat him as he deserves!" His eyes sparkled with rage, his hand involuntarily sought the hilt of his sabre; he was deaf even to the pleading of the tender Zutulbé.

"Hurt him not, my brother; you *know* how good and kind he has been to us; you *know not* how much I love him."

"What a pity," whimperingly remarked Lelamain, "that justice was not done you a day earlier; then I should not have been compelled to wed my child to *Il Bondocani.*"

Yemaleddin started at the name. "Did my ears deceive me? What name did you say, mother?"

"*Il Bondocani.* Read for yourself. Here is the heading of the contract, 'Marriage articles between Zutulbé, daughter of the widow Lelamain, and Il Bondocani.'"

At the sight of the document her son prostrated himself, and the old woman laughed long and heartily.

"So you, too, my hero, are afraid of him, like everybody else. Where is your unsparing sabre now? where your avenging wrath? Oh! the glorious name! the name of my son-in-law! Now I know it, if I fancy the rich treasures of the Mecca caravan, I have no need of weapons to attack it. I have only to shout, Surrender in the name of Il Bondocani! and every camel is my own. All the riches of the East are henceforth mine! Il Bondocani! Il Bondocani!" and she clapped her hands with delight.

"I am not ashamed to quail before a name which all on earth must pay reverence to, the name of the lord of princes, the *secret* name of our renowned and magnanimous sovereign, the Caliph Haroun Alraschid! For be assured it is he who has deigned to recompense me for my unmerited punishment by honouring my sister with his hand."

It was now the old woman's turn to feel awe-stricken, when she recollected how soundly she had rated the Caliph to his face, and what irreverent opinions she had unwittingly expressed of the conduct of the Commander of the Faithful. The advent of Mesroor, who came to announce a visit in state of the monarch, so added to the confusion of the old woman, that she began looking about for a place to conceal herself, and had she not been prevented by friendly force, she would have hidden herself under her own bedding.

Haroun now appeared in all the pomp of royalty, and the vivacious widow and her fair children prostrated themselves before him; he raised them from the ground, and his friendly affability soon dispelled the alarm of Lelamain. His glance rested fondly on Zutulbé, with whom he passed the remainder of his life in tranquil happiness. And many years did the old woman chatter about her Koran-reading, and her adventure with the Arab, to the amused denizens of the royal seraglio.

ZUMURRUD;

OR,

THE LOVING SLAVE.

LONG, long ago, a wealthy merchant of Khorassan, who had attained to nearly sixty years of age without the satisfaction of his ardent longing for offspring, was at length blessed with a son, who promised, as he grew up, to become all that the fondest of parents could wish or pray for. Scarcely had the youth reached manhood when old age began to tell upon his father, and the enfeebled sire took to that bed from which he never again rose. Ere life had departed, he called his son to him and imparted to him those counsels, through a steadfast persistence in which prosperity and the goodwill and respect of all the worthy (and why should we heed the comments of the base?) had ever betided him.

"Mark well my dying words, Ali, and slight not the loving advice of a father who is about to quit thee for ever. Be not impatient to gratify thy longings. Shun wine, wantonness, and mere gossip; speech was designed for prayer, for information, or for business only. Waste not thy substance, for by it art thou valued; once gone, thou must ask favours even of the meanest. Trust no man; for man's affection is but deceit; his religion hypocrisy. Shun those of ill-repute, even as men avoid a forge, the smoke from which taints the garments, even if the sparks should spare them. Consult the experienced; our own intellect is a mirror to show us the front; advice a second mirror to reflect the back. Deal not hardly with the lowly, and neglect no chance of benefiting a fellow-creature; it is not always in our power to do a kindness." As he feebly uttered this last apophthegm, death gently kissed him, and he fainted. For a while there was profound silence; then speech being granted for a prayer to heaven and the last profession of his faith, the shrewd but kind-hearted merchant expired without a pang.

Ali Scher, for so had his son been named, wept for, and sincerely lamented him; both high and low walked in his funeral procession, and every token of respect which might evince the estimation he was held in by his fellow-citizens was paid to his ashes. Ere long his wife—the mother of his child—departed likewise.

For one whole year did Ali devote himself to business and to solitude. So sedulously did he observe the precepts of his father, that life became insupportably wearisome to him; associating with none, and from his great wealth having no stimulus for exertion, he had no aim in life, no pleasure in mere existence. And then reaction commenced. "My father's counsels were doubtlessly well-suited to his quiet tastes and phlegmatic disposition, but suit not my more ardent temperament. I have tried his scheme of happiness, and this life is killing me with its dull monotony. The less wise seem the happiest; I will seek their society for a while, and, if I should find it evil, I can but quit it at my pleasure.

The life he now led was fascinating to him from its freshness; his long abstinence from pleasure, his wearisome loneliness, rendered the wild and reckless cheerfulness of his boon-companions inexpressibly exhilarating; and proud did he feel when they, and the licentious beauties to whom he was introduced by them, praised his open-handed liberality; indeed, it is very delightful to give, especially when one's purse seems inexhaustible. Moreover, there was sound sense in their ridicule of those ever-acquiring, never-enjoying automatons whom he used to sit beside in the public bazaar. So he gave himself up to the full tide of revelry, squandering the fair wealth his father had slowly and patiently toiled for, in as many months as it had taken him years to amass it. At last every sequin was expended, —his shop, his land, his every possession followed the same road; in the end he sold even his very clothes, all but the suit upon his back.

And then, at length, he began to estimate duly the folly of his past conduct; for vainly did he seek, from his associates, that liberality which had ever been the theme of their praise. "It was an excellent virtue in the opulent;" they remarked to him—*they*, alas! were too poor to practise it themselves. So not a single meal did he obtain from any one of them; how, indeed, could he expect it, since their entire energies were bent upon wheedling repasts from such weak youths as he had proved himself? Grief now possessed him,—grief mingled with indignation; hunger, too, threatened to gnaw his very vitals. Yet his raiment was still goodly, his features still comely, and his credit (had he chosen he might have abused it) among the dull merchants, whom he had once foolishly scorned, still unshattered.

One day he had sat from dawn until afternoon prayers without breaking his fast, when the urgency of his necessities made him resolve to reveal his utter destitution to a tradesman who had often shown him little kindnesses when he was a child. Proceeding to the market-place, reluctant, yet determined to avow all his past follies, he noticed a ring of well-dressed people, evidently intent upon something of interest that was going on in the midst of them. Curiosity is inherent in all of us, and though not always manifested, is ever latent; hence, Ali, who had, I own, no right to neglect so all-important a matter as filling his long-neglected stomach, was attracted by sympathy to the middle of the agitated throng. He there beheld, exposed for sale, a tall and graceful female, whose surpassing loveliness had attracted a multitude of would-be purchasers. The youth, not overwise it must be confessed, took his stand beside her, determined to see at what price she would be estimated.

The broker having stationed himself beside the damsel, commenced his duties. "Which of you rich merchants will open the bidding for this exquisite damsel, Zumurrud, the well-known embroidress? Be not ashamed to bid; the lowness of the first offer is no criterion of the spirit of the bidder or the value of the slave."

One of the merchants offered five hundred pieces of gold for her; a second bid ten more; an Arab sheikh, Rasheed by name, ugly, hoary, and blear-eyed, advanced a hundred; the second merchant again said, "And ten," and so on, until one thousand pieces of gold had been proffered for the maiden. The last bidder was the sheikh, for the merchants begrudged the high sum at which they must have purchased her. The broker now asked the girl's owner whether he would accept this handsome offer; in a loud tone he replied, "I would willingly, but I have solemnly promised never to dispose of her to any man, save by her own assent. Consult *her*, therefore, as to her determination."

The broker consequently thus addressed her, "Are you content, maiden, with this purchaser?"

The slave, shrinking from his leering looks and puckered visage, saucily replied, "The kisses of the toothless disgust the lips of youth." The sheikh scowled savagely, and shuffled from the laughing circle. Then a merchant would have taken her at the same high valuation, but she objected to his dyed hair, and refused a third for his squinting; and rejected a fourth, a tall swarthy old man, merrily comparing him to the nights of winter, "long, dark, and cold." At last, her owner, wearied with her frequent refusals, bade her select a purchaser at her own sweet pleasure; and she, having cast her roving, yet not immodest, glances around the circle, at length fixed her glittering eyes upon Ali. He was very comely, and the incorruptible goodness of his heart seemed stamped indelibly upon his noble-looking features. The grossness of debauchery had never possessed his soul; he had dallied with it; he had essayed the only two roads to happiness he knew of,—dulness and profligacy; he was alike disgusted with each; youth was still his heritage, and vice had not yet disfigured (and oh! how clear a stamp she impresses upon her votaries, repelling the pure by an intuition against which their reason strives in vain) his ingenuous countenance.

Her glance was prolonged, and seemed to read his soul. "He, and he alone, shall be my purchaser," said the girl, in decided yet not wholly ungentle tones.

Ali could not refrain from laughing. He, who was faint from involuntary fasting, to purchase a high-priced slave-girl! the idea was amusing. Yet it pleased him not to confess his utter poverty before his former equals; so he hung down his head from shame and embarrassment.

The broker, who little surmised the financial position of the heir to so ample an inheritance as that devised to him by his opulent father, vehemently pressed the damsel upon him by enumerating her merits.

"Not only is she beautiful, as you can see for yourself, but her wit is keen, her mind cultivated, and her hand so expert with the needle, that she gains for her owner, by her embroidery, more than six pieces of gold a day. I may term her, without exaggeration, a living treasure, a fountain of delight and wealth. What say you, my master, will you not buy her?"

And the girl, turning her full orbs upon him, faintly whispered, "Buy me, thou shalt not lose."

"A thousand pieces is too much; lovely as you are,

you are still too dear," was his answer; but his admiring eyes rested tenderly upon her.

"Purchase me, then, for nine hundred."

"Not so, my fair one; you are too costly for me."

"For eight hundred, then," she continued, and so abated her price, until it was lowered to five hundred pieces.

"Hearken to me, sweet girl," he whispered; "I am a ruined man, and have not a single piece of gold in my purse, else, had I thousands, I would freely expend my all for the joy of possessing you."

"Withdraw me for a while from this crowd, as though you would examine me more privately." Acquiescing in which suggestion, Ali was rewarded by a heavy purse of gold being quietly slipt into his hand, with the injunction, "Pay one-half of its contents as my purchase-money, and keep the rest for our subsistence."

He acted as she desired; and having paid the five hundred pieces of gold to the broker, repaired with the damsel to his desolate abode. It was clean, but bare; so that nearly one-half of the remaining contents of the girl's purse was expended in plainly, yet neatly, furnishing the lofty and spacious rooms of that once almost luxurious habitation. And wax-lights blazed once more, and the supper-table was again spread with savoury meats; and the night passed in a plenitude of happiness. Past sorrows were all forgotten in present bliss.

When morning came, Zumurrud bade her master provide her with a piece of woven silk, gold and silver threads, and floss silk of various hues. And from these materials she fabricated a richly embroidered curtain, working sedulously for the space of eight days; at the end of which period he sold it, by her directions, for no less a sum than fifty pieces of gold. And from time to time, as their need or their fancy prompted them, did the same transaction again and again occur.

Now a whole twelvemonth had elapsed, and the love which in its commencement was but sensual, had acquired strength and depth from increased knowledge of each other's goodness. But evil was impending; there is no escape from destiny, and Ali had not fulfilled that portion of suffering which is allotted to us all. The happier we feel, the more should we expect forthcoming sorrow; and that oftentimes from the most trivial of circumstances.

Ali had generally disposed of the precious product of her tasteful industry to the merchants of the city; but one unlucky day, when he had carried it to market as usual, his broker apprised him that a higher sum than ever had been offered for the curtains by a strange Jew, Barsoom by name, who was desirous of treating personally with him as to future purchases. After long bargaining, our hero obtained the great sum of one hundred pieces for the stuff, and departed homewards in a high state of exhilaration. His heart expanded towards the Jew, though he liked not the race; and when, after parting with him in the market-place, he again perceived him near his own door, weary-looking, and limping, as from great fatigue, he invited him to enter his abode, and put refreshments before him. This was the very thing Barsoom was aiming at when he paid so exorbitant a price for the embroidery. Certain of success—for he knew the beneficence of the young man—he had prepared everything beforehand for this contingency.

Having partaken of his hospitality, and established the bond of bread and salt (which should have been inviolate) between them, he took off the lid of a basket, and displayed some magnificent bananas to his friendly host. "I pray my lord's acceptance," said he, "of this fruit, the produce of my own garden, as some slight requital for his goodness to a poor Jew."

Ali would have refused, but when his guest forced the fruit upon him, by saying, "I fear you despise the gift; it is, indeed, unworthy of your acceptance," he took a banana, and as the look was very tempting, placed a morsel of it in his mouth. Scarcely had he swallowed it, when his head swam round; the giddiness increased to stupor; he fell senseless and prostrate on the floor.

It was not for robbery that this wicked act, this sin against hospitality, was perpetrated. Neither did Barsoom feel any malice either towards the young merchant or his slave-girl. But vanity urges many of us to commit actions which conscience disapproves, actions which entail no possible profit, and are, notwithstanding, attended by considerable risk.

You remember that an Arab sheikh had made the highest offer for Zumurrud, when her late master disposed of her by public sale. *She* had forgotten, but not *he*, her saucy rebuke of his aged amativeness; and chance now favoured him. His brother, Barsoom, was one of the most astute of mankind, and well skilled in the properties of every herb and poison. To him, on his return from a distant country, he had imparted the insult he had received (for the jeers of the bystanders had been bitter as wormwood to his cankered spirit), and lamented the impossibility of appeasing his vengeance.

"Impossible! nothing is impossible to the resolute. Had *I* been so treated, I would have had the girl against her will, and without the outlay of a single sequin."

Bold talkers are often taunted into achieving profitless feats, which they had designed for others; and Barsoom proved no exception to the rule. In an unlucky day for him, he cleverly carried out his own part in the nefarious plot; then taking the key of the saloon, he delivered it to his brother, Rasheed.

Had there been servants in the humble home of the senseless Ali, his labour would have been in vain, but what resistance could poor Zumurrud make, when the sheikh, followed by some trustworthy members of his tribe, seized her, stifled her cries by cloths, enveloped her in muffling robes, and bore her away to his own harem in the city. As to Ali, he was left unmolested, to sleep off the effects of the narcotic.

Immediately that he had secured his victim beneath his roof, the sheikh hastened to give vent to his long-repressed wrath.

"Impudent wench!" exclaimed he in savagely triumphant tones, "the toothless one, whom you sneered at for his age, is now your master; and that, too, without disbursing one of the thousand pieces he foolishly valued you at. You are now wholly in his power, for no man knows whither he has taken you. Expect the worst, then, for the insult you cast upon him; for Rasheed never forgets, nor forgives a wrong, however tardy may be his vengeance."

With weeping eyes she simply answered, "Heaven will requite thee, cruel Arab, for stealing me from my kind master. Is it worthy of thee to remember and revenge the foolish words of a petulant slave-girl?"

A little softened by her tears and humility, and inflamed by her beauty, which the tranqüil happiness in which she had passed the last twelve months had cherished and improved, Rasheed, with ogling looks and in a would-be tender voice, continued:—"Yet you are so handsome, that I will not punish your offence, if you will only renounce your religion,"—for he, too, was a Jew at heart, and only pretended to be a true believer to gain the privileges reserved to the followers of our Prophet,—"and yield yourself to my passion."

"Never! wicked old wretch," was her indignant answer. "Never will I become your mistress, or abjure my religion."

"Then you shall feel the pains I had intended for you," was the angry rejoinder; and in a trice, the poor girl was thrown to the ground by his eunuchs, and was ineffectually screaming for help, that came not, beneath the quick blows of a merciless stick.

After the spiteful old man had beaten her until his arm was weary and her shrieks had subsided into groans, he bade his slaves to thrust her for the night into an unfurnished room, and leave her without food. The next morning, when the muscles of his arm had been refreshed by sleep, the poor girl was again led before him, again firmly rejected his wicked propositions, and again writhed beneath his unsparing blows.

When Ali had recovered from the effect of the benj (for it was the essence of that potent herb, which would stupefy even an elephant, with which he had been drugged), he arose—faint, tottering, and scarcely conscious of the past—from his recumbent position. His first thought was for the safety of his beloved; and oh! the depth of his despair when he found her absent, and perceived traces of her forcible abduction in the torn fragments of her dress and the disarranged furniture of the room; she had struggled violently indeed, to escape from the kidnappers.

For the moment he abandoned himself to the wildest grief, and was crushed in spirit by the vastness of his loss. For *she* was all the world to him; from the hour she had become his, he had relapsed into that state of isolation from society in which he had passed the first year of his former bereavement. He had learnt, by sad experience, the value of his father's precepts, and thenceforth had observed them.

Yet his was not a nature to succumb for long to ill-fortune: calm reason reassumed her wonted sway; time, he knew, was all-precious, if he would recover his lost one; for else she might be removed for ever from his city and his country. So, by a mighty effort of self-control, he collected his thoughts and resolved what he would do. Women are ever apter in stratagems than men; it is their sole way of proving their claims to that equality from which the physical strength of man debars them. He betook himself, then, to an aged woman, one of Zumurrud's few acquaintances, whom she had often praised to him for her goodness, her experience, and her shrewdness. Having narrated to her, in few words, the tale of his grief, he ended by asking her friendly advice.

With ready promptness the old woman bade him to immediately purchase a shallow basket, well stuffed, and carefully lined with cloth and silk; to fill it with the most tempting baubles, such as bracelets, earrings, hand-mirrors, and other ornaments or knick-knacks affected by the sex, and to bring it to her house without delay. Meanwhile she attired herself as an itinerant vender of jewellery, such as frequent the harems of the opulent, and made a pad for her head, so as to be prepared for the basket when it should arrive. Ali made such haste, purchasing the wares without bargaining as to price, that he returned with them almost before the old woman was dressed for the task she had undertaken.

"With these I can find admission wherever there are women. I will obtain tidings of our dear one if I have to enter every dwelling in the city," were her parting words.

Wandering from street to street, and guided in her search by gossiping inquiries from the servants as to whether any new slave-girls had been just added to the harems of the neighbourhood, she at length arrived at the pavilion of Rasheed. It was built in a large garden, in a distant and unfrequented suburb, where the sparseness of the residents permitted him to indulge his sinful practices without detection. Groans were faintly audible as the weary old woman tapped upon the door. It was opened to her at once, for the distance to the bazaar was great, and the servants were glad to make their purchases without a long and heating walk. Besides, who likes not gossip? and the female hawkers are ever provided with the freshest of news. So she entered the pavilion, displayed her tempting wares before the women, and permitted them to purchase at such easy prices that she soon became a favourite.

"And now tell me," said she, after the first bustle from her arrival had subsided, "which of you has the toothache? (I have an unfailing specific for it, and very cheap) for I heard one of you moaning, I am sure."

In a minute every tongue was wagging. The master, who was feared, not loved, had just left his house for two days on a compulsory journey, and each servant dilated in her turn (or rather all at once) upon his brutality to the poor slave-girl. Each deprecated criticism as to her own share in carrying out the merciless orders of the skeikh (who, before leaving, had bade them fetter Zumurrud, and refuse her either food or drink until his return), on the plea of necessity. The gentleness of the victim had won upon their scarcely yet hardened hearts, although many a wicked action had they witnessed, and even aided, in that house of crime. When the hawker, therefore, had shown her own sympathy by weeping at their recital of the terrible scourgings the poor girl had undergone, they promised, at her request, to loose the luckless damsel from her bonds ("which you can easily replace," suggested the old woman, "before your master returns") and supply her with the food and drink necessary to sustain life. Moreover, while the old dame, adding example to precept, was fussily occupied in assisting them to unravel the knots which bound Zumurrud, she not only openly uttered such commonplace condolements as "Be of good courage, my child; pain lasts not for ever; Providence is good," and so on, but whispered, likewise, to the observant sufferer (who had recognized her features), "When you hear a whistle to-morrow night, whistle in return, and let yourself down to Ali by the ropes which are being taken off you."

Our hero was both grieved and rejoiced at the report of the old woman,—grieved, when he heard her tell of the tortures inflicted upon his loved one; rejoiced, by the certainty (?) of his recovering her. We should never exult in anticipation, for Fortune delights in baffling the best-laid schemes of the sanguine. Say only, "To-morrow I will eat, drink, and be merry," and you are inviting death to your banquet. For thus was Ali Scher, who had dared to assert that ere midnight to-morrow he would lead her safely to his home, punished for his vaunting.

From excessive excitement, and from cogitating how best, and most easily, he might accomplish his object, sleep, that night, refused herself to his wooing. Next evening, he became so drowsy that he lay down upon his couch to refresh himself by a short nap before night shrouded the earth with her dusky mantle. Sleep, however, like a faithless woman, often ruins those who trust her, and Ali, once locked in her embrace, could not withdraw himself from her fascination.

Two hours before midnight the impatient Zumurrud, having long and vainly waited for the expected whistle, saw an obscure form, with a large white turban faintly perceptible, continually shifting its position around the pavilion. So dark was it, that neither face nor figure, in the absence of the moon, were clearly revealed to her, but coincidence so strongly indicated that it must be her dear master that she whistled to him. The stranger, looking up, whistled in return to her signal, and she with bold hands grasped the rope, previously attached to a beam in her chamber, and courageously effected her descent. Moreover, she had tied to her side two saddle-bags of gold, which she took from the stores of the sheikh as an equitable compensation for the violence she had sustained. Scarcely had she reached the ground when she was disburdened quickly, but not roughly, from the weight of the saddle-bags, and hurried with gentle violence from the garden. Not a word was spoken, and the night was as dark as ever. The road appeared long to her; she stumbled from weakness and fatigue. Her companion seemed to comprehend her condition, and mounting her upon his shoulders, bore her carefully, yet rapidly, onwards, beneath arching boughs which drooped over a most rugged pathway. At times he, too, would stumble, and, at last, in dread of falling, she threw her arms around his head and closely clasped him. Horror! her smooth-faced Ali had a beard like a bath-broom; his neck was as hairy as a goat! "Holy Prophet! who are you?" almost shrieked the poor girl at this new catastrophe. "I thought you were my Ali."

"No, girl, I am Jawan the Kurd; I am Achmet's lieutenant."

"Let me loose, I pray you," said she, "and you may keep the two bags of gold I brought away with me."

Jawan laughed. "I suppose so, wench; I am taking both them and you to our cavern."

Jawan had been in luck that night. Whilst prowling about to discover a mode of entry into the pavilion (for he knew that its owner was away), he had heard a whistle; and kind Fortune (as he then thought her, yet it was ill-luck for him in the end) put both gold and a pretty girl into his power. He was one of that famous band of forty thieves long afterwards destroyed by Ali Baba; and had preceded his comrades to Khorassan in order to settle in their cave his aged mother, who, for many years their cook and general attendant, had now grown too feeble to any longer accompany her many masters in their roving forays.

"Cheer up, girl," continued the robber, observing her despondency; "there are only two score of us to wait on, and you shall be *my* favourite if you only reward me properly."

The increased weight of his burthen, who had fainted away, was his sole reply. At length the cave was reached. It was a natural excavation in some sandstone cliffs, rudely enlarged, and rendered habitable by the unskilful hands of the robber-horde. Buried in a wood which had so evil a repute that few but woodcutters (who had nothing to lose) ventured within it, its inner entrance was so concealed by a doorway of moveable rockwork, that the soldiers, who occasionally scoured the forest in search for the banditti, had failed to discover it. At present it was unoccupied, except by the infirm and peevish mother of Jawan the Kurd.

That very afternoon, before the robber, having with filial piety settled the old dame in her gloomy habitation started on his marauding expedition, he had chanced, on the outskirts of the wood, to light upon a richly-dressed officer, who, oppressed by the heat, had thrown himself beneath the shade of the trees for a temporary repose. He had fallen asleep, and he slept for ever; for Jawan cut his throat, stripped the body of its regimentals, and appropriated the horse, which had been browsing beside its master, to his own use. The Kurd had picketed the beast within the cavern, and there deposited, likewise, the clothes and arms of the murdered trooper. Having promised his captain to rejoin the band before daybreak, he now contented himself with telling his mother how he had brought her a slave; and having snatched a hasty meal, and left the bags of gold with the rest of his booty, he hurried off to meet his comrades.

When day broke, Zumurrud, who perceived how foolish it would be to wait for the arrival of her forty masters, bethought herself of a little stratagem by which she might possibly escape from her captor. Had she known the secret mode of sliding away the door, there was nothing to stop her egress; for the Kurdish woman was too feeble to oppose her; but she knew not its mystery. So she cajoled the old woman with honeyed words, and listened to her garrulous praises of her son, one of whose many achievements was recited with much unction.

"When we were in Egypt, my boy and Mustapha had

a dispute as to which was the more clever, and each agreed to exhibit a proof of his prowess. One of our band had proudly brought to our common stock a purse of silver which he had purloined from the abode of a money-changer, whose door had been carelessly left open by his thoughtless slave-girl. 'I cannot much commend your feat,' said Mustapha, who is a humane man, and never cuts a woman's throat if he can avoid the necessity; 'any sneak could have done as much; the poor girl will be beaten. This should have been avoided; you should have done the trick more neatly.' 'Do better yourself, if you can,' sneered the fellow. 'I will,' said Mustapha. So proceeding to the house of the money-changer, and rapping at the door just as the owner was about to chastise his slave for her negligence, he said, 'Is not this purse yours? My master picked it up in front of your shop, and bids me return it, and say, that had a stranger found it, he might have taken it away, and kept the contents for himself.' The money-changer was delighted, and clutched at the purse, which he immediately recognized. 'Not so fast, Sir, if you please,' said the pretended messenger. 'I am bidden to require a voucher that I have safely handed it to you.' So the money-changer withdrew to his saloon to write a receipt for it. On his return to the door, neither purse nor messenger was visible. But the slave-girl was not beaten; for her master believed it was his own carelessness. The night before this happened, my boy had met with great success in his vocation: he had cut open some saddle-bags in a khan, and abstracted from them a purse of gold. So cleverly had he crept out, that the judge of the city ordered the arrest of every denizen of the caravanserai, being certain that one or other of them had been the thief. At midday he had them all brought before him (his court was by the bank of the great river), with the intention of scourging them until the guilty one should confess his crime. But my boy approached the magistrate, holding the purse conspicuously aloft. 'Restrain your hand, my lord,' said he; 'these people are guiltless; I alone am the criminal, and I now restore the purse to its owner.' So he placed it in the hand of the merchant from whom it had been stolen, and laughing, continued, 'It was easy enough to steal; to regain it now would require far more wit.' 'How did you manage to steal it? said the magistrate. 'I saw this merchant receive the gold,' said Jawan, 'and followed him from town to town, until he entered the khan; then I lodged myself in the next bed to him, and watched until he snored; then I crept, *thus*, near him, cut open his saddle-bag, and snatched his purse, THUS!' So saying, he again seized the purse from the astounded merchant, plunged into the river, and swam up the mouth of an adjacent sewer; and as all the drains of Alexandria communicate with each other, got clear away. Then Mustapha owned my boy was his superior, for he had saved at least twenty from a beating, and the Captain made him his lieutenant. Ah! that was many years ago; my hair was jet-black then."

The old Kurd was pleased at the reverential silence with which her tale was listened to; and when the embroidress submissively inquired whether it would not be preferable to leave the gloomy cave and have her hair dressed in the cool fresh air without, before the heat became overpowering, all her little caution yielded to her womanish vanity.

"That is a good idea, my child," she answered; "these hogs (I don't mean my Jawan) are always dragging me about with them from place to place, and always keep me in some dismal spot where there is no amusement. I have not entered the public baths for more years than I can remember."

Sleep overtook the old woman under the soothing influence of the comb; Zumurrud was spared the painful necessity of pinioning her by force. The horse of the murdered trooper was hastily led forth from its hidden stable, his dress and weapons assumed by the tall and rather large-made woman, and the bags of gold firmly lashed to the saddle.

In her haste, for life and liberty were both at stake, she had galloped off without observing the direction of the road, and, after an hour's ride,—when she discovered that it led not to her home,—she dared not then return, lest she should meet the expected band. So she hurried on at the utmost speed of her charger, and the further she proceeded the wilder and more barren did the land become. Not an inhabitant was to be seen. A few uncultivated roots, and some over-ripe dates, fallen from palm-trees scattered here and there in the oases of the desert, were the sole sources of her sustenance. At length, after privations which would have proved fatal to one more delicately nurtured, she beheld afar off the glittering domes of a distant city. The land all around it was well cultivated, the climate agreeable, and the water—for the want of which she had pined in the sterile desert—flowing in a thousand rills.

Her heart had gladdened when first she gazed upon this smiling plain, but quaked a little when, as she drew near, she descried a large body of armed men advancing to meet her. Nevertheless, assuming a bold look (she looked like a handsome youth with a refined cast of countenance), she continued her approach, and was equally surprised and gratified by their salutation.

"Hail! O Sultan!" was the loud greeting of the nobles and officers who headed the array; the troops, brandishing their long spears, took up the cry likewise,—"Hail! O Sultan! long mayest thou reign over us!"

"What mean you, my masters?" she humbly inquired. "Are you mocking me? I am no sovereign prince, but only a traveller."

Then was the custom of that land explained to her, and she marvelled greatly at it. When the King died without direct issue, to prevent the contingency of civil war from the ambition of any subject, the whole army was stationed outside the gates, and the first stranger of noble blood who approached from the east, became the duly-elected monarch.

Nobility of soul was stamped upon the features of Zumurrud, and the saddle-bags of gold further attested the opulence of her family; so they hailed her their sovereign with universal acclamations, which became shouts of joy when she began to scatter handfuls of gold among the troops, until her bags were clean exhausted.

"He is a noble Turk," was the universal report, "who has quarrelled with his family, and journeyed forth to see the world."

She was too wise to contradict the rumour, and advanced with them to the city, at the gates of which she was met by a deputation of the magistrates and the principal citizens, who offered her refreshments and the homage due to her exalted rank. She courteously listened (though weary and faint with fatigue) to a list of their grievances under the sway of their last ruler, and in few but apposite phrases promised to redress them. She was then conducted to the baths of the palace, clad in royal robes, and led in regal state to the throne, before which all the nobles and spectators prostrated themselves.

Her kingdom was but a little state, which owed its security to its peculiar position. In the midst of a far-extending desert, and leading to no city of importance, no noisy caravan ever approached its verdant plain; strangers, except occasionally from Khorassan, to which land it was nearest, seldom ventured to traverse the wild paths by which alone it could be reached. The population was simple, hardy, primitive, and well-disposed. So Zumurrud had little difficulty in winning their hearts. Pure-minded and unselfish, as thrifty in the management of the public money as of her own private purse, she was enabled to lessen the already slight taxation without detriment to the State. Her people loved her, too, for her domestic virtues and example. Benevolent to the poor, just and affable to the rich, thoughtful not only of the interests but of the feelings and prejudices of others, firm though gentle in her rule, she became so popular, that any eccentricity on her part was regarded as emanating from an intellect too lofty for them to fathom.

Happy people! happy sovereign! Yet Zumurrud was not wholly so. Her love for Ali was too profound to suffer her to enjoy a comparative luxury, and the pleasure of command (and, oh, to a woman power is very sweet!), without sharing all with him. So she sent messengers to Khorassan to invite her belovèd to her new and princely home. After a while they returned with the tidings that Ali Scher was no longer in that land; he had sold all that he possessed, and set forth to wander over the whole world, until he should regain the object of his affections. For thus it had happened.

When our hero had arrived, a little after midnight, at the pavilion of the sheikh, he scaled the walls of the garden and whistled, at first softly, and then more loudly, beneath that turret which had been indicated to him as the prison of his beloved. Not a sound broke the stillness of the night in reply to his repeated whistlings; not a light was visible; all the household slept in careless confidence; for since the forty had quitted the cavern, more than a twelvemonth ago, not a single burglary had occurred in the city.

At length, hopeless of rousing her from a slumber still more profound than his own had been, and convinced that every chance of success, for that night at least, had vanished, he returned in sorrow, yet still hoping, to his forlorn home. Early next morning he betook himself to his adviser, and she, with friendly alertness, to the slaves of Rasheed. From them, quaking with terror as they pictured to themselves the wrathful sheikh, she learnt the simultaneous disappearance of the slave-girl and their master's gold. Back she sped to Ali with her tidings, and vainly, at his request, did she visit every harem in the neighbourhood. Worn out at last with the excess of his grief and the futility of his search, the despairing lover yielded to a devouring fever which almost brought him face to face with Azraal. From this attack he happily recovered, through the soundness of his constitution and the untiring attendance of the old woman, who, as soon as he regained some portion of his former vigour, bade him search through the wide earth for his lost one; less in the belief that he might thus regain her, than from the conviction that energetic action could alone dissipate his wearing melancholy. For he was one of those few who having once loved must love for ever. Death does not long separate such fervent lovers.

So he started on his difficult quest.

When the sheikh had returned from his journey, and was told of the escape of Zumurrud, and the spoliation of his treasures, he was mad with passion, and at first disbelieved the tale which his slaves, to avoid punishment, had fabricated. They asserted that a band of robbers, too numerous to resist, had burst upon them and carried off his gold and his victim, and had it not been for their cries, would have stripped the house of every valuable. When, however, he had ascertained that Ali Scher was hunting everywhere for his charming mistress, and the return of the forty thieves to that neighbourhood was proved by numerous outrages, he changed his opinion, and sent for his clever brother to hold counsel with him. By his advice, he engaged all the warriors of his tribe to accompany him; and Barsoom, likewise, armed his own male slaves and those of his brother with swords and slings, and they determined to search for the wandering horde, each in a different direction. So they, too, set out on their difficult quest.

When Jawan, who had boasted that he was the most cunning of all thieves, had related to the band how in one day he had acquired a horse, fine clothes, a lovely slave-girl, and two saddle-bags of gold, and had received the envious congratulation of his comrades, could not display the proofs of his prowess, he was so jeered at, so discredited, that he left the cave, vowing he would never return without the spoils he had been bereft of. He studied for a while the track of the departed fugitive; then he, too, left in his difficult quest.

Having again dispatched messengers in all directions to search for traces of her adored Ali, Zumurrud now devised a means by which every stranger who should visit her own city should be brought before her eyes. She issued an edict that no provisions should be sold there to any foreigner; neither should any one practise hospitality towards him, but that every day, at certain hours, a table should be spread before her palace, in front of her window, for all who might enter her dominions. All hospitality, she proclaimed, should henceforth be at her own royal cost, and not at the expense of her toiling subjects.

Now the fame of her liberality became spread abroad,

and many, whose sordid spirits preferred feasting from the purse of others to purchasing the necessaries of life for themselves, flocked thither. But Zumurrud endured them only for a while; the city was not made pleasant to them. The first month of this new decree, there appeared before her window a crafty-looking Jew, whom she recognized as the wretch who, having kidnapped her, had carried her forcibly to the pavilion of the sheikh.

Barsoom advanced and took his seat at the table; he greedily thrust forward his hand towards a dish of rice sweetened as in Khorassan; yet, before the food reached his lips, it was dashed from his hand by the attendants, who had received orders from the monarch not to permit the Jew to partake of her hospitality. Bewildered by this unexpected violence, he was led before the ruler, who sternly demanded his name, his business, and the purport of his visit to her country.

"I am a weaver, Ali by name, and seek employment."

"Bring me a geomantic tablet and a style of brass," said Zumurrud.

She then inscribed upon the tablet some mysterious-looking characters, strange curves, which impressed the spectators with admiring awe; then, fixing her eyes long and solemnly upon the shrinking features of the agitated captive: "Liar!" said she, "your name is Barsoom; you are a Jew and a kidnapper; you have come here seeking a woman who bas escaped you. Deny the truth and I will flay you alive, and burn your reeking carcase."

The detected criminal, smitten with terror at her awful power of soul-searching, owned to the truth and implored her mercy.

But Zumurrud replied, "Justice is the attribute of kings. Mercy to the kidnapper is cruelty to his victims," and left him to the sword of the executioner.

"What nation has so wise a king?" was the comment of the mystified spectators. "He can read the souls of men; he can call before his eyes the mirror of the past."

Before another moon had waned, Providence directed another of her enemies to her little territory. Jawan the Kurd, with a skill fatal to himself, had traced her to this remote district. He, too, beheld the tempting dish of rice sweetened as in Khorassan (fit for a prince or emir), and clutched at it with a paw like the foot of a raven. But the food reached not his mouth; his presence had been detected, and the guards led him to the divining monarch.

"Who art thou, man? What is thy trade, and wherefore art thou come to this our country?"

"I am a gardener," quoth he; "Osman by name. I am seeking some property which has been stolen from me."

Then she ordered her geomantic tablet and brazen style to be brought to her, and made mysterious figures, and pondered over them for a while; after which, raising her head: "Liar!" said she, "how dare you utter these falsehoods to a sovereign judge? Your true name is Jawan the Kurd; what you seek is not your own property; you are no gardener, but a murderous bandit. Own it, or tortures shall wring it from you."

The robber, fancying that his daring frankness might win him his life, and thinking, from her boyish appearance, he could terrify the King, boldly answered, "It is true,

I *am* the famous Jawan, one of the forty; and woe to you if you touch a hair of my head! We are sworn to avenge each other; and in the darkness of night the wakeful assassin is more than a match for the sleeping monarch."

"Vipers must not crawl unmolested through fear of our being bitten in slaying them, else many a traveller would perish from our cowardice. Take him, and flay him alive; stuff his skin with straw, suspend it over the principal gate of the city to show our contempt for his threats, burn his carcase, and defile the ashes of it. So shall the guilty learn that my habitual leniency proceeds not from the fear of man, but of God."

At this terrible sentence, the heart of Jawan shrank within him; his complexion became sallow, his teeth chattered, and, in the extremity of his terror, he cried out, "Oh, brave King! I said it but to try thee; none of our band save myself is within thy territory; I have abandoned my comrades; I have hurt none of thy subjects. Spare me, spare me, and I swear henceforth to lead an honest life."

"The leopard cannot change his spots. Thou art too old in crime to repent, not too young in years to die. I remit the tortures; but the sword of the executioner awaits thee."

Thus retribution overtook the murderer; and the people exclaimed, "What nation has such a ruler as we have! He is as brave as he is wise!"

Not many weeks afterwards the amative sheikh made his appearance in the city. Of all his train of followers not one accompanied him; some had been bitten by venomous snakes, some perished from want of water, and the rest had deserted him, wearied of the length of the journey and their many privations. He came limping and footsore; for his last camel had been slain to supply him with water from its stomach. Verily, he had suffered much; but his heart bounded with joy when he beheld the plenty that reigned around. He stopped before the shops of the provision merchants, for he had a store of gold and rich jewels upon his person; yet no man would sell him aught, for it was forbidden to sell food to strangers. The dealers told him there was a public table prepared for all foreigners; and the sheikh, unwillingly, for he was rich, dainty, and ashamed of his soiled and tattered garments, proceeded thither; for hunger compelled him.

When Zumurrud beheld him, she could scarcely recognize the haughty and richly-dressed Rasheed in the abject and miserable-looking wretch before her; but the memory of deep wrongs is eternal, and the voice and features of her oppressor were fixed for ever in her senses. So before he could ravenously swallow the peculiarly-sweetened rice for which he was yearning, his hand was seized by the guards, and not a grain of it reached his mouth. Conducted before the Queen, he fearlessly addressed her:—

"Wherefore am I thus treated? Was not the food designed for strangers? I sought not to steal it, for I am no thief, but a rich man." And he pulled forth his gold, and exhibited likewise his hidden jewels.

"Ere the bond of hospitality be established between us, I must learn from thee who thou art, and what is thy business in this our city. These may be stolen goods."

Rasheed, reassured, held up his head, for he knew he was neither thief nor murderer, and replied with dignified composure, "Although, through the perils of the wilderness, I am mean-looking and ragged, I am a rich sheikh, Rasheed by name; I was driven hither by destiny, whilst seeking for a treasure I had lost."

The geomantic tablet was again consulted, and after a little pause, Zumurrud, with slow and solemn utterance, thus continued, "Thou hast spoken truth; thou art the rich, but hard-hearted Jew, who forcest thy women to abjure their religion through dread of beating and starvation. Own all, for there is a witness of thy brutality in this city; else shall the agony of torture wring the secret from thee."

The recreant sheikh threw himself upon the ground before her. "Spare me. I will embrace the religion of the Prophet; thou knowest all things,—thou knowest I repent of my misdeeds."

"Repentance comes too late; deal with him as with a lapsed renegade." And the last of her enemies departed from the earth.

Yet another month passed, and sadness still possessed the soul of Zumurrud; for what availed it to her to be King, when her beloved shared not her dignity? But joy once more illuminated her countenance, when she beheld a comely and well-dressed traveller (for her lover had trafficked with success in his wanderings), whose profound melancholy of aspect impressed the beholders with commiseration.

Not greedily, but sedately, did he seat himself at the

table; and he, too, preferred to all other dishes the rice sweetened as in Khorassan. "Touch not that unlucky dish," was the advice of a pitying spectator, looking furtively at the watchful soldiers; "three, who have eaten of it, have resigned their souls to Azraal."

"Permit me," he rejoined. "Let them do unto me even as they will. Perchance I may be thus relieved from my miserable existence." Then he ate the first morsel, and Zumurrud longed to address him, but she reflected that he might be hungry, and let him appease his appetite. He ate not much, for his soul was very sad; he had heard no tidings of his lost one, and there was no enjoyment to him without her company.

The people marvelled to see him finish his repast, eating slowly and daintily, as was his wont; but when he had finished, one of the eunuchs bearing rose-water, wherewith he sprinkled him, courteously addressed him, "The King desires your presence. Let not your heart be troubled; he seeks but to make a few inquiries."

The bystanders looked askance at each other; one said, "I thought it would be so;" another, more acute, "No evil will betide him, for were harm meant for him, he would not have been permitted to swallow a single morsel."

The melancholy traveller respectfully saluted the ruler of the land, and kissed the ground in his humility. His salutation was returned; his reception honourable. To her usual questions he replied with dignified calmness.

"My name is Ali Scher; I am a merchant of Khorassan; I travel to regain a woman who is dearer to me than sight or hearing; to whose memory I have been faithful, though long bereaved of her."

Zumurrud seemed to consult her geomantic tablet. "Thou hast spoken truly," said she; "be not uneasy, for Heaven has decreed that you two shall soon be reunited."

Her chamberlain, by her orders, conducted him to the bath, attired him in princely robes, and mounted him upon the finest steed in the royal stable.

When evening came, he was again conducted to the palace, to the sleeping-chamber of the monarch. The excitement of the day had been almost too much for Zumurrud; she almost distrusted the actuality of her happiness, that she should pass that night alone with her long-lost lover; that, oh joy!—she could reflect no further. But woman's coyness, her delight at a surprise, prevailed over her more impassioned feelings, and she resolved to dissemble for a while longer. So she bade him rise from the humble attitude in which he had thrown himself (and the memories of the past blazed forth within her soul, as the sun, which rising above the horizon illumines and enlivens all things), and refresh himself with meat and poultry, with sherbet and with wine. "For after so long a journey it is needful to be invigorated."

When he had finished his repast, he obeyed her signal to draw near her. "I, too, am weary," said she; "come, therefore, and chafe my limbs."

And when, submissively, he began to chafe her feet and her legs, he found them softer and more lustrous than shining silk.

Her attendants had all retired. So, after jesting with

him for a little longer, she fondly smiled, and said, "Has all this happened without your recognizing me, Ali?"

"Who art thou, O King?"

"Thy long-lost slave, Zumurrud;" and the words had scarcely passed her lips ere they were stopped by his burning kisses; for, with the bound of a leopard, he had leapt upon his willing prey, and strained her to his breast with passionate ardour.

The following morning Zumurrud summoned all the lords and all the troops to a solemn audience. "Are ye satisfied with me as your sovereign?" she demanded. With one accord they all exclaimed, "There is none like unto thee, O King!" Then she continued, "Know, then, that *I* am a *woman*, and this stranger is my long-lost husband. Will ye that I should still reign over you?" And again the cry pealed forth, "There is none like unto thee, O King!"

Long did she rule, and happy were her subjects. There was no need for her people, when she sank into the arms of Azraal, to go forth from the city and look unto the East, for many and noble were her descendants.

THE SHAM CALIPH.

ALL the world knows that Haroun Alraschid was so fond of excitement, that when adventures did not occur of their own accord, he went forth to seek them. Giafar and Mesroor were his ordinary companions, and the former, more especially, not always his willing comrade. Of late the sovereign had been so seriously occupied with affairs of state, that he had not obtained leisure to divert himself with his wonted amusement; but a strange report had reached him, so incomprehensibly absurd, that for the sake of his own reputation he determined to trace it to its source. It was not merely rumoured among the people, but positively asserted by the police, that the Commander of the Faithful had forbidden his subjects to take their pleasure upon the water after dark, in order that his own royal diversions might not be interfered with. As no such edict had been issued from the palace, the Caliph determined to solve the mystery in person, although, of course, his officers might easily have saved him the trouble. I need scarcely observe that he anticipated some little sport from investigating the affair.

The well-known trio, clad as opulent merchants, strolled one evening to the banks of the Tigris, and hailing an aged waterman, bade him row them down the river.

"It is plain, my masters, that you are strangers here, or you would not have demanded an impossibility from me. At about this hour, or a little later, every night,"—and darkness was now erasing every object from their view,—"the barge of the Caliph floats down the river, in full state, the sovereign in his royal robes, his court in princely apparel; his benevolent vizier and his ugly executioner seated by his side."

Mesroor looked savage; he was conscious he was not good-looking, but not aware that others had detected it.

"In front of the boat," continued the sailor, "stands one who, in a loud voice, proclaims immediate death to whoever may be caught traversing the water from that hour until past midnight. Look! the lights of the vessel are faintly perceptible in the distance; before long it will glide past us."

It was a pretty sight to behold the pageantry. The barge was brilliantly illuminated by flaring cressets, which cast a rubeate light upon the principal personages of the group upon its deck. On a gilded throne sat a handsome youth, whose black garments were richly embroidered with gold; on either side of him stood figures, whose dresses had evidently been copied from the state robes of Giafar and Mesroor. A numerous body of armed slaves served as a body-guard, and flanked either side of the boat. Some well-dressed gentlemen, apparently boon-companions, were likewise visible, and the awe-striking proclamation was clearly audible.

"We must see into this affair," said Haroun to Giafar. "The imitation of ourselves is very passable; but if it prove not a freak of one of my sons, the pretentious offender shall pay dearly for his effrontery." Turning to the boatman, he continued, "Here are five pieces of gold for you, my good fellow, if you will venture to follow yonder barque: there is no real risk, if you only keep in the gloom; the lights of the vessel will serve to direct your course."

Even this tempting offer did not avail, until Giafar assured him that the seeming Caliph was a mere pretender, whom it was *his* charge to unmask, and who would sorely rue his insolence, should he molest any of their party. The waterman rowed quietly in the wake of the vessel, saw it anchored at a little islet, some way down the river, and, having safely landed his dangerous passengers not far off from the larger boat, received his promised reward. The islet was beautifully cultivated as a pleasure-ground; in the midst of it rose a graceful pavilion, embowered and partially concealed in the luxuriant foliage. As the pseudo-Caliph was passing beneath its sculptured portico, the enterprising trio pushed forward among the attendants, in order to obtain a better view of his mock majesty. They were rudely seized by the slaves, and led forthwith to a sumptuously-furnished saloon, at the door of which they were purposely delayed, until the sham prince and his boon companions had seated themselves at their ease. The pseudo-Caliph was sitting upon his throne, and was being waited on with all the ceremonial observances usually accorded to royalty, when the three intruders were conducted before him. Haroun did not wait to be spoken to, but impetuously addressed himself to the mock sovereign :

"What means this violence which has been displayed towards us ? We are three foreign merchants, who, naturally wishing to behold all that is beautiful in Bagdad, have landed upon this lovely islet. What harm can we have done ?"

"As you are foreigners, and have evidently not heard my proclamation, I spare you ; but woe to the citizen of Bagdad who may thrust himself upon my privacy. Excuse the roughness of my zealous servants, and pass this evening with me as my guests."

The banquet was served in regal fashion ; the dishes were delicate and savoury, the drinking-vessels precious in form and material, the party a merry one ; and as they gaily quaffed the sparkling wine, the hearts of all were expanded.

"Let each of you, my stranger friends," said the ruler of the feast, "tell us the most remarkable circumstance of his life ; or, should his own career have proved wholly uneventful, relate the most interesting tale his own experience can furnish."

There was no denying a request almost vociferously echoed by all the company, so Giafar thus began :—

ALI OF CAIRO, THE LUCKY PRODIGAL.

I cannot narrate any personal adventures, but my neighbour at Cairo obtained his great wealth in so singular a way that I would not have believed the story had I not heard the words from his own mouth. He had inherited a fair property from his father, which he had spent in dissipation, and, when almost destitute, quitted his family and native town for foreign parts, wandering from place to place, and obtaining the hospitality of the old friends and correspondents of his respected parent. He was passed on, as it were, from one to another, until at length he arrived at the gates of Cairo. He had but a few pieces in his purse when he halted there at sunset, just as the gate-keepers were closing the massive doors. He chatted with them as they admitted him, and, in answer to their inquiries as to who he was (for they perceived by his language and bearing that his station was superior to what his shabby garments would have indicated), he cleverly insinuated that, having ridden in advance of his own caravan to procure a warehouse sufficiently large for the vast bulk of merchandise he had brought with him, he had been intercepted by robbers, who had stripped him to the skin, but had mercifully thrown him the worthless clothes he now wore. "By good luck, I found stuck in the grimy pocket of this robe a single piece of gold, which will suffice to yield us all a tolerable supper." By this manœuvre, and by his affability and plausible frankness, he won both their hearts and their credence, so that next morning he was confidently introduced by them to the syndic of the merchants as a plundered but wealthy trader, who was seeking to hire a dwelling-place and stores in that commercial city. His winning tongue and specious manners corroborated the story of the gate-keepers, and secured him the hospitality of the worthy trader. After the bath and dinner, the host bade his slave to show his guest the two houses that were to let, and to deliver up to Ali the key of whichever he might prefer.

There were three ancient but well-preserved structures in a row, all of which were then unoccupied. My friend looked over two of them with a fastidious air, and then questioned the attendant respecting the ownership of the third. "That, likewise, belongs to my master," replied the slave, "but we no longer show it, for it is an unlucky house. Each tenant has perished the very first night he has slept within its walls."

Ali, however, persisted, and found the house more commodious, and far more magnificent in its decoration, than the two adjacent premises. "I will take this and none other," he persisted, for he hoped that he might thus be rid of his miserable existence, and the shuffling, scampish mode of living to which his necessities had driven him. "I may not let it you without the consent of my master," the slave remarked; "but of course it would be for his interest to have it occupied." They returned, then, to the owner's house, who, after osme little conscientious demur, agreed to accept him as a tenant, upon his signing a paper by which he acknowledged his own cognizance of the danger, and exonerated his landlord from all responsibility. The latter, in the extremity of his good nature, even lent the reduced prodigal the necessary furniture for that night, and sent him lights and a comfortable supper.

When Ali had performed the fitting ablution, had supped, and then (for the thoughts of impending death had roused him to repentance for his past profligacy and present knavishness) prayed fervently for a happier and a better life, should he be destined to survive the anticipated péril he calmly laid himself down upon his pallet, in a superbly-fitted saloon, where he purposed to pass the night. Scarcely had he extinguished his candle, when a lurid light seemed to roll like a cloud towards him, and a mighty voice roared in his ears,

"Ali, son of Hassan, shall I send down the gold?"

Not a whit dismayed, for his fortunes were desperate, his answer was bold and prompt.

"Ay, down with it, and the sooner the better."

Hardly had he ceased to speak, when, hurled as it were from a catapult, the gold descended from the fretted ceiling in one continuously-pelting shower, until the quantity was so vast as to endanger the stability of the flooring. Not any of it, however, fell upon himself; but the coins were piled up in a vast glittering circle all around him.

"Now that my task is accomplished, dismiss me to my pristine freedom," again roared the bell-mouthed voice, which shook the very walls by its reverberation.

"I adjure thee, in the most holy name of Allah, that thou explain to me the meaning of this marvel."

"From distant ages this gold was stored away for Ali, the son of Hassan, and delivered to my charge by one of his ancestors, a potent magician, that I might render it up to him at his demand. Whosoever, then, has ventured here, and been terrified at my voice, him have I slain; thou, on the contrary, hast fearlessly claimed thine own, and to thee have I now delivered it. There is yet another treasure reserved for thee in the land of Yemen, and when thou shalt have journeyed thither, it will be found by thee. And now free me, mortal, from my long servitude."

"Bring me that treasure likewise, and do me yet another service, and I will liberate thee for ever."

"Swear it!" solemnly tolled the awful voice.

"By him who framed the talisman which enthralled thee, I swear it. Gently bring hither my wife and children, so as neither to hurt nor terrify them, along with the other treasure thou hast spoken of, and henceforth thou art free for ever."

"Thanks, mortal; I go to fetch them. In three days expect thy family from Cairo. They shall enter this city with a stately procession, so as not to shame thee (for all things are known to me), and thy Arabian wealth shall be brought with them." And darkness reassumed possession of the apartment, for the spirit had departed.

The prodigal slept tranquilly until the morning; he arose early, and searched about the roomy mansion for a hiding-place for his golden heaps. Chance again favoured him; there was a discoloured slab, in the flooring of the saloon, which was connected with a turning-pin, and which, by a peculiar downward and then lateral pressure, could be made to slip away beneath the rest of the pavement. He had seen one of these in his old home, so fancying that the discoloured slab might be moveable, he tried the peculiar knack, and, to his intense gratification, saw the marble slide away, revealing to his eyes a capacious treasure-vault, to which access was obtained by a narrow-winding flight of stairs. Driving on the great circle of coin towards the aperture, and then shovelling down the countless gold with both hands, he barely contrived to stow away one-third of it before a loud rapping at the front door compelled him to withdraw from his energetic labour. Running to the street-door, determined to bar all ingress to the saloon, he found it was only the slave with whom he had conversed the previous day; who, seeing him alive, gave him a friendly nod, and hastened away to tell the glad tidings to his master. Harder than ever did Ali work to conceal his golden heaps from the expected visit of his host. The last coin was rattling down the vault, clinking as it fell, when the violent rapping at the house-door announced the advent of the owner. With a vigorous haul the slab was again replaced, and the perspiring prodigal flew down the grand staircase, apologizing as he ushered in his visitor, for his discourteous yet necessary delay.

Unwonted toil and a dirty floor had not improved the general appearance of Ali; so that his landlord, after having congratulated him upon his safety, and inquired whether anything disagreeable had disturbed his slumbers (to which question the tenant smilingly replied in the negative), drily asked, how long it would be before his goods arrived.

"In three days, without fail; my caravan is too well guarded to be despoiled; meanwhile, if I cannot get trust, I shall patiently submit to these filthy clothes and these unfurnished walls."

Assurance begets confidence. The trusting merchant introduced him to his own tradesmen, and having related his story in the public bazaar, presents of all sorts and from all quarters flowed steadily upon him. His kind landlord even lent him slaves to prepare a home for the reception of his family.

When the appointed time had come, the guardian spirit again appeared to the lucky one, saying, "Arise and meet thy treasure and thy harem, which are within a few hours' journey from the city. Part of thy wealth consists of costly merchandise; the rich clothing of thy family was taken from it; but the mules, horses, camels, slaves, and escort, are all genii."

Then Ali invited his friends and acquaintances to accompany him to his caravan, and requested them to bring their harems with them, that the females might be mutually introduced. So they all went forth together, and sat down to rest in one of the suburban gardens which looked upon the desert. They chatted and they joked, but from time to time gazed on the wide-spread sands. At last a dust rose like a moving column; then obscurely-defined groups seemed to emerge from it, and lastly these compound masses seemed to resolve themselves into clear and distinct individuals. The sounds of revelry, too, floated louder and louder towards them as the van of the cavalcade, with shout and song and dance, marched joyously onward. The leader of the escort rode forward to our hero, and respectfully saluting him, apologized for his delay; and then the merchants on their richly caparisoned mules and the ladies in their gilded litters joining the caravan, the whole formed one stately procession, which, traversing the streets, slowly wound its way to the courtyard of the haunted mansion. Its new master received them all with the most profuse hospitality, and whilst the gentlemen were wondering at the vast array of chests which had been unladen from the mules, the ladies were admiring the superb dresses of Ali's harem, suitable rather to Sultanas than to private individuals. Thus, in one short day, the fame of Ali's wealth and importance was spread throughout the city, and the traders who had given him credit when in rags prided themselves on their discernment.

As the prodigal wished to quietly dismiss the incarnate genii, he openly bade the leader of the caravan (the guardian of the treasure) to drive the mules and other animals, that very evening, a little space from the city, that they might be ready to start at daybreak on another journey. When night had buried all things in darkness, the genii, reassuming their spiritual essence, were wafted through the sky to the realms of ether.

I have little more to relate. Prosperity seemed to improve the morality of my friend, who, with every facility for indulgence from his almost illimitable wealth, has never relapsed into his early wastefulness; and of late, indeed, has become positively thrifty. I liked him better, I own, when he was more of a scapegrace.

Giafar paused, and one of the boon-companions scoffingly remarked:—

"Not a bad way that to obtain credit. I suspect the chests were empty, the beasts and escort hired for the day, and the treasure and its spirit-guardian the afterthought of a successful scamp. Now he *really* has property, he takes care of it. Well, so much the worse for his friends. Long life to the spendthrifts, say I."

The guests laughed at the conceit, and the pseudo-Caliph indicated to Mesroor they were waiting for his tale :—

NEAMEH AND NOAM.

Some years ago I guarded the purity of a king's seraglio. I am a eunuch, and have witnessed strange doings, which I might reveal for your amusement, but prudence forbids. The incident I am about to relate redounds to the honour of my lord, and I need not tremble to narrate it. It was not often there was a disturbance among our ladies, and never have I been compelled, in that palace at least, to execute the dread sentence of a mortally offended husband upon either wife or concubine. Once, and once only, did I find a man concealed in the women's apartment, and I will tell you what occurred. I was serving the Caliph at supper, when his sister, who had remarked his attentive observation of two of the slave-girls, thus addressed him :—

"Shall I tell you a tale, to-night, my brother? it is a simple, but a true one, which may interest you from your love of justice."

The Caliph nodded his assent, and the royal lady thus continued :—

"In the city of El Koofeh, there dwelt a youth, named Neameh, and a maiden, called Noam; they had been brought up in the same cradle, and loved each other from their earliest years. The girl was, strictly speaking, the slave of Neameh's father, who intended—such precocious beauty did she manifest in her childhood—to give her in marriage to his son. When they were both adult, they lived together as man and wife; yet both were very youthful, and *he* so fair and delicate, that but for his garb, he might have been taken for one of my sex. They were happy in their tranquil existence, but the beauty of Noam was so renowned, that it brought misery to their home.

"The governor of the district was seeking to propitiate the favour of his ruler, which had been gradually waning through the many complaints against his tyranny that had reached the throne from the oppressed people. As the sovereign was known to be amative, no gift could be more acceptable to him than a pretty and accomplished slave-girl. And as Noam was not merely beautiful but an exquisite musician, this despot, knowing her to be incomparable yet unpurchaseable, resolved to inveigle her from the house of her master, and transport her as a slave to the palace of his lord.

"It was needful to entice the girl from the home of Neameh, for open violence would not have been tolerated, even in a district which had been so long misgoverned. A handy tool was readily found by him, a saintly harridan who, under the guise of religion, would stickle at nothing which could gratify an open-handed employer. Women are so very easily deluded by pretensions to religion, that this seeming saint could penetrate any harem; so she had little difficulty in forcing her acquaintance upon the pious Noam, who willingly accompanied her to pray in one of the holy places. She was conducted, however, in her innocence, to the viceregal palace; and, thus entrapped, was forwarded at once on a swift dromedary to Damascus, there to abide the pleasure of the King.

"A letter, insinuating that her price had been ten thousand pieces of gold, was sent by the same channel, and the gratified Caliph hastened to view this costly damsel. But grief and fatigue had overpowered her, and though her features were exquisitely chiselled, yet the plumpness of health had deserted them, for she had sickened of a slow fever.

"Neameh was smitten with disease likewise; he pined for the loss of his beloved, and was helpless as a child under his affliction. His Persian doctor, a man of penetration, foresaw the dissolution of his patient should no remedy be found for a complaint which was rather mental than physical.

"Knowing the opulence of the father, he thus admonished him:—'If you do not value your riches more than your boy, you can save him; but the cure will be costly. He must accompany me to the capital; for although I cannot prove it (so cunningly has the abduction been contrived), I feel assured that Noam has been taken thither, and *she* is the heart and the life of your son. Give me four thousand pieces, and I will abandon my practice here, and take him with me to Damascus. Trust to my skill for success; I will not only save the life of Neameh, but restore him, also, his beloved.'

"What will not a father do for his only child? The parent not only acceded to the suggestion, but gave the physician more than he asked for.

"The youth journeyed to Damascus, where the Persian soon established himself as a mystic and cabalistic curer of incomprehensible diseases, with Neameh clad in garments of silk richly embroidered with gold, as his assistant. The costume of the sage was rich but sober, his deportment grave and dignified. His decoctions and ointments were stored in vases of gold and porcelain; his bottles and cups were of crystal, and a massive astrolabe of silver occupied a conspicuous place on his ebony shelves. Need I say that shop, proprietor, and assistant (for Neameh was very handsome), attracted universal attention?

"One day an old woman alighted from an ass, whose rich saddle and equipments betokened it was owned by a person of consideration. She described the symptoms of a maiden, whom she termed her daughter; and when told it was needful to mention her age and name, that the fortunate hours for the administration of her potions might be calculated, and to state her fatherland, that the remedies might be suitable to her native air, she rather unwillingly announced that her name was Noam, and that she was a native of El Koofeh. The agitated assistant trembled with emotion as he made up the medicine (an innocent one, that could neither cure nor kill), and wrote in Cufic characters on the outside of the parcel, 'From Neameh.'

"The girl, on seeing the writing, felt that she was saved; and marvellous benefit accrued to her health from the lover's remedy. The bloom revisited her cheeks, and the King, who longed for her recovery, sent a purse of gold to the physician that he might expedite her cure.

"'Keep it for yourself,' said the doctor to the old lady

who brought it; 'only help us, and more shall be forthcoming.' Then, under a promise of secrecy, he told her the entire truth, and the dame promised to procure an interview between the lovers. As the girl was not permitted egress from her chamber, the dame disguised Neameh (whose smooth visage needed not the razor) as a slave-girl, dyed the tips of his fingers with henna, and decorated his hair with ornamented strings of silk; then satisfied with his toilet, she exclaimed, 'You make a more charming woman than your mistress. Now mind your gait, move your hips from side to side, and sidle as you walk. Above all, avoid speaking;' and she drilled him, as it were, until he was perfect.

"He followed her in this guise to the palace, where the dame passed him through the sentries as a newly-purchased slave; but, from the exigencies of service, was forced to leave him for a while, after careful directions as to which chamber had been allotted to his beloved. Alas for the lover! he erroneously entered the saloon of the King's sister, who discovered his sex. She, however, pitied him when she heard his story, and sending for Noam, complaisantly looked upon their mutual transports, and assured them of her protection. But when the King knew all that had passed, he ruthlessly slew the youth, because he himself longed for the beautiful slave. Tell me, then, O fountain of justice! whether he acted well?"

"Most unroyally did he act. The lover deserved death for his violation of the laws of the harem; yet he only sought his own. A King should have pardoned him."

"My brother, you have delivered a verdict on yourself.

These two," and she pointed to Noam and Neameh, "are the innocent criminals, and to your sense of justice I abandon them."

We of the establishment prepared to seize them; but the Caliph, who noticed our approach, waved us back.

"I revoke not my sentence," he exclaimed; "leave them to each other."

And they departed unscathed.

A somewhat suspicious look was cast by many of the feasters upon the narrator; for few, besides Mesroor, could have known the secrets of a royal harem from his personal experience. The host, however, thanked his guest, and courteously intimated to Haroun that his turn was come.

MESROOR'S BARGAIN.

I know a little of the Court, and can vouch for the truth of the following anecdote. Indeed, I happened to be present when the *dénouement* took place.

There is a certain favourite eunuch of Haroun Alraschid, Mesroor by name, whose chief merit is his unswerving fidelity to his sovereign, but who has of late become infected with that spirit of rapacity which is the source of half the evils mankind is troubled with.

A few months ago he made a hard bargain with a professional joker, that for an introduction to the Caliph he should himself receive two-thirds of whatever the latter might bestow upon him; so, seizing the opportunity when his royal master could not sleep, from nervous irritability, he neatly suggested that El Karibee (for so was the wit named) should be sent for to amuse him. The idea seemed good, and the joker soon made his appearance.

"I warn you, beforehand," said Haroun, who was not in the best of tempers, "that, although a purse of gold shall reward you if you can make me laugh, should you fail, I will award you three blows with a stick for your sole recompense. Are you content with these conditions?"

El Karibee, confident in his skill, bowed his assent, and by comic gestures, funny tales, and quaint drolleries, such as might make a dying man to smile, vainly sought to cheer the Caliph, not a muscle of whose stern face unbent in sympathy. At last the patient grimly said,

"Mesroor, give the dull-witted fellow a blow with your *bâton.*"

The blow was well delivered, and the victim writhed beneath it. It seemed, however, to enliven his wit.

"Stop, your Majesty," he exclaimed, "I have had my share; the other two belong to Mesroor;" and he detailed his bargain about the two-thirds of the anticipated gift.

"Take his *bâton*, then, and pay your debt," said Haroun with a ringing laugh, and Mesroor's shoulder ached with the hearty return which was made from anger at the previous blow.

El Karibee carried off the well-earned purse, but whether Mesroor got his thirds of it I know not.

"The rascal never paid me," cried the excited eunuch, who had forgotten all but his own feelings.

At these words, the whole company, penetrating the disguise, fell into confusion. The sham Caliph threw himself before the real one, exclaiming,

"My aim is at length accomplished. I have met my sovereign, face to face, without the intervention of my too-powerful adversaries. Pardon, Sire, and justice: pardon for my personation of yourself; justice for the wrongs inflicted upon me by the sister of your friend."

"Your hospitality has atoned for your offence against myself," said the ruler; "your history will throw light upon your alleged wrongs;" and he sat in an attitude of attention, whilst his entertainer related as follows:—

I am the son of a very wealthy jeweller, at whose decease I inherited not only an abundance of precious stones, but a considerable estate in land and houses. Sitting one day in my shop, a lady, who, from the number of her attendants, was evidently of high rank, alighted from her mule, and requested to see my entire stock of necklaces. She was hard to please, for nothing but the finest of jewels and the most exquisite of workmanship would suit the refined fastidiousness of her taste; so she tossed aside, with a pretty disdain, nearly a hundred patterns, and seemed, indeed, to bestow more attention upon myself than on my wares. At last, with a languid air, she inquired whether I had nothing better to show her. "My father," I answered, "purchased an incomparable necklace for a hundred thousand pieces of gold; but, as its price is suitable to royalty alone, I seldom exhibit it."—"Price to me is no object," she rejoined, and the moment she had seen it she cried out with ecstasy, "This is precisely what I have longed for; take five thousand profit for yourself, and let me possess it."—"It is yours at cost price:" her full and lustrous eyes had enchanted me: "from *you* I care not for gain;" and I accompanied her to her splendid mansion, to receive payment for the superb trinket. I was detained some little time at the vestibule, and was then invited to enter the saloon. A drooping curtain of thick silk parted off the further end of the room, and shut out all objects from my view. In a minute it was withdrawn, and, seated on a gilded throne, I beheld a young but majestic woman, in whose handsome features, now openly displayed to me, I recognized my rich customer, and bent with deep respect. Rising from her seat, she approached me, saying, "Are all comely men bashful as yourself? Know that I love you," and, as she bent towards me, our lips met in a rapturous kiss. "Are you aware who I am?" she continued; "if not, I will tell you. I am Dunya, a maiden of repute, the sister of the Prime Minister; my hand is at my own disposal, and, if you can love me, it is yours." I joyfully accepted her proposal; we were duly, but secretly wedded, and I passed a whole month in her apartments, a month of ineffable felicity. At the end of that period she started for the bath, having solemnly charged me not to quit the suite of rooms until her return; indeed, with fond tyranny she forced me to swear so. Alas! for my resolution. Scarcely had she quitted me when I was summoned by the lady Zobeide to sing before her. In vain I pleaded my promise as an excuse. "Would I dare offend royalty?" replied the messenger; and, as I hoped to be back before the appearance of my wife, I accepted the imperious invitation.

Dunya had returned before I had obtained leave to withdraw from the lady Zobeide, and was furious with rage and jealousy. "Strike his head off; I want him no longer," she cried to her black slave, who advanced with his scimetar; but her female domestics crowded in his way, and implored their mistress to revoke so uncalled-for a sentence, saying, "He has done nothing worthy of death; he knew not your temper."—"Give him a sound beating, then, and turn him out," she cried; and so strictly were her orders complied with, that I could hardly crawl from the spot where the male slaves had cast my bruised body (it was some distance from her mansion) to my long-neglected shop.

Conscious that Giafar had too much influence with his sovereign to permit the exposure of his sister's shamelessness, I devised this stratagem of mock royalty to obtain a private interview with the Caliph. I have squandered much wealth in the scheme, but I have felt what it is to be a king (in all but power), and the enjoyment I have realized from my assumed state and dignity has almost repaid me for its costliness.

"Your wrongs shall be redressed," said Haroun; "but tell me frankly which you prefer—vengeance or love? Shall I restore to you your wife, or shall I punish her for her cruelty?"

"Despite of all, I love her."

"I will take care, then," rejoined Haroun, "that you shall possess in future the rights of an avowed husband, and be no longer subject to her violent temper. And now let us return, for midnight is approaching."

The stately barque was honoured that night with the presence of the real Caliph; but never afterwards did it float in its gorgeous beauty down the flowing river, for the pseudo-Caliph had abdicated for ever.

EL MULOOK AND HIS FRIENDS.

IN olden times there lived an aged sovereign, Suleiman by name, whose power was paramount throughout the vast regions of Northern India. All the lesser kings—and they were many—were either his vassals, his tributaries, or, if independent, virtually obedient to his legitimate influence; for all the rulers of the East revered him, so good and wise was he, so numerous and warlike were his armies. He had but one son, Taj el Mulook, whom, seeking to train up as a warrior (for the sword ruled all things in those days), he early instructed in the art of hunting, that his muscles might be developed, and his body inured to fatigue. As the youth grew up, such pleasure did he take in the chase, that for weeks together he would be absent from his home; and his parents, who doted upon him (for they were proud of his great comeliness), had less and less of his company as he advanced in years, until at last he remained away whole months in the jungle, slaying the lordly lion, the ferocious tiger, and the stately elephant.

Suleiman was growing old, and longed for grandchildren, that he might feel assured that his dynasty would sway the sceptre of the Indies after he and his son should have been gathered to their fathers. So, at one of the few opportunities which the almost continual roving of his son permitted, the sire thus addressed him :

"It is time to change this mode of life, which I designed as only a preparatory step in your training for a warrior, not as the sole pursuit of your existence. It is needful, I acknowledge, if the ruler of a great empire would be feared by other countries for the skill and strength of his armies, that his own soldiers should respect the individual vigour of his arm; but the arts of peace must not be neglected, else trade and agriculture, the true sources of revenue, will decay; and either his unpaid troops will perforce become banditti, or he will be driven to unjustly assail his neighbours. Think of this, my son, and stay at home with your aged father."

"And how shall I occupy myself in the city? In the wild solitudes of the interior of your dominions, where usurping man has not yet displaced by his tillage the wild beasts who are the natural owners of the soil, I pass my days in the glorious excitement of hunting; warring, not with the gentle gazelle and timid antelope, but with the tyrants of the hill and plain, their ruthless destroyers."

"I can sympathize with you, my son, for I, too, liked the chase when young; but oh! the weary days, when stormy nature rendered the chase impossible! Oh, the long and dreary evenings!"

"Thanks to Haziz and Hassan, who are far better story-tellers than hunters, my evenings pass as happily as my mornings; if you only heard some of their tales, you would almost envy me their companionship."

At these words the wise old King conceived a project, one both agreeable to his own feelings (for he dearly loved an amusing tale), and likely to further his great aim in life—the retaining of his son in the capital of his empire. He knew the influence of fiction upon the soul, how that feelings, and even principles, might be instilled by it, and fostered until they became motive influences. By its purchased aid he would so work upon the imagination of the Prince, so change the current of his thoughts, that the hateful chase should be abandoned for some new source of exciting enjoyment. So, having obtained the promise of his son to remain with him "one little week," he affectionately embraced, and dismissed him.

Immediately that El Mulook had departed, Suleiman sent a messenger to both Haziz and Hassan, commanding their instant appearance. They both promptly obeyed the urgent summons, and prostrated themselves before the King, who received them graciously in his private apartment. Both were good-looking and well-dressed; there was nothing remarkable about them, except the settled melancholy which almost produced a similarity in their countenances.

"For the last three years you have been the constant companions of my son, from whom, I fear, you have estranged me, by your tales. Interrupt me not," continued the monarch, who noticed their anxiety to exculpate themselves. "I seek not to punish, but reward. For the future narrate to him, not the baffled perils of the chase, not the glorious triumphs of victory over the enemies of our fatherland, but the fascinating intrigues of love; enervate his soul with wanton tales, and thus prepare him for the influence of woman."

For the sage monarch knew by experience (he too, had been a lover in his youth), how a beloved one could wile us from our dearest pursuits, could so absorb our whole thoughts and feelings, that everything unconnected with herself should prove unpalatable.

"This is beyond my power, O King," said Hassan; "for the joys of love have been long denied me; a cruel misfortune has incapacitated me for that passion which has been the source of my sorrows."

"I, too," said Haziz, "am equally unfitted to record the joys of love. I am unworthy of them, for I have caused the death of her who fondly loved me."

"Relate to me your histories," rejoined Suleiman; "that I myself may judge as to your capacity. And, perchance—for men call me wise—I may remove that sadness which is marked upon both your countenances."

At a sign from the monarch, Haziz thus commenced:—

REMORSE; OR, THE STORY OF HAZIZ.*

My life, O King, contains no incident worthy of being recited, but I will obey your command. My sadness arises from an incompetence to appreciate the depth of the passion when its intensity is concealed through the modesty of a betrothed. From a child I had dwelt in the

* From 'Haziz and Haziza,' part i.

same house with my orphan cousin, a sweet girl, of a gentle and retiring disposition; and as it was intended, when we had attained to our full stature and development, that we should be united to each other, none of the ordinary restrictions as to our intercourse were exacted. I felt towards her as a brother; I dreamt not that a warmer sentiment for my unworthy self lurked beneath the calm exterior of her loving nature.

When I became a man, my parents resolved that the marriage-contract between us should be performed; and, without in the least apprising me of their intentions (for I knew nothing of that prospective engagement which had been long ago settled by my deceased uncle and my father), began active preparation for the festivities. All this took place whilst my cousin and I were living together in pure and unrestrained familiarity; she, however, was conscious of the engagement, and attributed my brotherly fondness for her to a like knowledge of our destined union.

When, a few days before the Friday on which my father had determined that the ceremony should take place, he communicated his plans to me, I yielded tacitly to his will. Although new and warm impulses were beginning to stir within me, I had as yet beheld no woman on whom to lavish the fervour of my passion. My cousin was dear to me, so I felt neither reluctance nor ardour at the prospect of this union.

When all the preparations were complete (my father had proved no niggard in his expenditure), and our friends and relations had accepted the invitation to join us after morning prayers, I was sent to the bath, where I found, carefully laid out for me, a new suit of clothes of the richest description, a garment of white satin, interwoven with gold, and so perfumed with attar of rose, that I diffused a delicious odour as I sauntered quietly towards the mosque. It was too early for the ceremony, and I sat myself down upon a stone seat in front of a magnificent mansion, to repose there for a while. That I might not sully the freshness of my garment, I had thrown my handkerchief upon the bench; but the heat was so excessive that I exhaled a cloud of perfume from my raiment, and my face became moist from perspiration. I wished to dry it with my handkerchief, but I was in a dilemma, for I was using it as a cushion. At this moment an exquisitely embroidered and delicate white handkerchief fell softly upon me; and looking up to see from whence it had fallen, I descried, looking out from the brazen lattice-work of a projecting window, a woman, whose transcendent beauty kindled an instantaneous flame of passion. When she beheld my ardent gaze, she put her finger in her mouth, and then placed two fingers on her bosom (as one does in sighing); after which she closed the lattice, and withdrew wholly from my sight.

Vainly did I seek to comprehend her signals; vainly did I wait until evening (all things else, the contract, the mosque, my betrothed, forgotten or unheeded), in longing expectation of the reappearance of the enchanting vision. At length, long after sunset, I departed, carrying with me the gossamer-like kerchief to my father's house. My cousin was sitting up for me, and was weeping. As soon as she saw me she wiped away her tears, threw her arms around me, removed my damp outer garment, and gently inquired the cause of my unexpected absence. She told me how the guests, the cadi, and the witnesses had assembled in our house, had long waited for my presence, had eaten the wedding-feast, and eventually dispersed in despair of my coming. "Your father," she continued, "is positively furious with rage; he has vowed not to permit our union for a twelvemonth, so large a sum has he fruitlessly expended on these festivities."

I told her all, for I had none else in whom I could confide, and the tears ran down her cheeks from her emotion. Even then, had I known how she loved me, all might have been well; but I thought her feelings no more ardent for me than mine for her; that her tears were the sympathy of a sister, not the tacit complaint of a neglected bride.

"At least, then, we are reprieved for a twelvemonth. Aid me, dear girl, with your advice, and explain to me the meaning of those signals."

She looked piteously in my face, and exclaimed, "O son of my uncle, if you required mine eye, I would pluck it forth from its socket for you; so, then, however painful to me, I will aid you in the accomplishment of your desires."

She then explained to me that the first signal was the symbol of union; the second of her sorrow for the necessary delay of two days before that could be accomplished.

After two days I betook myself to the same spot where I had beheld the woman who so strangely fascinated me, and again by her signals did she defer an interview with me. For five days more did I wait, according to her will, and when at last her bewitching face appeared, not a word did she utter, but again made signals, which my kind cousin, who was continually weeping, and seemed wasting away from the excess of her sympathy for me, skilfully interpreted. And after more and more procrastination, at last I became sick with the deferment of my hopes, and loathed my food, and turned peevish and unkind to that dear girl who was ever solicitous for my comfort, and who bore even my ill-humour with smiling patience. She would perfume my garments when I sought an interview with my charmer, she would tempt my appetite with the most dainty of viands, she would cheer me by her conversation while I reclined my head upon her lap; and when, after nights of restlessness, I at length fell asleep in that position, she would not move from it, despite of her own inconvenience, and her own want of sleep.

At last, when worn out with want of food and restlessness, I had taken my stand beneath the alluring lattice, my charmer deigned to smile at my long devotion, and attracting my attention, hid a small flashing mirror in a sombre-coloured bag, pointed to some green shrubs, and then placed a lamp upon the top of them. These symbols, as interpreted by my poor cousin, indicated that when the light of day was obscured, I should enter her garden, and seat myself where I should perceive a lamp. And during that entire day she lulled my impatience with tales of devoted lovers; but they were mostly sad, sad as her own sweet face, sad as her hapless fate.

At the hour of nightfall I left my father's house, and proceeded to the entrance of the garden I had been invited to. The gate was left open. I entered, and walked stealthily towards a bright light, which was burning in a pavilion-like summer-house, opening upon the garden. The gilded lamp suspended from the middle of the dome, which was constructed of ebony inlaid with ivory, displayed to advantage the gold and silver embroidery of the thick silken carpets, the tempting viands reposing in costly dishes on a table of alabaster, the most perfect and luscious of fruits, the most fragrant and exquisite of flowers. A cup of crystal, too, had been placed near a silver beaker of yellow wine. Everything was indicative of opulence and luxury.

For hours I impatiently waited for my speechless charmer. All was quiet; not even a distant footfall disturbed the lone silence. The stillness overcame me; I had not slept for many nights; and at length consciousness left me. When I awoke (I had laid my head upon a cushion) I found myself upon the bare cold tablets of the marble floor. Day was near at hand, and I slunk back to my home, with anger and despondency in my heart; for I knew by the removal of the cushion that I had been visited and scorned. My sweet cousin, who had passed the night in jealous weeping, smiled sadly at my return, and congratulated me upon the accomplishment of my wishes. I struck her in my passion! That blow will never be eradicated from my memory. I struck *her*, whose every pulse beat in unison with mine, who was sacrificing her own fair prospects to forward mine. Thankless and blind that I was, I can never more look for happiness. Half fainting, and with dilated eyes, she murmured, "I forgive you; the delirium of a baffled lover is pardonable by one who loves him." And she kissed my forehead, and soothed me, and inquired of the past.

By her advice I wended my way that very night to the same spot, and the same tempting preparations for my coming greeted my sight. After waiting until past midnight, hunger possessed me, and I fed freely from the dishes, and quaffed the potent wine. In my enfeebled condition it was too strong for me; I slept, and on awaking found myself cast forth from the garden, and lying upon my back, with a sharp-pointed knife upon my stomach.

I learnt from my cousin that by this my charmer meant she would slay me if I dared again approach her. But when my despair became so intense as to threaten my reason, my wasted and weeping betrothed bade me, if the violence of my passion would kill if left unappeased, to dare all, and revisit the garden. "Yet remember," she warned me, "that sleep in that pavilion means death!"

That day I obeyed her injunctions; I laid myself down upon the couch, whilst she fanned me so gently that I slumbered until the evening. I then, by her directions, took a moderate meal of food and sherbet, and thus fortified against sleep and appetite, remained sober and awake, despite the loneliness and the seducing silence. After more than half the night had passed, I was rewarded for my abstinence. My charmer appeared, gorgeously attired in satin and gold, attended by ten female slaves, whose dress betokened the wealth of their owner. Radiant with delight,

I heard the first words she had ever uttered to me, "Now that you have preferred me to both sleep and food, I acknowledge and will requite the ardour of your passion." Then she signalled to her attendants to quit us; and when we were alone she kissed me, and pressed me to her bosom. The night passed in soft converse, in feasting, and in dalliance.

At dawn I left her, and returning to my cousin, found her prostrate with feebleness, and with long-continued weeping.

"I have triumphed, dear girl," I abruptly exclaimed; "she is mine for ever!"

The tidings were her death-blow; the feeble flame of life went out in the mute conflict of jealousy with unselfish love.

It was not until after her decease that my mother revealed to me the calm intensity of her love for me; her self-immolation was then manifest to me in all its quiet grandeur. Even my passion for my mistress was checked by the profundity of my remorse; I could not revel in the arms of another, while *she* who loved me to her own destruction lay in that grave to which my coldness and neglect had doomed her.

When, after long absence, I once more sought the lattice and the garden-gate, both were for ever closed against me; I lost, at one stroke, the woman whom I loved, and the woman who loved *me*. From that hour I have never smiled.

"Did you never learn the name of your warmly-disposed acquaintance?" inquired Suleiman with a slight yawn.

"Not from herself. But I ascertained that a Siamese princess, Indamora by name, occupied the mansion I had first seen her at."

"The very wanton who was the cause of my own incurable sorrow," cried Hassan, who thus took up the thread of the story:—

THE RIVAL BEAUTIES.*

It must have been shortly after the obsequies of Haziza (my friend's cousin, whom he is ever lamenting) that I first saw the seductive princess; from that brazen lattice-work, after having signalled to me her will, by symbols I had not the wit to comprehend, she let fall verses, which very plainly told me the ardour of her feelings and the length I might proceed to. I was, at that time, a very handsome fellow, of a warm temperament, and not unaccustomed to intrigue.

Admitted to the pavilion, no forbidden food or slumber delayed my transports. The princess yielded me at once all that the most favoured lover could ask for, and, for a time, I revelled in the alternating delights of feasting and of passion. My own good-nature proved my ruin. One night, whilst proceeding to my rendezvous, I was addressed by a respectable-looking aged female, who begged me to read for her a letter which she carried in her outstretched hand. It had come from her son, she said, a

* From 'Haziz and Haziza,' part ii.

wealthy merchant, who had been absent from home for ten years. From his long-continued silence, she had thought him dead; yet the letter was assuredly in his handwriting. Both she and her daughter were most anxious to decipher its contents, but, alas! they were not scholars; they must appeal to my benevolence.

A bright light emanated from the open doorway of a stately mansion; thither the old woman conducted me that I might see to read the open note. The house was so evidently the residence of a wealthy family that I entertained no suspicion of its occupants, and not being in a hurry, and ever glad to oblige my fellow-creatures, I passed beneath its portals. I was met by a damsel who was elegantly yet peculiarly clad in the same foreign fashion as that worn by the Princess Indamora, to whom, indeed, she bore a remarkable likeness. She was younger, however, and I thought her still handsomer; there was in her attitude and demeanour the same commanding forwardness, the same scorn for conventionalities: her gait and features were voluptuous, yet did not betray that utter abandonment of self-respect to passion which deteriorated the beauty of my mistress. I could not but admire her, and when she asked in dulcet tones such as neither before nor after have I heard equalled, that I would enter and kindly read the letter aloud, I respectfully advanced towards her. At that moment the door, which was lined throughout with sheets of copper, as though for protection against thieves, was violently slammed-to, the key hurriedly abstracted by the old woman, and the light extinguished.

"Fear not," cried the silvery voice; "no harm is intended; it is a little surprise, that is all. Take my hand, and I will conduct you to where there are lights in plenty."

The speaker approached me, and, in the darkness, passionately kissed my lips and pressed me to her bosom. I took her hand, reassured as to my safety, yet not quite pleased with my adventure. We passed through seven vestibules, and at length entered a spacious and brilliantly-lighted saloon, built of pure white alabaster, and furnished with cushions and sofas of the richest brocade.

"Which prefer you, handsome stranger," said the foreign damsel, "life with me in this luxurious home, or death and an unknown grave?"

"Life!" I briefly answered.

"Then marry *me*, for I love you;" and the witchery of her eyes, the music of her voice, the perfume of her breath, the soft pressure of her winding arms, all intoxicated me with desire, and I assented.

"Think not," she continued—and I beneath the spell of her voice fondly believed her,—"that *I* would have hurt you; but Indamora would not long have spared you. She is my cousin, and I know her well. She soon wearies of her lovers who sup and are seen no more. Her feasts are fatal. But I had seen you, my beloved, and resolved to save you. You will be mine, *willingly*, will you not?" And the look she gave me of love! of pity! of triumph! oh! it was indescribable. Suffice it, I was conquered, if not convinced, and, without either fear or regret, accepted the alliance.

The damsel clapped her hands, and the old woman, accompanied by four witnesses, the regulated number in that city, entered, saluted me respectfully, and took their seats.

The foreign lady formally acknowledged, in their presence, she had received an adequate dowry, declared me her consort (a declaration I reciprocated), obtained their signatures, as legal witnesses, to the marriage-contract, liberally remunerated them for their attendance, and courteously dismissed them. We were alone together, and I had no reason to complain of the coldness of my bride.

The next morning I proposed to withdraw myself for a while to my lodgings, and betake myself to my ordinary avocations. To my surprise, the street-door would not open. My wife was by my side in a minute.

"It is easier to enter here than depart, my husband. This door is nailed up from the outside, and once a year only are the fastenings removed. My cousin lets her pet birds go free, for she can lure them back; but I cage mine, that I may save them from her poisoned rice."

I was too well contented with my position to resist; indeed, I never wished to. Unlimited stocks of provision had been stored up for a twelvemonth's consumption; every imaginable luxury seemed daily provided for our wants, our appetites, or our whimseys. There was confinement, certainly, but the gardens were extensive, and not a wish or fancy left ungratified. Without relatives in the city, and without acquaintances worthy the name of friends, I was neither missed by them, nor missed them. My existence was passed in an earthly Paradise. The soul, perchance, was unsatisfied, but every requirement every desire of the body was gratified.

A twelvemonth sped away. I had become a parent, and scarcely cared to regain my liberty and revisit my former haunts.

"You are free this day," said my wife, as we heard the workmen outside removing the heavy nails from the fortified doors, and saw a host of tradesmen, with household requisites for the ensuing year, watching their progress; "but you must wait until evening, for the sake of decorum, before you depart; moreover, you must take a solemn oath to return before midnight, failing in which, to hold me exonerated, by the triple oath of divorcement, from the marriage vow."

I accepted the terms of release, yet sought not to free myself from my silken fetters. I scarcely cared to quit my Paradise, yet having left it curiosity impelled me to revisit the pavilion where I had been received so kindly by Indamora. It was not that I loved her, or preferred her to her cousin; although I appreciated too truly, as the event proved, the innate selfishness of my voluptuous wife, who kept me, as it were, for the gratification of her passions, I entertained no wish to change my vassalage. Neither of the women, indeed, was capable of love in its purer sense; but I, who could comprehend that the annihilation of self was the essence of that sacred feeling, knew I was unworthy, from the sensuality of my nature, of a more spiritual passion. I was supinely content because I dared not aspire to a nobler grade of sentiment.

I pushed the garden gate; it was unfastened. Indignant that my memory had so soon been forgotten,—for

I believed it was purposely left open for a subsequent lover,—I trod the well-remembered path to the domed summer-house, and there beheld a sight which melted my soul within me, dispersing all ideas of vexation and distrust. Indamora, the shadow of her former self, was sitting with her head buried in her lap: at the sound of my approach, she raised it; continual weeping had blighted the beauty of her once incomparable features.

"Praise be to Heaven for thy safety!" was her first salutation; "I thought I had lost thee for ever."

I hung down my head in shame (yet I was not to blame), and, in reply to her eager questions, detailed to her all the incidents of my capture and my marriage. I told her, too, that, in compliance with my solemn oath, I must leave her ere midnight. Then her tenderness vanished, her face became livid with rage, her eyes flamed with jealous fury.

"Traitor!" cried she, "dost think to turn me off like a discarded wanton! Shall my perfidious cousin enjoy thee, after having stolen thee from my arms? Never! never!" and thrice she violently clapped her palms, and her slaves flocked to her, and at a sign flung me upon the grass, and so clung to my limbs that I could not move an inch. Pausing, she exclaimed, "I will not slay thee, for it is *her*, whom I hate; yet no woman shall covet thee in future." Then whispering to her too zealous attendants, she turned upon her heel, and quitted me for ever. I may not narrate what followed; suffice it that henceforth unfitted to be husband or father, I fainted from anguish, and when at length restored to my senses, through some cordial administered by a slave more compassionate than the rest, I had slowly crawled, feeble from loss of blood, to the mansion of my wife, midnight had passed. In that luxurious home I was permitted to rest until my wound had healed, and was then cast as worthless from the portals.

"And these vile wantons, did you never see them more?" said the monarch, whose love of justice made him feel such interest in the narrative, that he longed to summon them before his tribunal.

"I was a stranger in the city, and powerless to avenge myself; I feared to expose my incurable calamity, and I left the land for ever."

"I thank you both for your narratives," continued Suleiman, "and commiserate your sufferings. I can neither bring the dead to life for you, Haziz, nor restore you, Hassan, to your normal condition; yet I can palliate the calamity which has befallen each of you. Power is the best substitute for love. You, O Hassan! shall lord it, as the chief of my eunuchs, over that sex which has so cruelly wronged you. Another passion, Haziz, with perilous adventure to give it zest (and *I* have a project full of romance), will banish from your memory the image of your lost Haziza."

"Thanks, gracious Sovereign, for your sympathy," they both exclaimed.

"Sympathize, too, with me, my friends," said Suleiman; "with an aged father, who seeks to retain his son by his side, and influence him by your tales to prefer the chase of woman to that of beasts. She is more difficult to subdue, but better worth subduing."

"My son," said Suleiman to El Mulook, "you told me you had some capital story-tellers in your company; so, as you are more fortunate than myself, for I have trained my own people to be wholly utilitarian, and have discountenanced the ideal as enervating and pernicious, I have enjoined their presence, that we may both of us be amused by their tales."

Hassan, duly cautioned to graduate his tales of love, commenced as follows:—

ABUSHAMAT AND ASLAN.

A merchant of Cairo had an only son, who, from his childhood, promised to be one whom any parent might feel proud of. The father, however, was superstitious, and fearing the magic of the evil-eye, brought up his offspring in a subterranean apartment, where there was no possibility that the envious eye of a fellow-mortal should blight the child by its pernicious influence. Whilst the pretty boy was changing to a handsome youth, many a time did his father visit him in the gloomy abode to which his timorous affection had consigned him; and incessantly did he strive, both by unusual indulgences and by the warm tenderness of his language, to prevent him from resenting so unusual a restraint. Moreover, as his wealth was great, he induced learned men, by liberal payment for their services, to visit and instruct him in all accomplishments necessary to sustain his social superiority. For the father was Syndic of the merchants of Cairo.

At the commencement of our history, the youth, despite of his confinement, had become plump and handsome, and his beard was already sprouting from his square-cut chin. Few women could have resisted his wooing, had he been warmly inclined; but his eyes had never lighted upon one of that sex, his mother in his infancy almost alone excepted. He had grown up with strange and unworldly ideas, for the Christian slave who had waited upon him had imbued him with some of those chivalrous notions of the sex which are peculiar to the barbarians of the West. This Christian had been sold to the merchant by some pirates who had captured him at sea.

One morning the trap-door of the airy and spacious vault in which Abushamat, the Syndic's son, had been so long immured was left open, as many surmised, from sympathy with the captive; for the Christian had disappeared, and was never heard of afterwards. Our hero availed himself of the chance, clambered up, sped along sundry corridors, and being pursued by the domestics, accidentally took refuge in the apartments of the women. The vision of a tall and vigorous youth, who, with panting chest and dilated eyes, burst suddenly upon the party, scattered the females in all directions; but his own evident amazement and hesitating timidity soon reassured them. There was a kind of farewell visit going on, the leavetaking of a very lovely maiden, who was to return on that day to Bagdad, in order to be wedded to a not too agreeable cousin. Her surprise was so intense that she omitted (perchance purposely) to adjust her veil, and her countenance, revealed to the admiring eyes of the youth, exercised an influence upon his fortunes that was reciprocated by the effect produced upon her by his own good looks. The apologetic explanation of Abushamat's mother soon removed all disquietude, and with one accord the whole party (the blushing damsel excepted) congratulated the parent upon the strength, grace, and beauty of her offspring. When the father returned from the business of the day, and gazed upon the ingenuous face of his son, who bore a striking but spiritualized likeness to himself, he could not resist the vehemently-urged request of the mother, that he would present the lad to his fellow-merchants as his acknowledged son and heir. The father felt proud of his boy, yet, naturally, made some merit of complying with the wishes of his consort.

The young man, half bewildered by the noisy bustle of the streets, which contrasted so strongly with the perpetual stillness of his solitary chamber, was at first abashed, but soon gained confidence from observing the respect paid to his worthy sire. Of course he attracted attention, for it was his first introduction to the mercantile world; and the younger members of it both smiled at his simplicity and triumphed in their superior knowledge of trade and its enormous profits. They boasted of their travels, and in so doing contrived to insinuate their immeasurable superiority over one so ignorant of the world as their Syndic's son confessed himself to be. He parted from them with the conviction that they looked down upon him as an incapable, one utterly unable to rival them in their undertakings.

It is galling to be despised; and Abushamat, who had his ideal of the capabilities that were in him, although his aspirations (fanned by a captive soldier, who despised the grasping acquisitiveness of trade) tended not to the sordid thought of mere gain, but sympathized with that spirit of enterprise which alone renders money-making not wholly degrading, returned to his home, galled to the quick by his suggested inferiority to those who were heirs to a lesser fortune; for he had learned, in that one day, to appreciate the position which wealth, even contingent, may confer.

Next morning, full of energy and will combined, he begged his father to start him in life. "My companions slight me," said he, "because they have realized their cent. per cent. by their ventures, and sneer at me as though I could not achieve what *they* can accomplish. I have been too long immured; you have wronged me by my compulsory inaction. Make amends, then, by providing me with the necessary outfit, and permit me to prove that not even *your* superstition has unfitted me to conquer in the battle for life."

"I am very wealthy, my son. I am the syndic of the merchants, and my savings will render you opulent beyond the risks of fortune. Remain, then, with me, my boy; you know not as yet the perils of the desert."

"It is those very perils which prove so captivating to me; it is the destiny of the noble-hearted to overcome danger, and in that solitude to which your credulity doomed me I have formed resolutions alien, I fear, to your own ideas of happiness, from which, however, no obstacles shall deter me."

It is difficult to oppose the headstrong plans of those we

feel affection for, and the resolute will of the emancipated youth was too much for the passive resistance of the tender father. The unprisoned energies of the son threatened to revolutionize the household; so the Syndic, in self-defence, not only yielded to, but forwarded the undigested schemes of his wilful son. Abushamat, who felt aggrieved at his long and foolish confinement, plainly told his sire that, should he refuse his request, he would assume the garb of a dervish, and thus live at free quarters with the devout, whilst wandering through the East.

"Be it so, then," at length said the Syndic; "you shall visit Bagdad, and not as a peddling trader, but as a rich merchant; for out of my vast stores I will provide you with fifty camel-loads of merchandise, each worth a thousand pieces of gold. Nevertheless, the perils of the road are not to be despised, for the Bedouins, the natural foes of the merchant, are numerous and daring."

Abushamat journeyed without any noteworthy occurrence until he had arrived within a few hours' distance from his destination. Despite of the objections of the leader of the caravan, who regarded this spot as peculiarly objectionable, and who urged that they should push on their beasts so as to arrive at the city before the closing of the gates at sunset, the stubborn youth insisted upon halting for the night, in order to attract more attention by entering within the walls at midday.

The night was very lovely; and our hero, who well remembered that the first and only woman who had ever charmed him resided in that city whose lights were faintly tinging the distant horizon, could not sleep. To get rid of his excitement, he strolled on foot a mile or two from the camp. Afar off he beheld some rapidly-advancing flashes; he knew they proceeded from the spear-heads of a marauding tribe of Arabs, and laid himself flat upon the sand. The glittering of steel in the moonlight, the rush of galloping steeds as they passed his hiding-place, were succeeded in a few minutes by the shrieks of the attacked. Resistance was hopeless, yet the assailed fought valiantly, and perished to a man. Abushamat was too far off to aid his little band, but he scorned himself for an inaction which alone preserved him. He saw the Bedouins lead away his reloaded camels, and, when they had gone out of sight, ventured back to the scene of butchery, in hopes of bringing succour to the wounded. He found himself the sole survivor of the little body of men who formed his caravan; and he who had designed to dazzle the inhabitants of Bagdad by the splendour of his cavalcade, was glad to trudge afoot to that city, almost without a coin.

So poor was he that he took shelter at night in the vestibule of a mosque. The conversation of two merchants, as they passed along the street, preceded by their slaves with lighted lanterns, attracted his attention. The younger, a harshly-expressioned man, was begging the elder to restore to him his cousin. His uncle (and father-in-law), for such was the relationship he bore to him, replied with sadness, "Did I not remonstrate with you when you were continually threatening her with divorce? yet, now that all is over, you regret your hastiness. Still, if she assent, it may not be too late to redeem the past." The speaker was aged, but comely; he looked so kind-hearted that Abushamat resolved to implore his temporary assistance. He stepped forward from his concealment, and confronted the friendly disputants. The abruptness of his appearance startled them.

"Who are you, and what is your business?" said the younger and more collected of the pair.

"I am the only son of a rich merchant of Cairo, and have been pillaged by the Arabs of a costly venture. At this moment I have not wherewithal to purchase food."

"What say you to receiving two thousand pieces of gold?" said the elder of the two merchants.

"As a charitable loan, or for what services?"

"My daughter Zobeide has been married to this young man; he loves her, but she is averse to him, although he is her cousin. In a passionate dispute with her, he uttered the irrevocable oath of divorcement, and they cannot be reunited without the intervention of a mustahall, or temporary husband. Now, in such a dilemma it is better to employ a foreigner than a native, who might boast hereafter of the favours of the bride; hence, I offer you this handsome sum if you will wed her to-night, and divorce her to-morrow."

Abushamat was sore distressed. A night's shelter and a liberal payment for a mere ceremony was far better than lying in the streets; so, despite certain qualms of delicacy, he accepted the offer, and, although the hour was very late for business, they at once proceeded to the residence of the Cadi, a good-natured magistrate, who would grant favours for a consideration. The elder merchant stated his wish to employ the stranger as a mustahall, and suggested a bond, by which ten thousand pieces of gold should be paid by the latter as a dowry, in the event of his refusing to repudiate his wife the next morning; if he did so, the old merchant covenanted to pay him two thousand pieces of gold, on condition of his immediate departure from the city. The bond was duly signed by both parties, and the damsel's father introduced him into the house of Zobeide as her temporary husband, the precaution having been taken of employing one of those convenient liars, a female friend of the family, to persuade both bride and bridegroom that the other was afflicted with contagious leprosy.

Curiosity baffled the well-laid scheme: the voice of Abushamat, as he chanted a chapter of the Koran after supper, was so sweet that it attracted the attention of the divorced. She eyed him from behind a curtain, recognized her youthful admirer at Cairo, detected the artifice of the friend of the family, and spurning the coyness of decorum, fearlessly entered his room, and reminded him of their former meeting. He needed not this: her features had been indelibly impressed upon his memory. He laughed at the accusation of leprosy, bared his own pure arm, gazed, not from suspicion but from ardour at the snowy lustre of her exposed skin, and forgot both past sorrows and future anxieties in the rapturous emotions of the present. It seemed to them that Providence had destined them for each other, and their mutual caresses evinced the passionate fervour of their feelings.

Next morning, ere they arose, Abushamat narrated all the incidents of his life to Zobeide, explaining how he had only one brief hour to linger with her. She inquired in whose hands was the matrimonial tie; and when he replied that the law, indeed, was in his favour as to retaining her, but that he neither possessed the gold for her dowry, nor even wherewithal to maintain her, she bade him be of good courage. "Take these hundred pieces of gold," she continued; "had I more I would give them to you; but such affection does my father entertain for his nephew, that he has removed all my property, even to my very trinkets, from this house to his own. Do not yield me, dear one; else, not being of age, I should a second time, against my inclination, be doomed to marry my hateful cousin."

"But how can I resist so moneyed an opponent as my father-in-law?" inquired the young man.

"By following my directions you can, at least, retard proceedings, and who knows what may occur hereafter? Be liberal with this money to the Cadi, and to any of the officials who can favour you; refuse to give me up; speak boldly of your resources, but plead for delay."

Scarcely was Abushamat dressed, when he was cited by a law-officer to attend the court of the Cadi. Putting five pieces in the hand of the summoner, he requested his advice, he himself, as he owned, being both inexperienced and a stranger to the laws of that city.

"Inquire of the Cadi, respectfully, by what code of laws it is ordained that he who marries at night should be forcibly unmarried in the morning."

The counsel seemed judicious, and was followed. Our hero, on entering the court, found his father-in-law awaiting him, advanced to the Cadi, and whilst kissing his hand, adroitly slipped fifty pieces into it. He then humbly inquired whether the law of that particular city compelled him to abandon the woman he had been legally united to; and when reminded of the alternative, the payment of the gold, pleading the difficulty of realizing, at once, so large a sum without sacrificing his goods, he obtained ten days' grace from the well-bribed justice.

Overjoyed with this reprieve, the young couple spent the evening in feasting, joking, and singing; for both of them had sweet yet powerful voices, and the lute-playing of the bride might have made the very stones to move in vibrating sympathy. The bridegroom was delighted with her performance; and not he alone, for scarcely had she ceased when four dervishes rapped at the door requesting admission on the score of their passionate love for music, which, to use their own expression, was spiritual meat and drink to them. Moreover, they asserted, they themselves were no mean proficients in poetry and singing.

There are times when our good-humour is such, that we would like all the world to share in our happiness. In such a mood were the two revellers, and, unusual as was the request, they welcomed the self-invited guests, offering them refreshments and chatting unreservedly with them. The time passed merrily with song and joke and mutual tale-telling. Abushamat, for the young are rarely reticent,—beware of the reserved, for such are ever on the watch to overreach the frank—related to them, before they left, his past history and his present dilemma.

" Be not uneasy as to the stipulated dowry," said one of

the dervishes as they quitted for the night; "for I am sheikh of a large community, and from our joint funds we will lend you the money, and wait for remittances from your father at Cairo."

Next morning, as the damsel lifted up the prayer-carpet, she perceived some gold that had been purposely left for her by their late guests, and being quick-witted, she prepared all things requisite for their entertainment that evening. They came and made a merry night of it; left a liberal recompense for their hospitality, and so continued as constant visitors for the first nine nights; yet no reference was again made to the promised loan. On the tenth, the last night of immunity from compulsory separation, no money had arrived, and the hearts of the lovers were too sad for singing. The dervishes, too, absented themselves from the house.

The dreaded morning came, and a loud rapping seemed to the fond pair to portend that their happiness had passed away for ever.

"It is your father," exclaimed Abushamat. "He has come to drag me to the Cadi: but what means the long train of loaded mules which block up the street?"

"We shall see," said Zobeide, who always looked to the bright side of things, and had some indistinct notion of its connection with the promise made by the chief dervish; so the old man was admitted; he came in smiling, accompanied by a fine-looking but dark-complexioned slave, an Abyssinian, who having respectfully kissed the hand of Abushamat, delivered him a letter. It purported to come from Cairo, and was to the following effect:—

"Having heard the tidings of your mishap, which has involved the loss of your entire venture, I have replaced it by another of equal value; and, as news of your marriage has likewise reached me, I forward you also by my trusty Selim, fifty thousand pieces of gold to defray your dowry and other necessary expenses. Accept, as marriage-gifts, a robe of sable from your mother (who congratulates you upon your union with her young friend Zobeide), and a gold ewer and basin from your loving father, Shemseddin."

Our hero was delighted, and embraced the old merchant; saying, "Now I can pay you your daughter's dowry, and whatever profit you can make above the cost price of my goods, I beg you to retain for yourself."

"Nay, by Allah!" was his answer, "I am not so mean; you shall have all they fetch in the market; and as for the dowry, give it to my girl yourself." For the father-in-law was now well pleased with the apparent opulence of the husband of his daughter. His nephew, however, from deep conviction that his own violent temper had lost him a woman of whom he was passionately fond, pined away and soon succumbed to a slight disease.

Who so happy as Abushamat, who could not comprehend the mystery of this opportune arrival of treasure, but accepted it carelessly as the bounty of Providence. That evening, when the tapers had been lighted and the music and singing of the loving couple sounded sweetly in the streets, the lute of Zobeide seemed a spell which evoked the presence of the dervishes.

"I have half a mind to exclude those fellows for breaking their word," exclaimed the husband as he heard their loud rapping; "they came not to console me when I wanted them last night."

"They were less wealthy than they supposed, poor fellows.; they were ashamed to show themselves without the gold; recollect what we owe to them," pleaded his more indulgent wife.

"Come in, you jolly promise-breakers," said the joyous Abushamat, who received them heartily; "no thanks to you that I am not in prison, for I would never have divorced my Zobeide;" and he ushered them into his saloon, and made them welcome as of old. Before they left, he accounted, at their request, for his escape from the clutches of the law, by narrating to them his reconciliation with his wife's father, consequent upon his receipt of the letter and merchandise from Cairo.

"But," said one of the guests, not the sheikh of the convent, "I cannot comprehend your statement. How many days' journey is it to your father's home?"

"Five-and-forty, or thereabouts."

"And what time has elapsed since your caravan was attacked?"

"Not a fortnight."

"So the work of ninety days—half needful for the tidings and half for the arrival of the goods—is magically performed in fourteen!"

"It is that which puzzles my brains. I would give half my fortune to solve the mystery!"

"It shall not cost you a dirrhem, my host," responded the questioner. "I am permitted by the Commander of the Faithful, who sits opposite us," and he pointed to the sheikh, "to reveal the whole secret to you. I am Giafar, and my two companions are Mesroor and Hassan, confederates of the Caliph in many a merry adventure. Chance led us to your street; your music attracted our attention; your frankness and liberality won the heart of your Sovereign, and to *his* munificence you are indebted for your rescue from ruin."

Abushamat prostrated himself reverently before Haroun Alraschid, and poured forth his gratitude with an unpremeditated eloquence which astonished even himself. The Caliph, who was as much gratified now by the evident warmth of his heart and the fluent choiceness of his language, as he had been amused by his previous simplicity and good-fellowship, raised him kindly, and briefly continued the explanation. "I concocted the letter from what I had gleaned from your conversation, and purchased the usual stuffs from Cairo and a slave from Abyssinia (for you mentioned your father had several from that barbarous land), the better to deceive you. And now the mystery has been solved come to my Court to-morrow, and you shall find that Haroun is no less your friend in his royal palace, than he has proved himself to be in your humbler residence."

The Caliph was as good as his word. He received Abushamat with gracious condescension, often invited him to the royal banquets, and, as years rolled on and his natural ability displayed itself, promoted him to high offices as they became vacant.

Haziz paused, and the hunter-prince, who evidently

felt no especial regard for a hero who, after the chivalrous aspirations of his youth, succeeded in love and fortune, through sheer good luck, thus commented upon him :—

"He was favoured by destiny, and did not merit her kindness. Somehow, in every story, the careless and the reckless find both friends and fortune."

"Is it not so in life?" responded Haziz. "All women, and most men, love to patronize: those who seek not to raise themselves are pitied for their helplessness, and hence regarded as the most suitable objects for compassion. However, when Abushamat had grown older and better, he too had his share of that suffering which is allotted to all of us."

"Relate, then, my friend, the rest of his career."

Haziz turned his eyes towards the face of Suleiman, who nodded his assent. He then continued:—

So long as Zobeide lived, all was well with Abushamat; wealth, power, the respect and regard of all he had dealings with, flowed upon him; he became the intimate of the Caliph, the friend of Giafar, and the benefactor of the poor. But Haroun was choleric and suspicious, easy of belief, and mercilessly just. He thought himself slighted, too, because, when the Sovereign, in a fit of good-nature, had sent Abushamat one of his discarded favourites to replace the loss of his bride, the now thrifty widower, unwilling to incur the expense of maintaining a mistress whose attendants alone numbered more than forty, had contrived to evade the ruinous gift by repeating the old adage, 'What is suitable for the master is not fitting for the servant.'

After a while the sense of loneliness prevailed, and Abushamat, having been presented by the good-humoured despot with ten thousand pieces of gold for the express purpose of buying a beautiful slave-girl, to erase, by her charms, the image of his lost wife, and thus restore him to his pristine cheerfulness (for the Caliph sadly missed the merry jokes and other convivial qualities of his depressed boon-companion), successfully competed with the Emir Khalid, the Wali of Bagdad, for the lovely Yasemeen.

That official, whose own experience of the sex would not have led him to purchase a concubine for himself, had attended the market under the following circumstances: —He had, by his wife Khatoon, an only son, who had been named Habazlam Bazazah. This child was the one great sorrow of his life; for the father, a fine-looking, noble-hearted warrior, could not hide from himself the painful knowledge that his son was hideous as a baboon, pusillanimous, half-idiotic, foul in person and in odour. He had now become a man, and the doting mother, aware that no woman would voluntarily accept her poor monster as a husband, enjoined her consort to purchase a slave-girl for his gratification.

Bazazah and his parent sought everywhere for a beautiful female, but none would hit the fancy of the former, save the exquisite Yasemeen, whose price, however, was so enormous, that prudence forbade her purchase by his father.

The disappointed youth had the sulks, took to his bed,

and easily persuaded his foolish and unprincipled mother that he would die if he could not possess the woman he was longing for. Khatoon knew that the noble Emir would never lend himself to any intrigue that should be unworthy of a man of honour; hence she consulted an old hag, who had often proved serviceable to her in matters of questionable propriety.

"In helping me out of *my* trouble, you will help yourself," said the adviser. "My boy, Ahmad Kamakim, is the cleverest rogue in the world, and once at large will accomplish your wishes, however difficult their attainment may prove. He is so bold a burglar that no house is safe from him; so still and cunning that he could steal the kohl from your eyelid without waking you! Only induce the Wali to let him loose, and Yasemeen is your son's."

It was not an easy task to prevail with the Wali, against the dictates of his reason; but there was no rest for him at home, until he had assented to her repeatedly urged request. Young wives seek to conquer by coquetting, old by worrying. Contrary to his better judgment, and willingly deluded by the assumed repentance of the imprisoned scoundrel (and this new piety, though distrusted, was the conscience-salve of Khalid, who knew he was wronging society by releasing an enemy to it), he besought the grace of the Caliph "for a poor wretch (the only son and support of a widowed mother), who had long pined in solitary confinement, and whose fervent regret for his past misdeeds was the best assurance that he would henceforth lead the life of an honest man."

Of this repentance, so repulsive was the gross expression of the criminal's countenance (for the robber had been led before him in chains and in his prison garb to stimulate his sense of mercy), the Caliph was not so sure; yet so rarely was he importuned by the Wali, that he not only forgave the canting scoundrel, but bestowed a small appointment upon him, that he might not be tempted to crime from inability to support his feeble mother.

Bad as the thief was there was nothing he would not do for his aged parent, who merited not his regard, since her own wicked example, and the evil principles she had unwittingly instilled, had vitiated his better nature. She told him the bargain she had made with the wife of the Wali, whose intercession had saved him from that perpetual imprisonment to which he had been condemned, and bade him devise some scheme by which both Abushamat should perish and Yasemeen become the property of Bazazah. The ruffian, a man of few words, nodded his assent, and that very night commenced proceedings.

His aim was to throw suspicion upon Abushamat, and thus did he accomplish it. He was aware that the Caliph passed the first night of the month in the apartments of Zobeide, and was in the habit of leaving his royal signet and a jewelled dagger upon the chair in the sitting-room, under charge of certain of his eunuchs. Ahmad Kamakim, although he dearly loved the juice of the vine, kept himself sober that evening, and waited with sullen patience until half the night was over. Taking a crowbar, some cement, a grappling-iron and cord, and a few other implements which might possibly be found requisite, he slunk, in the darkness, along the bye-lanes until he reached the garden-wall of the palace, which he easily crossed by the hooked end of the cord, and arrived before the private saloon of Zobeide. It was an outlying building that projected into the garden, and was easily accessible from above by a kind of trap-door in the roof, which had been constructed for the purpose of ventilating the apartment. To reach this elevation by his cord and grappling-iron was but the work of a minute for so expert a climber; to open the trap without waking the sleepers (he had rightly divined the eunuchs would not keep awake) required more care; but practice makes perfect, and, by the aid of his cord, he safely descended, secured the valuables, and retraversing the same route, left no trace behind him by which he might be tracked. Thence he hied to the mansion of Abushamat, who was tranquilly reposing in the arms of Yasemeen, broke in with equal facility, prised up a slab of marble with his crowbar, quickly secreted the royal signet beneath it, carefully cemented the edges of the stone, replaced it, and crept out again without disturbing any of the household. Retaining the dagger as a compensation for his disinterested services, he sneaked back to his foul lair, silently chuckling at his rapid success.

The signet was vainly sought for next morning, and the head of the police was summoned to the palace. Haroun was very wroth (as the eunuchs felt to their cost), yet knew not whom to suspect. The officer suggested, from so many other valuables being left behind, that the robbery was not the deed of an ordinary thief, but the work of some traitor of elevated rank, who purposed availing himself of the royal seal for forgery or some other nefarious project. He requested a search-warrant, which should enable him to enter the abodes of all persons whatsoever, however high might be their station, and, armed with this authority, departed upon his quest.

Upon the principle that a clever thief proves the best thief-taker, Ahmad Kamakim's small appointment had been in the police department. He had already exhibited such zeal and dexterity in his new calling, that his voluntary offer to trace the offender involved him in no suspicion. Bearing with him a weird-looking staff, the upper third of copper, the middle of bronze, the base of iron, which he used as a divining-rod, and followed by the Cadi and an adequate guard, he touched with it the doorstep of one of the ministers, listened to its sound, shook his head, and passed on to the residence of a second, then he came to the abode of his doomed victim. A sonorous clang, noticed by all the officers, issued from the rod as it struck the step; he entered, vibrating it gently to and fro, and seemingly following its guidance. Eventually he stopped before the marble flag beneath which he had hidden the signet, caused it to be raised, and lo! the lost treasure was descried by all the spectators. The immediate arrest and condemnation of Abushamat succeeded; his effects were registered as confiscated to the state; Yasemeen was surreptitiously removed to the harem of Khalid, and carefully kept by Khatoon beyond the ken of the Emir.

Among the many friends of Abushamat was the superintendent of the prisons, who felt perfectly conscious of the innocence of the former, and resolved to save him. The gaoler happened to have under his custody an avowed murderer, who in features, but not in stature or complexion, bore some passing resemblance to the late favourite of Haroun, and by the connivance of the executioner, who was bribed equally with himself, substituted that delinquent for the guiltless prisoner. When, the day after the execution, which was by hanging, the body was examined for the purpose of identification, the marked differences were too palpable to be lightly passed over.

"How is this? Abushamat was a shorter man than this corpse."

"The limbs become lengthened by suspension," was the reply.

"His skin, also, was much lighter."

"A body becomes livid from strangulation," was the answer.

"Let his heels be inspected."

Upon them was inscribed the name of Omar, a practice of the sect of the Rafidees, by which they evinced their contempt for that Caliph by continually trampling, as it were, upon his memory.

"Abushamat was a Sunnee; this man must have been of the rival creed."

"He who deceived the Caliph in one thing may have deceived us all in another," was the artful rejoinder.

It was rumoured, indeed, by many, that Abushamat, who fled to Cairo, and for very many years lived in secret with his father, was still alive; but no man cared to pry further into the matter.

Poor Yasemeen, when led to the bedside of the love-sick Bazazah, so strenuously refused to become his mistress or even his bride, that the indignant mother stripped her of her fine apparel, clad her in the garments of a menial slave, and degraded her to the service of the kitchen. The sweetness of her disposition, however, and her manifest delicacy, so affected the sympathies of her fellow-servants that they relieved her from the more degrading offices (such as fire-lighting, wood-cutting, and such-like coarse work) which had been allotted to her by the malice of Khatoon.

Not many months after these occurrences, Habazlam Bazazah died, and Yasemeen was delivered of a male child, whom she named Aslan, as beautiful as herself. When two years old the infant strayed, accidentally, to the spot where the Emir Khalid was reclining, and the childless parent, who was of a loving disposition, caressed him for his beauty and for his likeness to his old acquaintance, Abushamat. His mother ventured before her master to remove her stray darling, and, when questioned as to the parentage of the child, proudly acknowledged that he sprang from Abushamat.

"Henceforth, then," said Khalid, "I adopt him for my son; and when he shall be old enough to ask you the name of his father, remember to indicate *me* as his sire. It would be prejudicial to his future, that he should be deemed the offspring of a felon." She obeyed his wishes, and, under the kind tutelage of the Emir, the pretty boy ripened into the handsome youth, trained alike in the literary studies and warlike sports of the higher classes of that Moslem city.

It chanced, when he was nearly a man, that he accidentally encountered, in a public place of refreshment, the ex-thief, Ahmad Kamakim. The fellow was much intoxicated, and in a boastful way displayed a dagger, the hilt of which was adorned with precious stones of no ordinary value; an ornament which, for many years after its acquisition, he had not dared to exhibit, but which now, thinking it must have been forgotten after so long a lapse of time, he openly carried and tacitly bragged of.

"Whence did you procure so exquisite a dagger?" inquired Aslan, who could scarcely avoid coveting so splendid a weapon.

"Son of Khalid, to you alone may I reveal the truth; I earned this through the hot passion of your dead brother, Bazazah, for a pretty slave-girl;" and he fearlessly narrated the whole of his villainy, not doubting the secrecy of the supposed child of his employer, Khatoon.

Much disgusted with his associate, Aslan left the room, and having casually lighted upon the superintendent of prisons, related the whole story to him. His strong likeness to Abushamat immediately struck the official, who having elicited from him the name of his mother, told the young man truly, that Yasemeen, if pressed, would acknowledge he was the son of his beloved friend, Abushamat, who was still in the land of the living. Shortly after this *rencontre,* Aslan accompanied the Emir Khalid to the court of the Caliph, and was permitted to join his Sovereign in playing at goff. A heavy ball, apparently aimed at the Commander of the Faithful, and which, had it struck him in the forehead, might have proved fatal to him, was warded off by the young man, with such adroitness, indeed, that returning from whence it had been propelled, it struck the player between his shoulders and dashed him from his horse.

"Thou hast saved me, young man," exclaimed the monarch, "and whatever may be thy request, I will grant it in requital."

"Vengeance upon him who ruined my father."

"Is not he thy father who stands yonder?" said the Caliph, as he pointed to the Emir Khalid.

"He, indeed, is my second father; but he from whom I sprang was thy faithful Abushamat!"

"What, the felon who stole my signet and my dagger?"

"He was innocent. Ahmad Kamakim was the thief, and upon him will be found the dagger."

Then Aslan related the confession of the thief, who, when subsequently arrested and searched, at first protested that he had honestly bought the dagger; but when cross-examined as to his means of purchasing so costly a weapon, involved himself in such a tissue of contradictions, that he was judged worthy of death, and handed over to the executioner. He obtained his life, however, by a voluntary confession, which fully exculpated the falsely-accused parent of the Caliph's preserver. The remainder of his wretched existence was passed in solitary confinement.

Need I say that Abushamat was recalled from exile, reunited to his Yasemeen, had his confiscated property restored to him, was reinstated in his official posts, and lived long and happily in peace and affluence? As to Aslan, he passed his time alternately with each of his two fathers, whom he loved so equally, that he could never determine which he preferred.

Next evening Haziz in his turn essayed to amuse his royal patrons:—

THE MAID OF NINEVEH.*

In the early ages of the world, as our traditions inform us, three mighty empires were co-existent,—Egypt, Persia, and Assyria,—which were sometimes at peace, sometimes at war, yet always linked together by the golden ties of commerce. Of these, Persia was the youngest, the least in magnitude, and the least civilized; but her population, not yet enervated by luxury, the most hardy and warlike.

Sanharib† at this time swayed the sceptre of Assyria, and now passed his life in peaceful indolence; yet, when younger, few monarchs had exhibited a more martial prowess, a more vigorous intellect. His Prime Minister, Hicah, however, who was prudent, just, and able, was so attentive to the affairs of state, that the people missed not the active superintendence of their Sovereign; not having a son, he was not tempted, like many of his predecessors in office, to aspire to the crown. His whole affections were concentrated upon his only daughter, and it was the height of his ambition to wed her to some prince or nobleman, who might maintain her in the style to which she was accustomed. Unfortunately for his plans, she was of so ardent a temperament that her heart had yielded to

* From 'Uns el Wujood, Aboo the Lazy, and the Two Viziers.'

† Sennacherib.

love, almost before she had reached womanhood; and the object of her affection, however much he might have personally merited her hand, was neither in rank nor fortunes entitled to demand it. He was a naturalized Arab, an officer of that foreign cavalry legion which had so greatly assisted the King in his earlier campaigns.

It was a custom in those times, one which has survived even to our own days, to assemble together the royal armies for a grand review, and, after the whole of the troops had been counted and inspected, to proclaim gymnastic sports and exercises, with prizes for those who might distinguish themselves by their agility and dexterity. Preeminent among all was a very handsome youth, El Wujood by name, who not only carried off the highest honours by his skilful horsemanship, but bore away with him the heart of the impressible daughter of the Prime Minister, who, with others of her sex, had accompanied her parents to view the games and evolutions. From the lattice-work of her gilded litter she had beheld his smile of triumph, had eagerly questioned her former nurse as to his name, and despite of her seeming repugnance, forced her by mingled bribes and caresses, to convey to him a note, in which she displayed the warmth of her passionate admiration and her determination to be his despite of every obstacle which might impede their union.

Charmed with this epistle, and aided by the old intriguer, first a correspondence and then an assignation followed, a meeting which for ever affected the destinies of the young soldier; for so lovely was the girl, so fresh and unreserved in her impulsive artlessness, that no man could have quitted her without longing to possess her as his bride. Success makes us reckless of precaution. When their hearts had been inextricably knit together, the old nurse having carelessly dropped one of the many love-letters of "Rosebud"* (for such was the pet name her lover had given her), it was picked up by one of the attendants and delivered to the master of the house. The perusal of it painfully affected Hicah, for although its contents were such that no anxiety as to the purity of his child harassed his feelings, yet it breathed such ardent love, it evinced such an intensity of passion, that he felt assured that absence alone, and that not temporary, but permanent, could eradicate such deeply-rooted tenderness from the bosom of his daughter.

With a healthy mind, to resolve is to execute. Within four-and-twenty hours the damsel had been removed from her home, hurriedly transported to the seaside by the ordinary and somewhat rough arrangements for the government couriers, and, from thence, been more leisurely ferried across to a pretty islet, upon which the Prime Minister had erected a palace as an occasional residence. It was the sole abode, except a few fishermen's huts, permitted by him on that lonely spot; so desolate was it, that, although furnished with the extreme of luxury, and well stored with all that might tempt the palate, his dependants regarded their enforced retirement to it as a veritable exile.

Although El Wujood was both grieved and surprised by the girl's mysterious silence (so sudden was her departure that no intimation of it could be conveyed to him), he,

* El Ward fi l. Akmam.

nevertheless, was not the man to relinquish his mistress without an effort to recover her. He readily guessed the reason of her absence, but it was less easy to detect the precise spot to which she had been conveyed. Being in high favour with his Sovereign, he obtained leave of absence for six months, and devoted them to exploring every route by which she might possibly have been borne from him. After many a failure and much privation (for the country in parts was barren and deserted), he eventually, by diligent inquiries from stage to stage, traced the concealed journey of his beloved almost to the sea, and then by a not illogical deduction, conjectured that she had been taken to the summer retreat of her noble father. When at length, worn out by continual exertion and frequent want of food, he arrived at the beach from whence his mistress had embarked, he found the shore wholly deserted, not even the barque of a solitary fisherman being visible. Then desperation came to his aid; he felt assured, from the evidence he had previously obtained, that the maiden had been transported to that green islet on which the sun was now casting his rays in dying splendour. Alone (for he had no attendants) he could not hope to construct a boat sufficiently seaworthy to bear him across to the prison of his beloved; but he watched the ebb and flow of the tide, and perceived there was a current which would, in all probability, waft any light object to a pier-like ridge which jutted from the opposite rocks. So having collected some hollow gourds, he tied them together by a kind of network made from woody creepers, and, having watched the direction of the wind, he threw himself upon this fragile raft, and, though partially and sometimes wholly immersed, was safely, though slowly drifted onwards to the much-desired land. Poor wretch! fortune was still adverse to him; that very morning his 'Rosebud' had disappeared from her prison-home.

From afar off the young Arab had descried the white turrets of the castellated mansion in which his mistress had been immured; his eyes gazed intently upon them as passively he floated to and fro upon the calm ocean. Faint, wet, hungry, and weary, he scrambled up the rocks which led to the main entrance of the building, and staggered whilst he asked admission as a shipwrecked mariner. It was granted him by a kind-hearted eunuch, who, having ascertained that he was a fellow-countryman, took much interest in his sufferings. From him he learnt, what indeed he was already well assured of, the name of the proprietor of the solitary islet, and asked if the mansion was at present occupied. "It belongs to Hicah, the Prime Minister of the King of Assyria," was the reply; "and, until yesterday, his daughter, whom for some fault or other he had banished, dwelt in this dreary castle, and cheered us all by her sympathetic kindness. Yet, poor girl, she was very sad herself, and pined for the loss of a warrior she was attached to. We missed her last night and have vainly sought for her; we fear she has thrown herself in despair from the battlements."

At this annihilation of his hopes, El Wujood, man and soldier though he was, fainted; he had endured so much in his pursuit of her; he had tracked her so painfully to the place of her concealment that the utter failure of his plans at the apparent moment of success, was a shock too overwhelming for his enfeebled frame. When he woke up from his trance the foolish grin of a simpering idiot was fixed upon his countenance; utter oblivion of the past alone prevented a fit of raving madness. In those days, even among the Gentiles, he who was deprived of reason was befriended by his fellow-creatures (for Heaven has used the lips of these innocents as vehicles for prophetic revelations); so all the domestics treated him with kindness, attended to his wants, and watched over his safety.

The lost damsel, however, had not perished; her nature was too daring, her frame too healthy, to yield to the dictates of despair. She had, indeed, as was surmised, ascended to the roof of her luxurious prison-house, but so far from casting herself into the ocean, she had used every precaution to avoid injury in descending. Having knotted her garments and linked them securely to each other (and her ample store of raiment herein proved most serviceable), she had managed to reach the ground in perfect safety, and had stealthily directed her course, beneath the jutting cliffs, to a little inlet, towards which she had perceived the solitary boat of a fisherman was steering. Clad in her richest clothes and decked with her most precious jewels, her loveliness, her persuasiveness, and her liberal offers, proved irresistible to the boatman, who abstained from his intended fishing and bore her off immediately to the mainland. She had no definite project in thus escaping, but there was an all-pervading feeling, that thus and thus only could she again rejoin the man to whom she had given her virgin love. Poor soul! she was unwittingly flying from the very being to embrace whom she would have given half her existence. His improvised raft must have been crossing from the mainland at the very time her boat was rocking upon the water; for the wind had at first been contrary, and nearly two days elapsed before she reached the opposite shore. The storm which then raged had driven her barque far to the east, and eventually cast it a shattered wreck upon the coast of Persia. The ruler of that empire, a noble and generous-hearted man, chanced to be sojourning for a while at a palace near the sea, and to be present when the inanimate form of a richly-apparelled and lovely girl was dashed upon the beach. He caused her to be tended with every care, and, when she had recovered, listened attentively to a relation of her sorrows. Her beauty and her rank (for the superb balass rubies which adorned her tiny ears corroborated her claims to princely station) interested him in her behalf, and commiserating the distress of the love-sick maiden, he promised his active interference to promote her happiness. Accordingly he sent a letter to his then ally, the King of Assyria, and begged him to intercede with his Prime Minister for the pardon (if not the union) of his daughter.

The lord of Nineveh, who regarded El Wujood as the most promising of his warriors, and who was likewise desirous of gratifying his royal ally, sent messengers to seek for the former, and dispatched Hicah to the Court of Persia, to bring back his willingly-pardoned daughter. Nevertheless, that high official would not consent to yield his child in marriage to a portionless adventurer.

Luck, however, at length befriended the Arab. In

his semi-idiotic state he would stretch himself at full length upon the sand, and from morn to night stare listlessly upon the rolling waves. He would not abandon his position even to eat, and merely moaned when the cravings of nature urged him to appease his appetite. So the kind-hearted eunuch and his fellow-slaves would feed him as a child, and carry him to and from that shore which he ever unwillingly quitted. He had never told his name; and now he no longer spoke, but grinned in answer when addressed by the nickname some boys had given him—"Aboo the Lazy."

One day a ship of some magnitude approached the islet, as near as was consistent with safety; and then the sailors lowered a boat and rowed towards the mansion. The captain landed and threw his arms around the eunuch, saluting him as his long-lost brother. After a brief stay he took his departure, but offered before he went to receive any commissions for the far West which the household might intrust to him. Each slave risked some little sum as a venture, and at last it was suggested that the money found in the pocket of the idiot should be used in his behalf. Only a few pieces of gold were found in his purse, which he allowed them to abstract without troubling himself to move; yet from these few pieces sprang such a harvest of wealth that he was rendered independent for the rest of his existence.

It happened thus wise. The ship had been hired by certain traders who, having but a limited capital, roamed from port to port bartering away what they had procured from one country for a different cargo, which they knew would be saleable in some adjoining one. By this mode, their returns being very quick, they often realized large sums by a single voyage; yet as their chief gains were made by trafficking with savage or semi-civilized races, who paid very heavily in raw produce for manufactured articles, their risks were commensurate with their gains.

The captain had invested the little sum he had received as the venture of the idiot in the purchase of a large ape, which had become a general favourite with the sailors, and which evinced a most remarkable sagacity. The rough mariners had taught it many tricks, and the captain hoped to sell it when trained at a considerable profit. Circumstances rendered it so precious to all of them, that it was retained out of gratitude. A violent gale had blown the vessel, far away from its intended course, towards an island wholly unknown to all on board. The harbour was fine, and as vegetables and fresh water were urgently required by the crew, the ship was anchored, and the whole of the merchant-adventurers, wearied of their long confinement, landed to refresh themselves.

The foliage was luxuriant, the air balmy, and the general aspect so delightful, that none remained on board excepting those whose services were absolutely required for the management of the ship. As no vestige of a hut or cabin met their eyes, and neither man nor beast was visible near their landing-place, but all was still and alluring to their senses, they dispersed themselves in scattered groups, gathering the wild fruits from the tangled woodland. On a sudden they were simultaneously set upon by an almost pigmy race of naked blacks, who swarmed down the trees (by the foliage of which their nest-like huts had been concealed) and clung in crowded clusters upon the venturous individuals who had trespassed upon their domain. Resistance was hopeless: all yielded to the legion of little blacks, who had taken them by surprise, and were now menacing with shining daggers those who refused to be pinioned. One seaman alone dared to oppose them, and him the curly-haired cannibals not only slew upon the spot, but ere his body was cold grilled slices of it upon a fire, and ravenously devoured them before his shuddering comrades. Aboo's ape (for so it was designated) had been landed with the voyagers; he was an amusing companion, and had grown so tame and been so petted that no one feared he would wish to escape. Swinging himself from bough to bough, he merely grinned and chattered at the negroes, while they were assaulting his friends, and kept himself at a safe distance from their clutches; but when night came, and the savages having tightly-bound their collected captives to the trunks of some lofty trees, had climbed to their elevated huts, the faithful beast crawled in the darkness to his master, the captain, unloosed the ropes of fibre by which he was bound, and then aided him likewise in setting free his shipmates. Their release was effected without noise, and the whole party retreated, without interruption from their captors, to their boats, thrust them from the shore and silently rejoined the vessel.

Whilst fervent gratitude for their escape was the prevalent feeling, and money was of no account compared with their safety, the captain proposed a general subscription for the benefit of the poor idiot, whose money had purchased the animal which had preserved them. All gave so liberally that the capital of the absent Aboo became the largest of the whole company of adventurers. The entirety of this sum was risked by his proxy, the captain, in the pearl fishery, and so remarkable was the luck of the divers when exerted on his behalf, that Aboo's stock of pearls was such as princes might have envied him.

All these events occupied many months, during which El Wujood had been removed to the Persian coast by the thoughtful Hicah, who anticipated that the sight of his imbecility would prove an effectual cure for the undesirable passion of his daughter for so poor a match.

Strange to relate, in place of disgust for his mental feebleness being the effect produced by an interview between the blooming girl and her fatuous lover, she was all commiseration for the noble mind wrecked from love of her; whilst both memory and intellect partially revived in him, as he wistfully gazed upon her well-remembered face. And day by day his brain strengthened, and in a very brief space Aboo the Lazy became again the active El Wujood.

Between this happy crisis, and the previous banishment of 'Rosebud,' events had occurred at Nineveh which seriously affected the life and fortunes of Hicah. Considering that his daughter had for ever disgraced herself by her imprudent advances to the Arab officer, that great statesman resolved to replace her in his affections by adopting another heir. In vain did his wife implore him to desist from a project which to her seemed not only fraught with wrong to their own child, but pregnant with danger from the known duplicity of that nephew whom he intended to adopt. Men of the world invariably prefer unscrupulous ability to conscientious mediocrity; hence Hicah trained Nadan for his future successor and occasional substitute, in the confident belief that his recommendation of so astute a politician to his Sovereign would redound to his own credit and convenience.

For a while Nadan conducted himself with the most prudent decorum. By a chilling reserve he concealed the profligacy, the rapacity, and the intense selfishness which were his natural characteristics, until circumstances permitted him to openly practise them with impunity. He had improved his intellect, which was far from contemptible, by studious application, and had acquired those business habits (a combination of punctuality, memory, shrewdness, and alertness) which are needed alike by the statesman and the merchant. So long as Hicah was present Nadan was useful and subordinate; but when his patron had left the capital to bring home his daughter, then the natural malignity of his disposition broke forth, and he manœuvred to immediately eject his uncle from his post, and be substituted in his place.

To effect this, he first ingratiated himself with his royal master by cordially sympathizing with his pleasures, and enabling him to indulge his indolence by his own assiduous application to business. Then, when his services had become indispensable, he gradually insinuated doubts as to the fidelity of Hicah, and revived the old jealousy of Persia (the natural enemy of Assyria, as he termed her) in the bosom of his Sovereign. At last he crowned his treachery by so crafty a trick, that the monarch, despite of twenty years' fidelity on the part of his minister, may readily be pardoned for having mistrusted him. He counterfeited the writing of the Prime Minister, whose seal had been left in his charge, and attached an impression of the latter to forged documents addressed nominally by Hicah to all his traitor friends, but in reality to all those nobles who, having penetrated the fawning duplicity of Nadan, had become his political opponents. This paper, which purported to emanate from the head of a vast conspiracy, comprehending among its members all the most honourable of the aristocracy of Nineveh (so that Nadan might sweep away all his adversaries by a single blow), apprised the supposititious correspondents of the early approach of a host of Persian troops, bade certain tributary princes to raise their vassals against their sluggish Suzerain, and other parties to open the city gates upon the assault of the invading army. The cleverest part of this iniquitous scheme was the mode in which the trustworthy and incorruptible courier of Hicah was forced to become an unwilling witness against his master. A facsimile of his dispatch-bag was fabricated, and by a dexterous exchange effected by a hired confederate (a thief who was liberated expressly for the job), the forged documents were substituted for the real letters of friendly gossip which the old minister had forwarded to his friends. When the courier had been arrested, at the suggestion of the adopted son, he acknowledged his having received the contents of the bag from the hands of his lord.

The enraged monarch, who could not withstand such incontrovertible evidence of the treachery of his minister, would have confiscated his property and put him to death had he been then in his dominions; but at the request of Nadan, his near relative, who did not wish to lose a rich inheritance, and who urged that poverty and exile combined would be a full equivalent for capital punishment, contented himself by pronouncing a sentence of perpetual banishment upon Hicah, and by conferring his wealth and office upon the nephew, with a strict charge (only too readily obeyed) that no portion of the riches of his predecessor should be forwarded to him.

The arrival of messengers from Assyria, who announced to Hicah his banishment and utter ruin, and the return of the eunuch's brother, who brought home such unexpected wealth for El Wujood, occurred almost simultaneously. Then the Arab showed the sterling nobility of his soul by proffering all his newly-acquired riches to the impoverished minister, who refused to accept them as a gift, but wedded him to his daughter, and ever after lived with them as their cherished guest.

Once free from the moral control of their aged adviser, the ruler and his new minister wholly abandoned themselves to festive enjoyments, regarding the people committed to their charge by Heaven as mere machines for providing means of gratification to their lord. The sinews of government were relaxed; oppression and corruption became the rule, not the exception; the troops were unpaid and became demoralized; the cultivators refused to grow crops which were taken from them by the tax-gatherers; there was no employment for the peasantry, and universal disaffection prevailed throughout the country.

Pharaoh of Egypt resolved to snatch so favourable an opportunity for annexing the whole, or at least a portion, of Assyria to his fertile realm. Such was the prevailing discontent, that he believed, and with reason, that he might seize Nineveh itself without serious opposition. Yet wishing for a pretext to cover his violation of the existing treaty, he wrote as follows to the potentate whose dominions he had resolved to appropriate :—

"*Pharaoh of Egypt to Sanharib of Assyria, greeting.*

"The gods of Egypt have intrusted me with irresistible power solely that I may benefit my fellow-creatures.

"No people can be happy who are ruled over by the ignorant. It is my duty, then, to depose all incompetent sovereigns. It is asserted by your subjects that you are both silly yourself, and have none but the foolish around you. Either disprove this statement by sending me one talented enough to accomplish what I have written at the end of this letter (and he who fosters talent I own to be worthy of rule,) or descend from a throne of which you must be unworthy. I, reverentially, will provide a successor who shall carry out my designs for ameliorating the condition of mankind."

The postscript was equally terse and decided.

"Send me an architect who can build me a palace the foundations whereof shall not rest on earth. I will provide the materials."

Sanharib was terror-stricken upon the receipt of this demand. He abandoned at once and for ever his luxurious supineness : his old energies seemed to gush forth afresh. But it was impossible to reorganize his army, and to arm and discipline raw levies in time to resist such well-trained hosts as the King of Egypt would hurl upon him. He resolved, then, to attempt the aerial structure, and issued peremptory orders for the attendance of all his ministers and chief priests at a general council. In those days all learning was confined to the priestly order, and to the very few nobles who had been instructed by them.

Without an exception, all acknowledged their inability to accomplish the required task, although the boastful envoy, who had brought the letter, positively asserted that his royal master was too just to demand an impossibility, and that the builder of the royal pyramid would himself indicate how the feat might be achieved, to prove to all nations the national inferiority, and hence justifiable subjection, of the Assyrians.

A woman saved the nation from despair. The daughter of Hicah had returned to console her mother; her father, as I have narrated elsewhere, was well and prosperous. She demanded a strictly private audience with the King, and thus addressed him :—

"Leave, Sire, the conduct of this affair to myself; I will answer with my head for the successful solution of this enigmatical problem. The wit of woman is keener than that of man. Boldly reply that the builder is ready to commence operations, but that the workmen who are to lay the foundations being employed in the most distant region of your widely-spread empire, cannot possibly reach his capital for the next six months. Offer him any number of noble hostages he may demand for your peaceable abdication of the throne, if your architect should fail in so easy a task. At all events, the interval gained by this reply will enable you to offer a more protracted resistance to his invasion than the state of your army now permits, and who knows what good fortune (perchance the aid of Persia) may be hereafter in store for you?"

The advice was good, for delay was all-important. The King would have showered rewards upon her who had relieved him from his terrible embarrassment; she refused, however, every recompense but one, the pardon of her father, whose return she urged as absolutely essential to the success of her plans. His thoughtful wisdom, she declared, would carry out her crude project; the idea was her own, but the details, upon which everything depended must be devised by him.

Before she quitted the royal apartment, the magnanimous though misguided Sanharib assured her that he would in no event hold her responsible for her necessary failure, but felt deeply indebted to her for a subterfuge, so plausible that the lord of Egypt could not, without loss of prestige, refuse his acquiescence with the needful delay. It was settled, moreover, that Hicah should return in disguise, and that Nadan, whose neglect and incapacity were now apparent to the roused monarch, should be kept ignorant of all their schemes.

The Egyptian envoy was staggered by the easy nonchalance which marked the demeanour of the Assyrian ruler; he acknowledged the reasonableness of the required delay, and returned to his country bearing with him a hundred hostages, all carefully selected by 'Rosebud' from the adherents of Nadan; for she doubted not that the man who had betrayed his benefactor would betray his Sovereign likewise. She was not wrong in her mistrust, for Nadan had written to Pharaoh (though neither the damsel nor her royal confidant surmised it) that Sanharib only procrastinated to victual his fortresses upon the frontier, and to complete his preparations for a determined resistance. He had proffered the aid of himself and partisans to assist in overthrowing his present master, provided that he should be permitted to occupy the vacant throne as a tributary prince. He was actually base enough to offer to assassinate Sanharib, by means of his confederates, the timely removal of whom baffled a scheme which the Egyptian monarch would scarcely have countenanced, although he would not have hesitated to profit by the crime.

'Rosebud' now applied herself with diligence to the procution of her design, and was zealously aided by her husband upon whom devolved the difficult and perilous enterprise of procuring her the fitting instruments. She had heard that certain islands in the Southern Ocean were frequented by the colossal Rok, a bird whose strength and magnitude were such, that when adult it could carry off the calf of an elephant in its talons. These stupendous creatures seem to have been extirpated; for nowadays few if any travellers assert that they have seen them. Our heroine indulged the daring idea that it might be possible to train the unfledged young, if they could be successfully taken from their nests and subjected to a loving control. The risk was terrible; the destruction of the bold adventurer who should plunder the nest inevitable, should the parent birds surprise him; but El Wujood had the courage of a lion, the perseverance of an ant, and the craft of a fox; he was aided, too, by his ape, who proved an efficient coadjutor, and success crowned his efforts. He returned to Assyria with two immature birds, and both he and 'Rosebud' tended them with such affectionate care, that they became obedient to her signals. As soon as they could fly, a little boy (who was wont to feed them) was strapped upon the back of each, and directed his course by reins attached to the talons of the monster. After some little practice, as the ride was made preparatory to a meal, the birds readily permitted the children to mount them, and rose or descended in obedience to their voices.

Hicah had now returned from his exile, and under the name of Abicam the Sage, took upon himself the conduct of the embassy. Empowered by his Sovereign to order all things suitable to his dignity as an ambassador, or needful for his design, he started for Egypt with a retinue composed of the most stalwart men of the Assyrian nation, in order to convey the impression upon Pharaoh that he would meet no ignoble adversaries, should he persist in his scheme of enslaving the land of Nimrod. His escort was composed of many races, that he might demonstrate the vast extent of territory ruled over by Sanharib, and a cloud of wiry Arabs, under the command of El Wujood, surrounded the elephants which bore the trained birds within their towers, and guarded them from the prying eyes of curiosity.

The caravan reached Memphis without any unusual difficulty, and having announced the long-expected arrival of the Assyrian architect, received orders to await the presence of Pharaoh in that ancient city.

The priests of Osiris, the favourite god of the Egyptians, assured the monarch that, although the solution of the difficulty might possibly be guessed, the laying of an aerial foundation was practically impossible. Their statements encouraged the despot, who, after an interview with Abicam, had conceived so exalted an opinion of his ability, that he believed nothing was too arduous for the sage to accomplish: moreover, from his conversations with that clever politician, who represented the alleged disaffection and distress in Assyria to have been partial only and grossly exaggerated, the supposed facility of subjecting that realm to his sway appeared somewhat doubtful. And, in truth, six months of incessant vigilance and exertion had so altered the face of affairs, that the march of the Egyptians to Nineveh would no longer have been bloodless and triumphal.

But the time had now come for the commencement of the aerial palace. On a wide plain, within view of Memphis, near the site of the eternal Pyramids, there was collected so vast a throng that, even in that populous land, the like had rarely been recorded. From the mouths of the Nile to the frontiers of Ethiopia troops had been gathered together in readiness to start for the projected expedition (for none believed in the promised abdication); and besides this martial array, there were wains filled with building materials, a compact body of artisans, and a crowd of credulous spectators, who had flocked thither to behold a marvel. They were not disappointed, for long was that day remembered in the annals of Egypt. The King appeared in full state, accompanied by the principal members of the hierarchy and nobility, whose vast retinues formed an army of themselves.

On a little eminence stood Abicam and his small group of Assyrians, in the midst of which, conspicuously arranged in a triangle, were disposed three enormous elephants, whose gilded tusks and housings of purple and gold increased the admiration of the multitude. They looked like giants to men, when compared with the puny race of Africa; for not only were they of the bulky breed of Asia, but had been carefully selected for their strength and magnitude, to impress the Egyptians with a sense of awe for their possible adversaries.

When the trumpets proclaimed the coming of Pharaoh, the Arab horsemen who had kept the populace at a distance from the elephants, wheeled right and left, and left the beasts fully exposed to the sight of the Egyptians. Abicam rode forward towards the King, and having saluted him respectfully, but with dignity, thus spoke—

"My workmen are ready, and await the orders of your Majesty."

"Let them begin," answered Pharaoh; and there was the silence of death throughout the masses.

Abicam waved his hand, and at this signal the cupola of gauze which surmounted the central and further elephant was suddenly torn away, and displayed an enchantress standing aloft upon a silvery platform. She bore in her hand a jewelled wand, which sparkled in the glaring sun; a tiara of diamonds upon her calm and lofty brow reflected the light with painful brilliancy; her cloud-like drapery was azure, starred with gold. In her countenance were mingled the softness of woman and the dignity of man; her eyes flashed with excitement; there was consciousness of power in her every gesture; her port was majestic.

The daughter of Hicah (for it was she who enacted this part) thrice waved her glittering wand; and then in clear, distinct, and solemn tones were heard these words,— "Slaves of Sanharib, lay the foundations of an aerial palace for the friend of your master."

In an instant the towers upon the backs of the other elephants fell to pieces, and a loud rustling smote the air, as the roks, flapping their spreading wings, rose with their youthful riders. The children, beautiful as the star of the morning, were almost nude; garlands of flowers decked their hair; their scanty garments were of floating gauze, and of rainbow hue. Thrice circling round the area to display their terrific steeds, they soared aloft, and in a minute were lost to sight.

"What magic is this?" exclaimed Pharaoh. "What unknown gods are these? I recognize them not among our known divinities."

"These are mortals, not spirits," replied Abicam; "but thus potent are the subjects of Sanharib. See! they return."

And, as if responsive to the renewed waving of 'Rosebud's' wand, the dark spots, which were barely perceptible beneath the clouds, rapidly enlarged, and the two birds, far apart, descended with stately motion. A broad floating ribbon was suspended between them, and the children, displaying their golden trowels, directed the flight of the roks towards the King of Egypt.

"*Our foundation is laid,*" they cried; "*send up your promised materials.*"

"You have conquered, O sage," said Pharaoh. "It is I, now, who cannot fulfil the conditions. I am content: for he who is master of such beings as I have beheld this day, is designed by Providence to rule over a nation. Henceforth I become the faithful ally of Sanharib, the unswerving friend of Assyria."

To prove the sincerity of his words he placed the treasonable letters of Nadan in the hands of the disguised Hicah, and loaded him with presents both for himself and his lord.

Proudly did the successful politician meet his grateful Sovereign. He was reinstated in his office of prime minister, and passed the remainder of his happy life in the society of his bold son-in-law and his spirited daughter. As to Nadan, he died in prison.

"Such a girl would be worth wooing," exclaimed El Mulook at the end of the tale; "she is worth fifty of your Zobeides. If I *must* marry, and I suppose it will be my duty some time or other to provide a successor to my throne, I would I had the luck to meet her like."

Haziz seized the opportunity to oblige Suleiman.

"Character is stamped indelibly upon the countenance. Nature writes legibly, but few there are who can decipher her meaning. Nevertheless, as this tale is a truth and not a fiction, the portrait of the heroine has been handed down to us. Seek her likeness among women of every rank, and when you have found it, wed the maiden, whether she be princess or peasant."

The crafty old monarch chuckled with delight as Haziz graphically described the features, aspect, mien, and voice of the Princess Dunya, the very lady whom he had selected as a fitting bride for his son, and whose portrait he had exhibited that very morning to the obedient tale-teller.

"I must be off to-morrow," were the parting words of the princely hunter, "and should I bring back a plebeian wife, her soul at least will be noble."

"Figs spring not from brambles," said Suleiman; "such faces are not bestowed upon the vulgar herd. Good night, and pleasant dreams."

THE RAJAH'S DAUGHTER.*

At break of day El Mulook departed. Under the apparently artless guidance of Haziz, he wandered on from land to land, vainly seeking the image portrayed upon his memory, until he arrived opposite the Islands of Camphor, the Princess Royal of which bore the reputation of being the most beautiful woman in the world. She was noted, moreover, for an unaccountable repugnance to marriage, insomuch that she had vowed to slay the man who should wed her against her will, (a custom too prevalent with us Orientals), and to perish afterwards by her own hand.

To tame such a Tartar, to master so lovely a tigress, was

* From 'Taj El Mulook, and the Lady Dunya.'

the most attractive lure that could have been held out to the hunter-prince. Upon hearing this report he immediately crossed the strait that led to the Camphor Isles, and sought an opportunity of beholding the man-hater. Being well aware, as she had already refused many an eligible offer, how fruitless it would be to ask her hand (a measure he was by no means prepared for, without personal comparison of her with his ideal portraiture of a heroine), he determined to have recourse to stratagem to obtain an interview with her. Accordingly, having hired one of the handsomest shops in the city, and deposited therein the costly merchandise he had brought with him, he attired himself and his companions in rich and elegant apparel, and sat down in the midst of his many servants, all conspicuously clad in their native costumes, on the skins of the rarest beasts, bordered around with a deep fringe of bullion.

The distinguished look of El Mulook, the luxurious appointments of his shop, the novelty and rarity of his goods, naturally induced a run of business; and all the women whose fortune and whose leisure permitted them to indulge their fancy and their curiosity, made a point of ransacking the stores of the handsome foreigner. One day an aged crone, well dressed, and evidently of respectability, though not of rank, requested to be shown the most precious stuff he might possess, as her mistress, the Lady Dunya, whom she had reared from a child, had commissioned her to purchase the materials of a sumptuous dress. He smiled, as he bade his slaves take the wrappings off a roll of embroidered stuff, so valuable that he had never yet displayed it to any customer; and when asked the price, declined mentioning it, indicating his wish that she should accept it as the medium of introducing him to the Court. "For," he remarked, "amusement, and not profit, was his sole motive for visiting the islands." The bait caught, and his unparalleled beauty, his gentlemanly deportment, his unmercenary feeling, were the constant themes of panegyric from the nurse to her royal mistress. "You admire the beauty of his wares," she would say; "ah! you would not think of them, if you could only see the man; your whole senses would be absorbed in gazing upon him; so graceful a form, such exquisitely chiselled features has Nature lavished upon him. No woman could resist him; it is lucky for me I am old, for my virtue could not withstand his wooing, if he fancied me." And by thus continually harping upon his perfections, she excited the curiosity of the princess.

Soon, by his liberality, the Prince induced the supple messenger to convey some love-letters from himself to the Princess, who although indignant at him for his presumption, yet naturally felt some interest for a nobleman (for such she had learnt he was) whose daring evinced the ardour of his passion. Her replies, however, were so chilling, her rebukes so unmistakable, that bolder measures became necessary if he still cared to obtain an interview. The difficulties he had experienced had piqued his vanity, and the chase he had originally commenced as a mere amusement, had gradually become invested with an extrinsic importance. He had ascertained from the nurse that the Lady Dunya was wont occasionally, but at uncertain intervals, to divert herself by strolling in the gardens attached to an old and dilapidated palace that formed part of the royal appanage. Acting upon this hint, he cultivated the acquaintance of the head-gardener, and soon became (thanks to his urbanity, and still more to his purse) such a favourite with him that he obtained permission to enter the grounds whenever the usual notice of the intended visit of the Princess should not have been received.

"Permit me likewise," he said to the gardener one day, "to indulge my taste by redecorating the entrance-hall of this fine old palace at my own cost. An acquaintance of mine, a fresco-painter, seeks to display his abilities in restoring the building to its original beauty. His attempt, if successful, will prove an excellent introduction to remunerative employment." The favour was most willingly granted, and an artist instructed by the Prince depicted two tableaux upon its walls; one showed a female dove abandoned by her mate, fluttering and struggling vainly to extricate herself from the net of a fowler, who was just about to twist her neck; the other exhibited the male dove winging his way to assist her, but nearly overtaken by a hawk, and about to perish from its merciless assault.

These pictures were designed to counteract the influence of a peculiarly vivid dream upon the imagination of the handsome cold-hearted Princess. Dunya, when young and impressionable (as the garrulous old nurse related), had dreamed that a female pigeon had, at the risk of her own life, rescued her entangled mate from the snare of a fowler, but had subsequently been caught herself, and abandoned to her fate by her craven helpmate. "All males are thus base-hearted," had been the comment of the girl, and the moral had been so graven in her memory, that thenceforth she conceived a settled aversion for that unknown sex.

After these paintings had been completed, and the nurse had sent word to the Prince that, on the morrow, her mistress proposed to stroll through the pleasure-grounds of the deserted palace, the next morning, El Mulook, having arrayed himself in his richest clothes and most splendid jewels, repaired to the garden, and as, thanks to his colleague, the customary intimation of the visit of the Princess had been omitted, was admitted as usual. He had not sauntered about long, when there walked in from a private gate that lay between himself and the more public entrance, the Princess Dunya, escorted by a large retinue of merry females and sedate eunuchs. The bustle they made attracted the attention of the gardener, who, running to the Prince, urged him to conceal himself, as egress was now impossible. In a spot which was fast relapsing to its natural wildness, where the unpruned creepers offered many a nook for concealment, to hide was far from difficult, and his wary and efficient coadjutrix, the nurse, faithfully earned the frequent largesses he had bestowed upon her, by suggesting to the Princess that she would feel less trammelled by courtly etiquette, and could yield herself more freely to the impulse of her own sweet will by dismissing her train. The idea was approved of, and El Mulook, even if discovered, ran no risk from the scimetars of the eunuchs.

The unveiled Princess passed and repassed the hiding-place of El Mulook, and the latter, when he beheld in her features the reflex of his dead heroine, almost betrayed his presence by the excess of his emotions. Oh, joy! the object of his ideal passion, and she whose coyness had stimulated his habit of seeking to subdue all who might oppose him, were one and the same being!

At length the lady entered the newly-decorated hall, and beheld the frescoes.

"Marvellous!" she exclaimed; "this is the unrevealed finale of my dream. The male bird, then, *did* design to save his mate, and death alone forestalled him. Ah! I have wronged the sex by my obstinate assertion of its heartlessness and ingratitude." And from that moment all her prejudices against man were dissipated, and the softer ideas natural to youth and womanhood assumed their place.

When Dunya, after this revolution in her sentiments, had quitted the building, she sauntered by herself, wrapped in sweet reverie, musing on the passionate letters she had so coldly replied to, and wondering whether he who had indited them was the paragon so graphically depicted by her nurse. The latter, whose peering eyes were turned in every direction to detect the lurking-place of the liberal foreigner, who she felt convinced would take advantage of her communications, loitered behind, and soon descried the Prince, although safely hidden by the shrubs from cursory examination. She bade him walk boldly forth, as though unconscious of the presence of the royal lady, and then hurrying on, rejoined her mistress. With a start of surprise, Dunya, as she retraced her footsteps, confronted the noble-looking Prince, and blushing at his rapturous gaze, shrouded her sweet features with the cruel veil.

"Begone, bold youth!" said the crafty nurse, with simulated anger, "or the eunuchs will return and slay you. I neglected to apprise the gardener of our coming, so your fault is less heinous in thus trespassing on a royal domain, but withdraw quickly ere the wrath of the Princess be aroused." The apology of El Mulook for his intrusion was so gracefully worded, that the charms of his tongue, added to the beauty of his person, so fascinated the woman, whose heart was predisposed to love from her recent reverie, that the warmth of her feelings was revealed for the moment in her eyes, which shot forth tenderness and passion as they rested on his comely features.

"He was the writer of those letters you so scolded me for conveying," was the whisper of the cunning dame, who thus linked together the past and the present, and those ardent aspirations which, when written, she had rebuked, seemed now to flow unuttered from his lips in pleasing symphony. Their tongues were silent, but their looks betrayed the secret of their hearts, as El Mulook, obedient to the renewed injunction of the nurse, sadly withdrew from a garden which had become converted into Paradise by the presence of his Dunya. As to the greedy old woman, who easily read the expression of the artless lady, she chuckled as she thought of the future, and counted beforehand the wealth which would accrue to her from avowing so perilous an intrigue. For in love as in commerce, the greater the risk the greater the gain. So skilfully did she foster the incipient warmth in the bosom of her charge, that, the very next evening, she was dispatched with a message to the Prince, that Dunya would receive him in her mansion if his courage should not fail him. He was to be dressed as a female slave, and passed through the guards by the aged crone, who was an adept in such intrigues, and had the pride of an artist in their successful achievement. I need scarcely remark that, despite the dissuasion of Haziz, the heart of El Mulook did not quail, but bounded with rapture at the thought of peril.

The guards were not suspicious, or his manly gait would have betrayed him; he was stopped, however, and eyed suspiciously by the head eunuch, who indeed, at first, refused to admit him; yet, when menaced with the anger of his royal mistress, who, as the nurse alleged, proposed to purchase this *foreign* musician, he became blind to the peculiarities he had noticed in the stalwart slave, and was willing to attribute them to her distant origin. Nevertheless he retained his suspicions that all was not right in the matter.

The old woman having conducted El Mulook through the crowded saloon of the harem, to the private boudoir of her mistress, considerately left the enamoured pair to themselves (for various tasks had been allotted to the domestics to prevent intrusion upon the privacy of the Princess), and carefully, yet with seeming negligence, mounted guard outside the apartment. Apart from all mankind, and with daylight fast closing upon them, the lovers abandoned themselves to expressions of mutual tenderness, and embraced each other with mingled purity and passion. All the long cool summer night they toyed and prattled with innocent dalliance; and the Prince, to her great delight (for his rank would prevent opposition to their legitimate union) narrated his past history, spoke of her marvellous resemblance to the "Maid of Nineveh," and revealed his true position as heir to the Suzerain of the Indies.

Yet, although there could be no obstacle to their ultimate marriage, a long interval would elapse before a messenger could reach his father, and an ambassador return to publicly demand her hand, in accordance with state etiquette. The thought of being severed from each other for six long months was unendurably bitter; so they schemed how they might pass their lives in each other's society during the interim. Each morning, ere break of day, Dunya was to withdraw to another chamber, where she would resume her ordinary occupations, see company, transact business, and chat as usual with her attendants, for she was a kind and affable mistress. In the evening, as early as might be, she was to return to her boudoir, which was thenceforth to be the acknowledged abode of her favourite musician. Well did El Mulook keep up his professed character, for he was a skilful player, and at night the sounds of minstrelsy echoed sweetly from his closed door; the nurse was their sole attendant, and her hoard of gold and jewels increased so rapidly as to more than compensate her for incessant vigilance. So a whole month glided away unnoticed, amidst song and music, chaste caresses, and protestations of undying love. Absorbed with the novelty of a passion hitherto unknown to him, the intended message to his father, and the natural anxiety of Haziz for his absence, were wholly forgotten by the thoughtless Prince. Haziz, poor fellow! whose heart had foreboded evil from the hour when his impatient friend had preferred the romance of passion to the quiet course of a diplomatic marriage, and who dreaded that a sudden blow might lay the heir of Suleiman low before his rank could be surmised, had long before this period abandoned all hopes of the existence of El Mulook. The cessation of the previous almost daily visits of the aged nurse (who was at present too busy with her dangerous charge to attend to shopping) augmented his dismay; so, not daring to inquire at the palace as to the fate of his friend, he no longer doubted, from his protracted silence, that (together with the veteran intriguer) he had fallen an unknown victim to the rash and unnecessary course he had adopted. Near the close of the month he departed, with his merchandise and all his companions, from the hateful islands; for, since his longer sojourn could not (as he erroneously supposed) benefit his lost lord, he held it advisable to return immediately to the Court of the Indies, lest perchance, by his own unexpected death, all traces of Suleiman's heir should become obliterated. So he journeyed without delay or hindrance to the bereaved father; and feeling how vain it was to condole with him upon so irremediable a calamity, partially succeeded in diverting his thoughts from a grief which would have borne him speedily to the grave, by urging him to avenge his child. War was proclaimed throughout the vast empire; and so adored was the wise monarch for his benevolence and his equity, that not only did the people of his own realm flock in thousands to his standard, but the sovereigns of adjacent countries lent him their armies to aid his righteous quarrel. Stimulated by the thirst of vengeance, which temporarily restored him to the vigour of youth, he started with half his troops (a countless host), leaving orders for the rest to push on after him, as soon as the necessary preparations for their transport and provisionment could be completed.

Meanwhile the loving pair, wrapped up in their own felicity, and forgetful of the world without, were heedless of the passage of time. For six months had El Mulook remained in the harem, a prisoner to love, and during that period the ardour of his passion had so increased, the warmth of their mutual affection had grown so intense, as to carry them beyond the bounds of prudence and of caution. A combination of two most trivial circumstances put an end to their bliss. It chanced that one night the old nurse, who guarded the boudoir by reposing on her mattress outside the door, slept so profoundly that she neglected to apprise the lovers of the approach of day; and the chief eunuch having been charged by the King, who had risen unusually early, to deliver to his daughter a precious casket of jewels he had just received, passed the chamber before which the old woman was loudly snoring. He roughly shook her, and the horror of detection overwhelmed her palsied senses as she cowered before his piercing eyes.

"What mean you, sluggard, by lying here until this late hour of the morning?" said the stern official, with lowering countenance; for his suspicions were aroused by finding her posted, like a sentinel, before the chamber of the musician. "I must enter here," he continued, "and judge for myself the reason of your conduct."

"I have not the key with me," she shrewdly replied, "but I know where it lies, and will go and fetch it;" and she shuffled away from the searching looks of the tyrant of the harem, and, snatching up her hoarded treasures, quitted the palace. Kind fortune alone saved her from pursuit, and from the condign punishment awarded to the betrayer of her trust.

Impatient of her tardiness, the suspicious potentate so quietly displaced the door from its sockets, that he beheld the half-conscious Princess and her sleeping lover reposing in each other's arms. One glance at the exposed face of the latter told him all; despite of the proffered bribes, the agonized supplications of the distracted Dunya, who, waking at his entrance, implored him to conceal what he had noticed, the stern but incorruptible guardian having again secured the door, returned to his Sovereign, and declared that he had found a handsome youth in the same chamber with his sleeping daughter. Full of wrath, the indignant parent hastened thither, and at the sight of El Mulook such was the violence of his rage, that he would have slain him with his own hand, but Dunya, caressing her sire, threw herself before the Prince, exclaiming, "Kill me first, O my father, for he is my husband, and I dare to avow it;" for she was resolved not to survive him.

The fond father, however, would not hurt his child, but having chidden her, sent her to another room, where she was closely watched, lest, in her distraction and despair she should lay violent hands upon herself.

When the lady had been removed, El Mulook, drawing

nimself up proudly, confronted the Rajah with calm dignity.

"I am in thy power, O King," he exclaimed; "slay me if thou wilt, but my sire, who is far mightier than thou art, will amply avenge my death. Indulge thy rage, and the curses upon thee of thy slaughtered subjects, their ravaged fields, their desolated homes, will result from thy gratified malice."

"Who art thou, then, who crowest thus boldly?" said the perplexed monarch.

"Thine equal, at the least; the heir of Suleiman, the suzerain of the Indies," was the confident answer.

At these words the petty ruler of the Camphor Islands paused in his design of forthwith crucifying the daring violator of the sacred harem; and having inquired of the Prince as to who in that city could confirm his assertion of kingly rank, remanded him for a while, that he might ascertain the truth of his pretensions. He at first felt disposed to believe the arrogant claim of El Mulook to a station so exalted that policy demanded oblivion for an offence he was willing to repair; for the habit of command had so stamped its indelible impress upon his visage that he looked every inch a prince. Yet the departure of Haziz and his retinue, to whom the captive had confidently referred as testimonies to his royal extraction, so militated against the truth of his claims, that the Rajah resolved that he should expiate the past by a comparatively painless death, one which even a prince might endure without degradation.

And now the prisoner was firmly bound, and upon his

knees awaited the descending sword; the executioner had already raised his sinewy arm until the armpit was exposed, and fixed his calm cold eyes upon the Rajah, expecting his customary nod, when loud cries of alarm and the violent slamming of doors and shutters, and the tramp of many feet, as it were of fugitives, induced the despot to arrest the stroke.

"What means this unusual disturbance?" he demanded; and the voices of the throng without responded,—

"An army numerous as the sands of the ocean has crossed the strait, and your troops have fled before it."

Then, while all quaked with fear, and the executioner with uplifted scimetar still hovered over his victim, a compact body of horsemen, strangely but richly clad, attended by an honourable escort of the King's cavalry, galloped their foaming steeds to the porch of the palace, dismounted with unceremonious haste, and pushing aside all who would have impeded them, thrust themselves into the presence of royalty.

"We have hurried hither," said the envoy of Suleiman, after most brief salutation, "as messengers of peace or war, according to your past doings: of peace if the son of the great suzerain of the Indies, who, disguised as a merchant, has sojourned in your city, be still alive; of war even to annihilation, should he have been slain by your order, or his fate be still shrouded in mystery."

At this confirmation of the royal lineage of his captive the Rajah trembled, and would have removed him from the sight of his people, that they might not witness the indignity he had put upon him. But Haziz, who had accompanied the embassy, sprang towards the doomed one, and, clasping him in his arms, hastily unbound him, and wept with joy at their opportune arrival. Then the Rajah humbled himself before him whom he had condemned to die, crying,—

"Pardon, O youth, the harsh treatment which proceeded from the wrath of a justly-offended father. Suffer not the warriors of thy sire to desolate my poor dominions."

"If thou hast not harmed my bride," replied the magnanimous Prince, "I forgive thee all our misery, for I regard thee as my father-in-law; but if thou hast hurt her—"

"I have dealt with her," interrupted the Rajah, "with the forbearance of a fond yet aggrieved parent; no evil has betided her, as thou mayest see for thyself."

And having led him to the bath, and arrayed him in the garb of royalty, he conducted him to the chamber of his Dunya, who in a tumult of joy and sorrow, of tears mingled with smiles, stretched her arms towards him, crying,—

"I thought they could not slay thee, my own, my beautiful—thee, the son of a king; but, oh, my heart has been very sad from the loss of thee." And she kissed, and clung to him, and embraced him openly.

Then the Rajah closed the door upon them, and left them to each other. But he himself hastened to dispatch rich presents to his dread invaders, and with all his court repaired to Suleiman, and prostrating himself before him was reconciled to him.

And after the ceremonials of marriage between the hunter-prince and his perilously-won bride had been completed, the noble pair and their terrible escort returned to his native land.

The cherished wish of the renowned Suleiman was fulfilled, for his issue still sways the sceptre of the Indies.

HASSAN OF BASSORAH.

"SO then you have no father, and I no son; you have a mother, and I no wife; you are in straitened circumstances, though skilful in your calling; I, though wealthy, and acquainted with an art which princes have implored me to impart to them, have no home, no relatives; my very isolation inclines me to you." Thus spoke Bairam, a well-clad, somewhat aged, but sinewy-looking Persian, who, having eyed our hero, a comely youth, as he deftly plied his trade, and by the commendation of his workmanship contrived a pretext for addressing him, entered into, friendly converse and elicited his family history. The father of Hassan had been wealthy, but had died. Mismanagement on the part of his mother or his brother (the lad knew not which) had reduced him to the necessity of earning his livelihood as a working goldsmith. "His spirit," he said, "was above his condition. He felt he was destined to nobler deeds; but he must toil to live; there was no one who cared for him;" and so on.

Such were the facts and feelings the astute Magian gleaned, by his sympathizing looks and honeyed words, from the guileless youth. The young, the aspiring, the discontented, the adventurous, were the tools he sought. He thus continued :—" I am aged and childless; my soul seems to cleave to you, for you are spirited, clever, and very comely; such an one as I would adopt, if your docility should prove filial. Some day I will teach you the rudiments of the inestimable art of transmuting copper into gold; but this must be done in secret."

" At once I pray you," cried Hassan eagerly; and the Magian yielding, after some little pressure, to the urgency of his request, bade him close his shop, prepare his crucible, fill it with any clean scraps of pure copper he might possess, and urge his bellows until a green fume should ascend from the fused mass. Then, when the fitful tint flashed radiantly from the liquid metal, the alchemist let fall some intensely yellow dust into the bubbling fluid, and having stirred it incessantly with an implement of steel, let the fire gradually cool beneath it.

" Leave it undisturbed for this evening, my son, and to-morrow, having assayed it, sell it through a broker. And now farewell; I will revisit you in the morning."

There was no sleep for Hassan that night; he rose early, tried the rich-looking mass with file and touchstone, found it virgin gold, impatiently started for the market, sold it quickly for a large sum, and smiled as he showed the proceeds to his bland patron. " Let us make more," he said, " there can never be a glut of gold."

" It would look suspicious to sell that precious ore too frequently," answered the alchemist; " be guided by me. Live frugally, and practise this art but once or twice a year. The transmuting powder is hard to be obtained."

"What is it composed of?" inquired Hassan.

"Not too fast, friend; I must first try your obedience before I communicate the grand secret."

Yielding, however, to his importunity, the sage promised to consume the last small portion of his precious powder in transmuting some more copper, at nightfall.

"Each drachm of this dust, the sole ingredient by which copper differs from gold, will transform twenty pounds of the commoner metal into the rarer. I have only three ounces left; this time you shall do the work yourself: it is the second lesson."

Then he proposed to the youth to effect the great operation at his own house, which was in the country; but when his pupil demurred (for there was a something sinister in the expression of his teacher's countenance which filled him with forebodings of evil) he smiled contemptuously at his manifest timidity, and having recommended him to secure the heavy bag of silver he had realized by the sale of his ingot in his private chamber at home, offered to instruct him there that very evening. "But, remember," he continued, "none living, not even your mother, must be within earshot of my words. If this art should become common, how would it profit us to make gold?"

There was reason in his words; so when, after sunset, Bairam knocked at the private residence of the young goldsmith, all was prepared; the metallurgic apparatus in due order; a simple yet appetizing repast spread before them, and the widow far away in a remote apartment.

"You have been thoughtful, my son," said the visitor;

"have you been wary, likewise, and hidden the proceeds of our secret operation?"

"It is here, my father," answered Hassan, pointing to a flagstone, "safely deposited with the small residue of my father's savings. And now partake with me of this supper, that there may be the bond of bread and salt between us."

The Magian smiled dubiously, but ate. "It is not every one," said he, "who duly estimates the sanctity of the tie."

The supper removed, they set to work; that is to say, the pupil operated, the sage noting time and quantities. A huge lump of gold resulted from the correct nicety of the admixture: one grain too little of the powder would have spoilt the entire mass; all beyond needful of that fearfully-gained drug would have been wasted. They both exulted at their success; and the Persian, in high glee, offered some sweetmeats to his pupil, saying, "I have eaten of *your* food, now eat of *mine;* such is the custom of my country." Then Hassan ate, and became stupefied, for the sweetmeat had been drugged. Whilst he was unconscious, the Magian packed all the gold, silver, and other valuables of his victim into one chest, and thrust Hassan, bound neck and knees together, into another. Porters, ordered beforehand, conveyed these burdens to a vessel, which had been chartered by the Persian, and the wind being favourable, and all prepared, she sailed that night from Bassorah.

When all danger of pursuit was over, Bairam loosed his victim.

"Why have you thus treated me?" said the latter.

"What harm have I done you, that you bear me a captive from my home?"

"'Tis for your own good," answered the former. "I have a lovely daughter, and design you for her; but he who weds her must worship the same pure element which I do. See it blazing brightly before us;" and he pointed to a fire kindled from the sun, and prostrated himself reverently before it. "I hate the Moslems, those fanatical followers of a false prophet," he continued, "and use them for my tools that they may sell my gold for me and I myself avoid suspicion; yet forswear your religion, and I will fulfil each promise I have made you."

"Never," replied Hassan; "you have been false to the sacred tie of bread and salt, and I scorn both you and your Pagan rites."

Then the Magian was very wroth, and his slaves beat the poor youth with plaited thongs until he fainted.

But the mariners permitted not a continuance of this cruel treatment; for, although they had been hired by this Persian, they were not of his creed. Moreover, their superstition was enlisted on behalf of the captive; for when, shortly after this brutality, a hurricane burst on them, they heard in the howling of the wind the wrathful reproof of Heaven for their having supinely permitted an Infidel to attempt by violence to pervert from the truth his Moslem slave. They were a graceless set of fellows, yet still respected the religion of Islam.

Consequently the Magian changed his tactics, and sought to bend Hassan to his will by friendliness and cajolery. He treated him kindly, arrayed him in fair garments, and thus apologized for his roughness towards him :—

"Loving alike my own religion and yourself, it was natural, and surely pardonable, that I urged you, even with violence, to embrace it; yet since you are so firm in your convictions, I will respect your scruples, and even show you the ingredients of my powder, if you will boldly aid me in obtaining them."

He spoke persuasively. In his heart Bairam cared no longer what tenets might be professed by his victim; only just at first, he would have spared the youth had he yielded to his will; and procured a substitute for him. Now far advanced on his voyage, he was glad that the being whom he had devoted to destruction should be a worshipper of the Prophet who had denounced his creed. Since, however, it was essential to the success of his project that his pupil should be docile, and he felt he could no longer enforce obedience by brute force, he did his utmost to cajole him, and so far succeeded, that Hassan, left alone without friends or money, clung of necessity to the man who pretended a regard for him and kept him from want.

After a voyage of three months' duration, they both landed on a desert spot, with very little luggage, and slowly proceeded from the coast inland, until the ship was out of sight. The Magian now produced a small kettle-drum, which he commenced striking with a plectrum of silk worked in gold with talismanic insignia; small as it was, the air was sensibly agitated by its vibration, and the far-apart palm-trees seemed to shake violently as the waves of sound reached them. Far, very far in the distance, a dust arose, and that dust rapidly advanced, and as it neared them three she-camels might be descried, two of which permitted themselves to be mounted, and the third bore their slender stock of food upon her back. For one whole week they swiftly and incessantly travelled over a sterile region, which bore nothing that might sustain life in man or beast; then they came to a fertile plain, where both they and their steeds refreshed themselves for a while, and then again they mounted their beasts, and as the ground continually rose, slowly and painfully ascended hill after hill, until they seemed in the region of eternal clouds. Afar off might be dimly discerned a palatial residence, and as their provisions were almost exhausted, and the incessant fatigue began to tell upon both of them, Hassan proposed that they should crave hospitality.

"Not so: it is the abode of evil spirits," replied the Magian; "we must hurry past it, and in a few hours your journey will have ended."

Before long they arrived at the foot of an abrupt mountain, to the top of which there was no visible footpath. As far as the eye could reach, the sides rose precipitously an upright wall of more than a hundred feet high. No practicable access to the summit could be descried, and yet to that peak the Magian pointed his skinny finger, joyously exclaiming,

"At length, my son, we have arrived at the goal of all our labours; upon that height grows a shrub the burnt ashes of which are alone needed to convert the baser metals into virgin gold. All the mysteries of alchemy are now revealed to you: you have become joint inheritor with myself of that inestimable secret which thousands of sages have vainly pined for. To gain this shrub, one thing alone (disagreeable, I own, and apparently, yet not really, dangerous) is necessary. No mortal foot can surmount the rocky barrier which Nature has interposed between our wishes and their fruition. Stratagem, therefore, must be resorted to. Those monstrous creatures, the rok-vultures, build their nests on the crags above these impregnable cliffs, and if you have courage enough to conceal your form within the skin of a camel, you will be borne aloft by the parent birds, who will be scared by your shouts when you cut yourself free from the fur which hides you. For man, the lord of fire, can terrify by his voice every living being with whom he may come in contact."

The youth submitted himself, trembling all the while, to the will of the alchemist, without whose co-operation he could not hope to regain the port where he supposed the vessel was still at anchor. So one of the camels was slaughtered, and Hassan encircled by its skin, and borne aloft by the stooping rok, gave utterance to such shrieks as the bird alighted near its nest, that, startled from its prey, it soared away into the boundless sky.

Then the voice of the Magian was heard from below, shouting out, "Throw down six bundles," which order the lad obeyed, picking up the wood which he had cut from amidst a rotting pile of human bones that nourished the shrub as a rich manure.

"Thanks, fool," was the parting salutation of Bairam to his victim; "I brought you here to gather this precious harvest. Now get down if you can. Pray to your Prophet to help you; even *my* God could not save me, were I where *you* are perched." Then smiling grimly, he mounted one camel, packed his treasure upon the second, and with a scornful nod rode off into the desert on his homeward route.

Hassan had always distrusted the wily Persian, yet this utter abandonment of him seemed a horrible dream: he could not at first realize his awful peril: when he comprehended it, he ran at full speed along the mountain plateau, until it suddenly terminated where it overhung the surging waves of the heaving ocean. A speedy death was better than a lingering one; there was the chance, too, that he might survive the fall, and make his way back to some inhabited portion of the globe. So, with a fervent prayer for aid, he cast himself down from the cliffs, and after much buffeting with the waters, was cast ashore in a state of unconsciousness, far away from the spot from whence he had precipitated himself. When he recovered his senses, he found himself close to the palace he had previously noticed, and which the Magian had asserted was the abode of evil spirits. In his present mood he would have faced Eblis himself; for, without food and shelter, his life could no longer be sustained. With the courage of despair he entered the unguarded portal, expecting each moment to be pounced upon by some hideous ogre or malevolent genius. The only beings he encountered were two beautiful girls, who were playing at chess, and who evidently regarded his arrival as a pleasant interruption to their loneliness.

The younger, starting up, clasped him by the hand, exclaiming, "At last I behold a human being: bear witness, O my sister, that I adopt him for my brother;" and she provided him with food, and fresh garments; and after he was refreshed, inquired of him how he had discovered their solitary home. He told them the simple truth; and they continued:—"You are the first man who has escaped this cold-hearted monster, who, to gratify his quenchless thirst for gold, has, year after year, for longer than we can recollect, sacrificed some trusting youth to the horrible death of gnawing starvation."

"Pardon my curiosity," said Hassan, now thoroughly refreshed, "but how does it happen that you dwell in so solitary a spot, separated, as it were, from all mankind?"

"You may well marvel at this," answered his sister, "for no woman would dwell alone willingly. Our father, however, who is a Prince of the Genii, is so jealous of our affection for him, that he isolates us by almost impassable deserts from all mankind, lest we should love any but himself. At long intervals he sends for us to his court; but usually we dwell alone, surrounded with every pleasure, except society. The grounds are charming, and prolific; most ample stores of all that may conduce to our convenience await our wishes; but our life is very dull, and we are really delighted at your coming."

Thus kindly and frankly was he received by the two girls, who were the sole occupiers of the spacious palace; and when their five sisters, who had been out hunting, returned from their sport, they vied with the other two in their gracious hospitality. Time passed quickly in their company. Hassan, as soon as he was restored to health and vigour, accompanied them to the chase, and a year sped onwards so rapidly that our hero, whose manners and tone of feeling had become refined from intimacy with these noble females, was only made conscious of its passage by the sight of his old enemy. He was chasing the antelope with his fair companions when he beheld him, almost on the very spot where he had abandoned himself, torturing a young Moslem, to force him to enter within the skin of a slaughtered camel: the young man was tightly bound, and submitted to his cruel usage with sullen patience. "My sisters," said Hassan, "aid me in avenging humanity by ridding the world of this execrable monster. Allah will hold it a good deed, and recompense us for it hereafter." They were all armed, and well mounted, so that their sudden onslaught struck the Magian with dismay; ere he could recover from it, the sword of the avenger had cloven him asunder, and his soul was hurried to that fire which on earth he had loved so well. His intended victim was mounted on his betrayer's camel; and being well provided with provisions, and all things needful, returned in safety to his friends and country.

Not long after this occurrence the sky above the desert became darkened, at which sight the damsels hastened to conceal their cherished guest. Soon there arrived a guard of honour, sent by their father to escort his daughters to a marriage festival. "We shall be absent, dear friend, for two or three months," said his sister by adoption, as soon as an opportunity for visiting Hassan permitted her to bid him farewell. "Here are our keys; use all things freely, only do not open the door you see yonder. This little favour—and we request it as much for your own sake as for ours—I beg you to grant me by that sacred tie of brotherhood that is established between us." Then they departed, and Hassan was left alone in the deserted palace.

The solitude was unbearable. No human voice now greeted him; the rooms which had so lately echoed with the lively prattle of the laughing girls, were now silent and gloomy. He had not a neighbour within hundreds of miles. He had no occupation, he felt no interest in anything. In the bustle of life we act; in the dead calm of compulsory indolence and solitude we think, we theorize. The thought, however rebuked, would again and again recur, "Why am I forbidden to enter that apartment? does it contain some terrible secret which they wish to hide from me? Even though death should follow my intrusion, I *must* venture within it to unravel the mystery." He had uttered his thought aloud, and the sound of his own voice seemed to inspire him with daring. The key was turned, the door flung widely open. Scimetar in hand, he paused at the threshold, half expecting to witness some ogre, or foul spirit that would oppose his entrance. All was calm within. The apartment was empty; it was a mere anteroom, with a flight of stairs leading to the roof of the palace.

He bounded up the steps; he had never yet looked from the roof upon the splendid landscape of wood, water, hill and plain, the commingled aspect of which he felt would be magnificent; for the strange life he had led of late had called all the latent poetry of his soul into existence. He gazed with tranquil admiration on the prospect around, and noticed more especially a small private garden exquisitely laid out, and filled with every sort of odoriferous shrub and sweetly smelling or brightly-coloured flower. Surrounded, except in front, by dense masses of foliage, rose a graceful pavilion of lattice-work, built of the most precious materials, and enclosing a spacious marble basin of limpid water. Whilst he was still admiring it he perceived some large snow-white birds winging their way towards it, as if thirsting for its waters. He watched them, himself unseen, as they alighted before it, and witnessed, to his intense amazement, that they ripped open their breasts with their talons, and emerged from their dress of feathers as lovely maidens; plunging into the bath, they disported themselves merrily, and frolicked with all the innocent gaiety of unobserved privacy. For who in such a solitude could witness their gambols save the seven damsels who dwelt there, daughters of a vassal of their own father, the sovereign of *his* tribe of the genii? So they romped like children, and splashed each other with water, and in their unadorned and statuesque beauty assumed such graceful and alluring attitudes, that passionate longings throbbed in the breast of the youth; and he, to whom love in its more earthly sense had been hitherto an unknown feeling, became so inflamed by the loveliness of one of these sprightly girls, that when they had flown back to their distant home after their delicious bath, his previous gloom became a settled melancholy; he loathed his food, and pined away before the voluptuous images in which his fancy dared to revel.

Time passed on. Again a dust arose in the desert, and

the prattle of many voices reanimated the echoing chambers. He knew his fair protectors had returned, yet could not rise to meet them; he was so prostrated by his love-fever, that he had grown helpless as a child. His adopted sister, who felt an earnest tenderness for him, and affection enables us to divine the thoughts of the being whose heart beats in unison with our own, quickly penetrated his secret, whispering softly, "You have used that key; you have viewed what is forbidden to your sex to look upon, and perchance we shall all perish through your indiscretion." A faint deprecating smile was the sole reply he could make: his voice was gone from utter feebleness. So she excused his illness to the six as the natural result of his long solitude; and while they hunted and amused themselves as usual, she bore him from his couch in her soft yet vigorous arms, as a mother would a sick child, and consoling him with hope, nursed him so tenderly that health speedily revisited him.

When he had nearly recovered, yet was still sad at heart, she reverted to the scene he had beheld, and explained that on the first day of every month the daughters of their king, the ruler of a certain tribe of the genii, were wont to bathe in that secret pool; "and since you assure me," she continued, and your illness confirms your words, that your life depends upon your union with one of them, I will aid you, heart and soul, to gain her. It might, indeed, be the ruin of us all were my complicity detected (for my father is the vassal of their sire), yet come what will, I must not let my brother pine to death, even should I imperil all our lives to save him. Be cautious, active, vigilant, and your success is certain. When next they come hither contrive to abstract the feathered robe of the girl you most long for, and leave all else to me. Conceal it carefully—for who knows the future ? yet never acknowledge you have preserved it ; let her fancy rather that in the madness of passion you irretrievably destroyed it that she might become yours for ever." Thus she cheered him ; and the prospect of such happiness so revived his spirits, that every trace of sickness soon left him. He was again the merry-hearted creature whose society so enlivened the exiled seven.

On the anxiously awaited day having found a hiding-place beneath a spreading bush which bloomed in close proximity to the haunted pool, he had furtively removed and secreted the robe of feathers, which had enabled the wearer to speed through the air with the swiftness of an arrow ; and now all but the youngest and loveliest of the late merry group had flown away ; her sisters had left her vainly seeking the stolen garment. Weeping at her inexplicable loss, and crouching through maiden shame as she beheld a figure approaching her, she was charmed to hear the sympathizing voice of the sister of Hassan. "Dear girl, I have observed all that has occurred from the roof of our palace. I know your dilemma, and have brought some clothes with me to guard your charms from the profane eyes of the bold youth who has disrobed you. He did so from mad passion ; a month ago he accidentally beheld you, and almost pined to death from despair of gaining you. I say not he is worthy to possess one so exalted as yourself ; but he is handsome, gentle, chivalrous, and refined. He honourably seeks your hand; permit him then to approach you, since thus only can you discover whether he has destroyed your plumage. Should he fail to win your affection, you may perhaps influence him by your entreaties to restore you the sole means of returning to your father."

The sweet damsel did not make this long speech all at once, but communicated her ideas little by little, in the lulls of the storm of sobs which ever and anon burst irrepressibly from the captive maiden. Her words were not wholly ineffectual; hope revived; she had found a friend; she would cajole the wretch who had dared to deprive her of her liberty. So, after a day or two, she permitted Hassan to plead his cause; and he was so handsome, so eloquent, so respectful, that she almost pardoned him. But, of course, she pursued her plan of wheedling from him what had been done with her feathery encasement, and, being quite a tyro in guile, actually deluded herself (by simple reticence on the part of our hero) into the belief that he had wilfully destroyed it. Such zealous confederates had Hassan in the seven sisters (who I fear were less scrupulous in deceiving the lorn maiden than he was), that when all hope of returning to her home had left her, she made up her mind to accept her daring suitor. So, after a brief but ardent courtship, she yielded her heart to him, and in the absence of a legal official to celebrate the marriage contract, was wedded to him through the intervention of one of the sisters. For forty days joy and festivities pervaded the palace; all the seven sympathized with the transports of Hassan and his bride, who, however, were destined soon to leave them.

A vivid dream excited his remorse. His mother, wasted with sorrow at his long absence, seemed to reproach him for his careless happiness. Tears were in his eyes as he related the vision to his amiable hostesses; and they, divining his wishes, not only bade him return home without delay, but presented him with such abundance of gold and jewels, that the means of living in opulence were ensured to him for life. Then, when obedient to the mystic tones of the Magian's drum, whose piercing notes reverberated far and wide over a vast expanse of country, camels mad with sympathetic excitement flocked thither from all quarters; they loaded the submissive beasts, some with treasures, others with all sorts of provisions, and courteously escorted their late guests far upon their journey. When, at length, they parted from him (not without many an invitation to return), the youngest, who had adopted him as her brother, lingered behind, and clasping him to her breast, fainted with the excess of her emotion. I am not sure the gentle girl did not love him more ardently than she would have owned; if so, what magnanimity she had evinced in aiding him to wed another!

There is no need to tell how Hassan and his bride traversed the deserts and crossed the sea; suffice it, they arrived safely at Bassorah, and rejoiced his mother by their coming. At her suggestion (for she was a prudent woman) they quitted their native town, where, the previous poverty of the family being well known, the enjoyment of their recently acquired fortune would have been attended with disagreeables, if not with peril; for the wealth would have been attributed to alchemy, or to some other nefarious or illegal practice.

They journeyed, therefore, to Bagdad, and there resided in ease and luxury.

After three years had elapsed, Hassan determined to keep his promise of again visiting the seven sisters; so, seeking to manifest his gratitude to them, he purchased every object of interest or novelty which the market of that emporium could provide.

Before he left home, he strictly enjoined his mother to show all due respect to his high-born wife (the history of whose capture he had already narrated), but not to permit her to quit the house during his absence. He then proceeded to relate that he had never destroyed her dress of feathers, but had concealed it in a chest in a certain closet, fearing that the sight of it would tempt her to abandon him. Alas! for this confidential communication; it was fortuitously overheard by Menar es Sena, his lovely wife, who had passively yielded herself to him, because she had hitherto imagined that flight from her plebeian bridegroom was impossible. Hence, no sooner had her husband uttered his last farewell, and started on his route, when she importuned her guardian for permission to visit the public baths, and so vehemently insisted upon her rights, that she gained her point and proceeded thither. When she was undressed, the exquisite symmetry of her proportions and the refined loveliness of her features excited universal admiration, insomuch that a favourite attendant of Zobeide, the wife of the Caliph, who had chanced to behold her, reported to her mistress the surpassing beauty of the stranger, declaring that in all Islam none could be found to vie with her. Thereupon Zobeide resolved to inspect this marvel of perfection, and invited the wife and mother of Hassan to visit her in her palace. The unsought-for honour could not be refused; the beauty was admired, petted, and eventually asked, being a foreigner, whether she had any rarities at home which were worthy of being viewed. With feigned simplicity she answered promptly, "Oh, such a wonderful dress of feathers! you would take me for a bird if you could see me in it, but my mother-in-law, who never leaves me, has locked it up in her private closet; so I can't show it you." Then Zobeide became imperious, and, despite of the asseverations of the old woman, who denied all knowledge of its presence, sent Mesroor in her company to fetch it; and he, guided by the directions of the lovely bride, soon found it, and returned without delay to his mistress.

Menar es Sena carefully examined the skin. It was perfect as on the day when she had left it before the pool in the desert. Donning it quickly, and imitating a bird, she strutted about naturally, and plumed herself gracefully, like a snow-white swan; then she tried her wings, and now feeling confident in her powers, she soared aloft, bidding her mother-in-law tell Hassan that the loss of herself was but a mild penalty for his former subtlety and his present neglect. "Should he so fondly love me," she continued, "that he cannot exist without me, he must seek me in the far off Isle of Women, near Borneo, and then, perchance, I may pardon him." Having uttered this farewell message, she spread her wings, and flew with the rapidity of the wind to the home she had so long quitted.

What tongue could adequately describe the despair of

Hassan, when, on his return, he heard of the flight of his loved one! His close custody of her had been based upon his humble conviction of his own demerits; his apparently neglectful absence had resulted from the gratitude he entertained for the dear sister whose unselfish affection had procured so peerless a bride. What was life to him now, without her? He loved her; would follow her to the world's end. So he started in haste for the Indian Archipelago.

I have no time to relate the perils encountered in his long and painful enterprise; how that, at length, through the favour and connivance of a neighbouring potentate, he contrived to land in an island where women ruling as masters, forbade the approach of all foreigners of the male sex (their own mates being too submissive to be dreaded); how that his deep humility and the sad intensity of his love for his lost bride won him the commiseration of the general of these Amazons, who had offered him any maiden in her army whom he might select as a substitute; how that having refused the kindly solace, he proceeded to the Court presided over by his wife's sister, who, at the urgent request of his protectress, had spared his own life, but incarcerated his bride for the shame she had brought upon her family by this degrading misalliance. Scarcely yet assured of his own safety, he had departed from the palace, and now, devoid of fixed plan, was walking disconsolately towards the most solitary spot he could descry. It was a narrow dell, shut in between mountains and a foaming torrent; not a living tree was visible, no human being could be discerned who might indicate what route he should pursue. Gloom and silence reigned supreme; the melancholy roar of struggling waters could alone be heard. "No wonder that such a spot is avoided by all mankind," he was thinking, when the shrill and angry tones of boyish voices in loud quarrel disturbed and disproved his reflections. Two lads were tussling with each other, and the blood upon their faces and their stained garments showed that blows had been freely exchanged between them. On the ground, at their side, lay the objects of their dispute, a metal wand, inscribed with strangely-fashioned letters, and a leathern skull-cap studded with triangular plates of iron engraved with similar characters. The value of neither seemed worthy of so savage an altercation, for hatred even to the death flashed defiantly from the eyes of each, as, like Cain and Abel, they fiercely contended with each other. The weaker, with a cry of relief, exclaimed on seeing the stranger, "Let *him* decide between us," and as his panting opponent likewise assented, our hero agreed to act as umpire.

"Each of us wants the wand, and neither cares for the cap," said the former speaker; "and our father, a mighty magician, who dwelt in this desert and is but just dead, and as yet unburied, has neglected to will them to either of us."

"What, then, are the hidden virtues of each?" asked Hassan; "intrinsically, they seem worthless."

The other lad explained that the wearing of the cap merely produced invisibility, but that he who should wave the wand had seven tribes of genii for his vassals.

Judging that those who neglecting the corpse of their

parent, would have slain each other for the acquisition of power, were wholly unworthy of possessing it, and believing that Providence had cast this chance in his way to enable him to succour and regain his imprisoned wife, Hassan bethought himself of a stratagem to acquire both treasures for himself. "Lads," said he, "it is impossible to fairly divide your inheritance; the value of the objects is too different. Suppose, then, you race for the choice; let him who first reaches this coloured stone," and he cast a large and conspicuous one as far as he could hurl it, having shown it previously to them that they might recognize it from the peculiarity of its shape and colour, "and brings it back to me, take the wand, leaving the cap to his brother. Now—off!"

Intent solely upon victory, the rivals forgot the inestimable objects they were leaving behind them; scarcely had he finished when they started at full speed, the hindermost clinging to him who had got the start to retard his progress. A fight ensued when they reached the stone; but when the elder, who had stunned his brother and taken the prize from him, triumphantly turned his face towards the umpire, the cap was on the head of Hassan and the wand within his hand. He had become invisible; so the young savages lost their treasures, and brotherly affection once more returned to their hearts, for the sense of mutual wrong engendered a mutual sympathy: their loss eventually proved their gain.

Our hero thus armed and shielded returned to the city, and having entered the dungeon where his wife was immured, heard her (himself unseen) deploring her folly in having left the man she really loved, from a baseless jealousy of his avowed affection for his sister and a natural indignation for the trick which had been played her. She was weeping violently, for her wrathful sister had caused her to be beaten, and had now issued orders for the recapture of her husband.

"I both can and will save you, dearest!" said Hassan showing himself; "forgive me for my wrongful capture of you, for passion urged me to that violence: I should have died had I not possessed you. To make amends I will restore you, should you bid me, to your father, or else take you to my own dear sister; for I have power more than equal to the rulers of this land."

"Where thou goest I will go, and never more will I leave thee!" was the fond reply.

I shall not relate how they quitted the prison, were pursued and overtaken by the winged troops of his involuntary father-in-law; how his own tributary genii valorously defended him; how that the contending spirits scorched each other with breaths of flame; how that, after a long conflict, his own dread warriors were victorious, and the conquered father and the cruel sister, as much vanquished by his generosity as by his arms, became reconciled to the plebeian mortal who had dared to mingle his human blood with that of their kingly race.

When all strife was over and solemn oaths of eternal amity had been exchanged, our hero dismissed his terrible army and returned to his native land. On his road he visited his adopted sister, and, in token of his gratitude, left in her hands the source and emblems of his magic power.

Neither he nor his wife craved for exalted station, accompanied as it ever must be by peril and responsibility; so being very wealthy, thanks to the liberality of Menar es Sena's family and the rich gifts of the seven sisters, they purchased houses and lands at Bagdad, and lived at their ease in that fair and luxurious city. Their descendants dwell there in opulence to this very day.

KHALEEFEH THE FISHERMAN.*

"NINE times have I let down this accursed net, and nine times have I dragged it in empty. There's a spell upon it, and no luck has ever betided me since I refused to sell my fish to that sorcerer Jew. Well, here it goes for the last time;" and that hulking, needy varlet, Khaleefeh the fisherman, cast his net again into the muddy Tigris, hurling it this time with such angry vigour, that it fell further out into the stream than previously. He waited for a while, and then slowly hauled it towards him. The net did not feel heavy, yet as it neared the bank there was something alive and struggling perceptible, which proved that the tenth venture would not be wholly without issue. When at length it had been landed and carefully uncoiled, nothing was found therein but a scabby, one-eyed, limping, undersized ape. In the anger of his disappointment the peasant seized a stick, and was about to strike the animal; but when the beast spoke —ay, actually spoke—he dropped his bâton and stared stupidly at it. "Don't strike yourself, Khaleefeh," said the

* Including 'Abdallah of the Sea.'

little monster. "I am your luck, your *own* luck, master; so leave me alone, and cast the net again into the river."

In went the net, hurled, if possible, still further from the bank than last time. A little pause, and it was hauled towards the bank. This time it was heavier than the last; so weighty, indeed, that it needed the exertion of every muscle of his stalwart frame to land the contents securely. "Another ape!" he exclaimed as he discovered a great red beast, with a handsome blue tunic around its loins, and its eyelids stained with kohl, like a woman's, cradled serenely within the net. "Why, Heaven seems to have changed all the fish to monkeys, just to spite me. I am always unlucky; but take *that,* you brute, for walking into my property;" and he whirled the bâton around his head, intending to belabour the ugly intruder. "Don't agitate yourself, man," said the beast, in the *nonchalant* tones of a supercilious dandy, "I'm *luck,* not your luck though, but Abu Saadat's. Take the matter quietly, and your fortune's made."—"Eh! What? my fortune's made! Tell me how, and I won't thrash you."—"I flatter myself," said the complaisant beast, as he eyed his fine blue tunic with an air of pride, and smoothed his abundant yet somewhat ruffled fur, "that I'm rather a different sort of creature from *your* ape; I am a luck-bringer, and whoever owns me is sure to gain ten sequins a day at the least. Of late I have permitted myself to be appropriated by Abu Saadat, the Jew money-changer, but I think I'll patronize you. Now, under *my* protection, cast in your net again."

The fisherman was confounded at the cool assurance of

this ugly beast, yet obeyed its order. He was rewarded by catching one of the finest and most delicious fish that the river had ever yielded. Pleased with his success, he inquired of his shaggy adviser, "What next?"—"Of course you would like the honour of owning me, and I don't mind humouring you," said his strange patron; "only it is needful that Abu Saadat should voluntarily transfer me to you. So lay this tempting fish daintily on fresh green grass; carry it quickly in your basket to the market-place, and show it, in all its freshness, to the money-changer. Refuse to sell the dainty to him for any less equivalent than *me* and his luck; I know the greedy epicure would resign his very soul to gratify his stomach." Both apes then, swinging their bodies to and fro on a young elastic bough, to give themselves impetus, suddenly loosed their hold of it, and flew, as it were, far into the centre of the sullen stream. When they had disappeared beneath the bubbling waters, the past *rencontre* seemed to the bewildered fisherman so like the incidents of a dream, that he began to fancy that he had not wholly slept off the hashish he had indulged in the previous evening. At all events, however, he would proffer his fish to Abu Saadat, the reputed sorcerer.

The market-place was crowded when the fisherman, having unpacked his prize, displayed it to the money-changer, who, greedily coveting it, tossed a piece of gold to the vendor, and bade his servant carry the delicacy home, and order it to be dressed in such-and-such a fashion (and he openly specified the mode, for he had set his heart upon the dish). Now the price was a fair one, and Khaleefeh longed to accept it; yet the ape's advice (and surely that *rencontre* was a reality?) was buzzing in his ears. So he fumbled the coin about, and scarcely had the servant carried off the basket, when he banged the coin down on the changer's table, crying, "Halloo! what do you mean by walking off with poor folk's fish?" The Jew, suspecting it was an attempt to screw more money out of him, threw him two more pieces and, without disturbing himself, went on with his business. "Three pieces of gold for one fish. Well, that *is* a price. But the ape said I was not to take money. What shall I do?" and in the excitement produced by his unwillingness to abandon a larger sum than he had gained by a whole month's toil, and the growing conviction that the mysterious ape was the arbiter of his fate, he advanced and receded at least half-a-dozen times in front of the table of the money-changer. At last, throwing down the coins with a clash, he again roared out, "Halloo! what do you mean by walking off with poor folk's fish?" The Jew was very angry, but thinking this a trick to pick a quarrel with him, and being very adverse to a brawl with a true believer, pushed two more pieces of gold towards the rough fellow, meekly inquiring whether he was still dissatisfied. "I don't want your money at all. Just say out loud, 'I give you *my* ape for *your* ape, and *my* luck for *your* luck,' and the fish is yours without purchase." Wearied with his blustering and laughing at his whim, the Jew uttered the suggested formula. From that hour he waxed poorer and poorer. But Khaleefeh went on his way rejoicing, though he had not a single coin in his possession; for he had firm confidence in the promise of the luck-bringer. Full of hope, he resumed his fishing, and ere nightfall his gains amounted to no less a sum than ten pieces of gold. It seemed as though he had only to cast his net, and the fish were doomed to enter it. He had an unseen co-operator, who scared them to its meshes; it was the invisible agency of the mysterious being who had been unwittingly transferred to him by its unconscious possessor. Philosophers smile at luck, but to what else can we attribute the prosperity of the reckless, the penury of the provident?

Day after day did the same occur; but unwonted riches made sad work with the brain of the once poor peasant. "A hundred pieces of gold! yes, I have them secure, but I shall be robbed of them to a certainty. Where can I hide them? If I bury them in the ground I shall not dare to leave my home, lest rogues discover them; if I place them in a purse, armed thieves will lay wait for me, and take it by force. I have it! I will stitch my money in a fold of my garment over my chest, and none will think of that." He started as usual with his nets; but his luck seemed to fail him. His late good fortune made him impatient, for his wrath began to rise when again and again he had drawn his empty meshes to the bank. At last, with an imprecation, he dashed his nets so violently into the stream, that he jerked out his hoard of gold from the fold he had coarsely stitched up in his garment, and the shining pieces flew in all directions into the water. To strip was but the work of a moment; he was diving in all directions, disinterring his much-loved gold from the muddy bottom of the river. Very little did he recover. His whole thoughts were absorbed in his anxious occupation; he saw nothing that took place on the bank, where a prowling scamp was carrying off, half in fun, half in earnest, the squalid raiment of the diver. When, worn out with his exertions, he raised his dripping body from the ooze, he found nothing but his nets to cover his nakedness. But from the bank there was watching him a well-dressed gentleman (no less a personage than the Caliph Haroun Alraschid), whom he naturally imagined must have removed his dress. "Come, none of your nonsense, give me back my clothes," said Khaleefeh, who had wrapped his coarse nets around his huge frame, and was brandishing a stake. "Don't fancy you are going to make a fool of me, you little fellow, for I won't stand it; be quick now, or you shall taste my cudgel." And he whirled his heavy stick around in so menacing a way, that the wayfarer felt convinced that a single blow would annihilate him. "Don't strike me, friend," he quickly answered; "I know nothing of your own garments, but you are welcome to my cloak."

Now the Caliph would not have objected to a pleasant adventure; but a personal struggle with a rough and powerfully-built peasant, too ignorant to believe his rank should he assert it, was by no means to his liking. So he yielded his cloak with a good grace, for the weather was very hot. He had ridden out that day, to distract his thoughts from an *amour* he was half ashamed of. Having lately purchased a beautiful and accomplished slave-girl, Koot El Kuloob by name, he had become so enamoured

P 2

of her that for an entire month he had never quitted her apartments, save for the Friday's prayers; hence public business had been wholly neglected. But his minister, Giafar, being a privileged person, had ventured that morning to respectfully remonstrate with his Sovereign, and by his representation of the injury that was accruing to the State from his continual absence, had induced Haroun to withdraw himself for a while, on the plea of hunting, from her too fascinating society. The Caliph was to be weaned by degrees from his amorous indolence.

Immediately after the Friday's prayers, the two companions had mounted their mules, and started on their expedition into the waste country, where the game was most likely to be plentiful. The Sovereign cared little for the sport, and dallied behind with his favourite minister, until the more enthusiastic hunters were far ahead, and eventually out of sight. The weather was very sultry, and Haroun became thirsty. In the distance he perceived an almost stationary figure, which he supposed to be some gardener or peasant, from whom he might obtain water; so bidding his vizier remain where he was, in order to collect together the scattered hunters, he cantered on in search for liquid. Having reached the Tigris, and quenched his thirst from the running stream, his attention was attracted, whilst watering his mule, by the uncouth figure of the savage-looking fisherman, who with long dishevelled locks floating wildly over his strange covering of network, was rolling his fierce and bloodshot orbs in every direction, angrily seeking the practical joker who had secreted his garments. Their eyes met, and the presumed offender was roughly accosted by the enraged peasant, who, now appeased by the gift, dropped his stick, and contented himself with grumbling at the exchange.

"It's a flimsy affair this; cost twice as much as mine, I dare say, yet not half so strong and useful. It's all silk, and finery; no substance in it; still it's better than nothing."

Observing that his ill-humour was allayed, Haroun ventured to remark that he should not be too ready with his cudgel, since, judging from his sinews, his blows would fall hard.

"As to that," replied the fisherman, "I think *I* ought to know better than you; for I have been thumping myself half the night, just to ascertain how I could stand the bastinado, should the Caliph, wanting my gold, order me to be beaten that I might say where I had hidden it. It's all gone now, though: it's down in the bed of the river; so he can't get it. And I have had all my pain—and I hit pretty hard, I can tell you—for nothing."

Whilst thus narrating the assay of his powers of endurance, he was altering the robe to his liking, by cutting it with his knife wherever it slightly pinched him. Tolerably pleased with his performance after looking at his reflection in the water, he now eyed the stranger with a familiar stare.

"You seem a good sort of fellow, and have a soft and pretty voice; tell me frankly, don't you belong to the Court?"

The Caliph nodded.

"I could see that with half an eye," continued Khaleefeh;

"I knew you at once to be one of the singers, or pipers, from your little mouth and your puffy cheeks. Now, how much a month do you get? ten pieces, eh?"

And our 'rough,' who had grown consequential from his easily-won gold, looked with a patronizing air on the Commander of the Faithful, who again nodded his assent to his conjecture.

"Now *I*," continued he, "earn that sum every day by *my* trade, and if you like to be my man, I'll teach it you. It's better than piping. What say you?"

The Caliph resolved to carry on the joke.

"Don't be a hard master, and I'll do my best," said he laughing. Then, obeying the orders of his instructor, he tucked up his skirts within his girdle, and having arranged the net according to the mode prescribed him, hurled it with all his force into the bed of the river. When it was time to withdraw it, he tugged and tugged with all his might; yet, even when Khaleefeh condescended to assist him, their united force scarcely moved it.

"You ill-omened piper! If my net should be spoilt through your clumsiness, I'll not only take your mule as a compensation, but beat you to a mummy, just to teach you not to hurl your net further than you can draw it back."

The Caliph, with this prospect before him, would gladly have put an end to the adventure by announcing his dignity; but so ignorant and brutal did the fellow seem, that he felt convinced he should merely be disbelieved, and roughly treated as a pretentious braggart.

So, having vainly scanned the horizon in the hope of

beholding the approach of his retinue, he buckled to the task, and by such strenuous exertion that the sweat streamed down his face in rivulets, contrived, by the aid of his herculean master, to safely land both net and cargo.

The multitude of fishes was so great, that Khaleefeh was in excellent humour.

"You're an ugly chap," said he, "but when I've trained you, you'll make a decent fisherman! Now ride off to market and bring back a couple of big baskets. Then, when we have strapped them on your mule, and stowed the fish in them, we will trudge back to town, and you shall hold the scales and sell them, and I'll take the money; nothing can be easier."

I need not say that the Caliph rode away with gladness in his heart at escaping from such an ogre. He succeeded in finding his escort, and merrily narrated to his courtiers his initiation and progress in the art of fishing. At his suggestion they rode on to the Tigris, and emulously bought up the produce of their lord's instruction. So liberal were their payments, that when Khaleefeh returned home at night he reckoned his earnings that day had even exceeded the high average he had lately received.

Meanwhile Zobeide, the legal wife of the Caliph, had taken advantage of his absence to gratify the jealousy she entertained towards the new favourite of her husband. She had prepared a pretty collation, and infused an opiate into one of the most dainty of the dishes. Koot el Kuloob had been invited to amuse her Highness by her minstrelsy, had been offered refreshments, had partaken of the drugged sweetmeats, became insensible, and in that state been incarcerated in a large chest, which was then locked and removed from the harem.

"Let the closed chest and its unseen contents," said Zobeide to one of the eunuchs, "be sold for any price they may fetch in the public market. Whatever sum may be realized retain for your services." She commanded, moreover, that a report should be spread abroad that the ruling favourite, having been accidentally suffocated while eating, had been deposited by her orders in a tomb, which she had caused to be erected to favour the deception.

Haroun was moved even to tears by this sudden catastrophe. He expressed not what he suspected. He was aware that poison was too often resorted to by jealous wives; yet could not believe that one so good and gentle as his cousin Zobeide could have sullied herself by so criminal a deed; he doubted not, however, that the tomb contained the fair charmer who had so enthralled his senses, and abandoned himself, consequently, to unrestrained grief.

The morning after these occurrences, Khaleefeh, for the first time in his life, entered the palace of the Commander of the Faithful. He had given credit on the day before to one of the eunuchs, who, in the scramble to obtain the produce of the royal fishing, being without money at the moment, had requested him to call at the palace, where he would be liberally remunerated.

Giafar observed and recognized his uncouth form in the gateway, and fancying that the Caliph might be amused by an interview with him, and his sadness be dispelled by the quaint oddity of his notions, he bade the attendants detain the fellow for a while, that he might ascertain the pleasure of his Sovereign.

"Your master has come to scold you for not having brought his fish-baskets," said the vizier; "shall I conduct him here, or shall I turn the rascal out of doors?"

"The brute shall raffle for his fate," said the Caliph, whose limbs ached from his forced labour on the previous day. "Write on twenty slips of paper the various grades of punishment, from death to the most trivial of penalties; on another twenty, the various government offices, from the meanest to the highest; on a third set, sums of money, from one to a thousand pieces of gold. He has tempted his fate by his bullying conduct; verily, I will carry out to the uttermost the sentence which Providence shall allot him."

This was not the answer the kind-hearted vizier had expected; but he consoled himself by reflecting, that the chances were two to one in favour of the fisherman. So he led Khaleefeh through room after room until he arrived before the great curtain which veiled the Sovereign and his Court from the outer world. Giafar watched the peasant with curiosity, expecting to see him awe-stricken when he beheld the Caliph in full state, surrounded as he was by his brilliant retinue; but he erred in his judgment.

As the massive curtain was raised to admit them, the eyes of the fisherman lighted upon his late pupil, and he loudly exclaimed, "So you've returned to your old trade: a nice fellow you are, surely, to make a bargain to help me, and to leave me in the lurch, after I had taught you to fish." But his vituperation was checked by the dread silence that prevailed, and the unsympathizing aspect of all around him. There was so cold an impassibility in the features of the Caliph, as he simply pointed to the folded papers, and bade him select his fate, that even the stolid impudence of the bully quailed before the calm dignity of the ruler, and he obeyed his orders with a shaking hand.

"Read it for him," said the Caliph to Giafar.

"One hundred blows with a stick."

A nod, and the doomed one was writhing beneath such stripes as, proud of his brute strength, he was wont to threaten to those less vigorous than himself.

"Maledictions on you all! I'm none the worse for it; I can stand a deal of beating. Let me try my luck again." So cried the enraged fisherman, as, smarting from his punishment, he snatched another paper from the bowl.

"Refrain," said the dark-browed Sovereign, "for should your death be decreed, the full penalty will be exacted."

"I care not: read it, master," replied the flushed peasant, handing the slip to Giafar.

"Nothing."

"Nothing! I'll try my luck once more."

"For the last time then," said Haroun, whose anger was appeased by the repeated ill-fortune of his harsh instructor.

"One piece of gold," was the wording of the paper.

"A hundred blows for a piece of gold: I don't like your terms of business; it's the last time I come here, or my name's not Khaleefeh." And the burly rascal left the presence-chamber without the least show of respect to any one, and hastened to the vestibule, muttering to himself,

"This is the first day of ill-luck since I caught that ugly ape."—But the morning alone had passed.

Just as he was quitting, the eunuch who had bidden him call at the palace to receive the price of his fish, laughingly called out, "Well, friend, how much has your pupil paid you for teaching him your trade?"

"One piece of gold, and a hundred blows of a stick; would to Heaven I had never trusted you for fish! I had better have given it you, than have come hither." And the humbled bully fairly gave way to his feelings, and blubbered outright.

Now the eunuch was a kind-hearted man, and had been so liberally requited by the Sultana Zobeide for some perilous work he had surreptitiously performed for her, that on the spur of the moment he threw his well-lined purse to the fisherman, saying, "Take this to console you." It contained a hundred pieces of gold: the spell of good-luck still beamed upon Khaleefeh.

Roughly yet fervently expressing his gratitude, he proceeded homewards, but not being in a hurry, for he was not going to work with so much money in his pocket, he loitered in the slave-market, where he perceived a little knot of men assembled round the broker, who was offering for sale a large chest and its unknown contents, the latter supposed to be valuable, as they came from the palace of the Sultana. "Bid, noble merchants; it is a fair speculation, and will be sold a bargain: that which comes from the home of royalty must surely be precious. Did you say twenty? Thank you." And the biddings soon rose to one hundred pieces.

Then Khaleefeh, trusting to the influence of the mysterious ape, roared out "And one." The merchants burst out laughing at his impudence, for, to judge from his appearance, he had not even the single unit, and the joke went round, "Let him have it, and see how he will get out of the scrape." No one, therefore, competed with him, and when with a burlesque dignity he had thrown his purse into the hands of the broker, and bidden him count the pieces, he shouldered the huge chest, and, amidst the quizzing of the jeering crowd, trudged homewards, staggering beneath its weight. His back ached; he was very weary, and having vainly essayed to break open the lock without tools, he put off the task until the morrow; and having stretched his mattress upon the top of the chest, for his quarters were very scanty, was soon in the land of dreams.

It was dusk when he awoke. There was something moving beneath him. Was it a wild beast within the chest, or was it an imprisoned ghoul which would devour him if it could escape? Nonsense! it was mere imagination. So he settled himself once more upon his bed. Again there was a violent struggle, and this time a more desperate one, to raise the lid. All was dark; Khaleefeh was so neglectful of household matters, that he had no means of striking a light. His hair stood erect; a cold perspiration poured in large beads from his forehead; his limbs shook with terror as he started from his couch; his knees were so relaxed with vague dread, that they refused to bear his body from the scene of horror. The noise within the chest soon ceased; and then, on hands and knees, he crawled from his narrow chamber. "Help!

neighbours, help! the devil is in my room, and I have no light to see him; lend me a lamp." It was not late, and though they laughed at his absurd mode of expressing himself, they readily provided him with a lamp, and the means of breaking open the chest.

Courage returned with light. The unseen is always terrible. Khaleefeh worked with furious energy, and though the lock was too strong to break, the lid was soon forced from the sundered hinges. It was no savage animal, no hideous ogre, that lay crouched at the bottom of the coffer, but a lovely woman, who having, under the agony of suffocation, struggled violently yet vainly to release herself, had again relapsed into insensibility. The air revived her; a minute later, and Earth would have lost one of the fairest of her daughters.

I will neither dilate upon the astonishment of Koot El Kuloob (for she it was) upon finding herself in a wretched hut in place of a royal palace, nor upon the reluctance of the fisherman to abandon a prize for which he had ventured nearly all his gold. Woman's tact, however, prevailed; the hope of reward proved more potent than the fire of passion, and at her request he absented himself from the house until morning. The accomplished beauty penned a note to the merchant who had introduced her to the royal harem, and Khaleefeh, the bearer of it, was rewarded with a thousand pieces of gold for returning the damsel to her friends.

Nor was this all; for, in her gratitude, she insisted upon an interview between the Caliph and Khaleefeh; and the former, being in high spirits at the recovery of his lovely mistress, listened graciously to the quaint recital of the fisherman's adventures, and bestowed such favours upon him, that the rest of his life was passed in ease and plenty.

He had no need any longer to work for his livelihood; but occupation is needful to all men, and when the irksomeness of idleness oppressed him, he would go down to the great ocean, and cast his nets where none could recognize him as the well-to-do *protégé* of the Commander of the Faithful.

His last adventure was a strange one, and displayed a virtue in him which is daily growing rarer,—I mean gratitude.

There were times when he liked to be alone, and ponder on the past: the comfort of the present was enhanced by a recollection of former hardships. He had selected a very lonely spot for his fishing-ground, one where probably no man for centuries, if ever, had cast his net from. It was the narrow extremity of a ridge of rocks which jutted far into the ocean from a barren district, where the inhabitants were few and unenterprising. Its solitude, the great depth of water, and the quality and size of the finny tribes which disported in the dark-blue element, were most attractive to his mood. One day he fancied his usual seat was already occupied; but the figure, whatever it might be, had vanished long before he reached the extreme rock. There was a dusky mass, perhaps a large fish, perchance a small shoal of them, perceptible within cast of his net, and he so directed the latter that, spreading as it fell, it encircled the object in its meshes.

The creature did not struggle, but was very heavy. When landed and partially unwrapped, it addressed him in a human voice, saying,—

"I am Abdallah of the Sea, and have let myself be caught in order to confer with you. Return, friend,"—for Khaleefeh was springing from rock to rock to escape from the supposed Afreet, who, he thought, was bent upon devouring him,—"for I, like you, am a child of Allah, and seek only our mutual benefit."

The fisherman looked back; his late captive was in the water to his waist, and undistinguishable from the children of the earth. Khaleefeh was no coward, though he dreaded evil spirits more than his fellows did; so he resolved to brave the encounter, "for was he not as muscular and active as the unknown?" He took, then, his former station upon the rock, and listened to the words of the man of the sea.

"I am tired of eating raw fish; and the fruits of the sea, though pretty, are salt and unpalatable. When, from afar off, I have beheld the clustering grapes and the swollen melons, I have longed for them. Bring me some, child of Adam, and I will requite you with the loveliest products of the sea, such as our women like to deck themselves with, but which we males smile at."

Khaleefeh gladly consented to this exchange, and promised to bring his new acquaintance the fruits of the season, but not until the next day, for it was not easy to obtain them by purchase in that uncultivated land. On the morrow they again met, and the fisherman handed to the merman a basketful of grapes and melons, and the man of the sea, on his part, pointed to a little pile of scarlet coral, lumps of gold, large pearls, and other treasures of the deep, which he had amassed in anticipation of the return of his friend. Both were pleased at the barter, for the fruits of the land were as rare to Abdallah as those of the sea to Khaleefeh. So, after each had expressed his mutual satisfaction, and the latter had concealed the valuables in his net, they conversed together on the peculiarities of their respective elements.

"Would it be possible," inquired the fisherman, who longed to behold the habits and customs of the denizens of Ocean, "to visit your abode?"

"Yes," was the answer, if he should permit his body to be smeared with oil from the liver of the Dendan, a predaceous monster of the deep, he would temporarily assume their own nature, and be enabled to breathe the air that was mingled with the water, even as they did. So he undressed himself, was anointed, and walked and respired on the bed of the sea as freely as on dry land, and very shortly all things were as clearly visible to him as in the light of the sun.

The water seemed as densely peopled as the earth, and its human inhabitants were similar in front to the children of Adam, but were furnished behind with a broad flexible caudal appendage, like the hinder extremity of a fish. They dwelt in vast caverns, had no traffic with each other, wore no clothes, did not sell their labour, as the children of earth do, but every one, whether male or female, caught with facility as many fish as were needful to sustain life, and munched them raw as a child would a cucumber. They had neither amusement, interest, nor occupation, but lounged about sadly, neither hoping nor craving anything. The females were beautiful, but very pert, laughing and pointing at Khaleefeh as they passed him, and crying aloud, "See! he has lost his tail!"

It is not pleasant to be jeered at, especially by the sex, and our hero was glad to return to land, for existence seemed monotonous and insupportable in that cheerless element, where equality displayed itself in the universal absence of all that was pleasurable. And so did the inhabitants seem to regard life; for the only sounds of revelry which he heard, were the loud shouts of triumph which greeted the death of one of the natives. The fisherman looked so astonished at this apparent want of feeling, that his guide inquired whether the children of Adam did not act similarly on so joyful an occasion.

"Assuredly not," he answered; "we mourn and grieve; our women shriek aloud, slap their faces, and rend their garments."

Abdallah seemed shocked: he uttered not a word until they had regained the rock. "Farewell, for ever," he then cried, "I will have nought to do with a race which either believes not in a more blissful existence hereafter than we experience in this wretched life, or, if believing it, enviously laments the future happiness of the departed."

They never met again. But as to Khaleefeh, he presented all his ocean treasures to the Caliph, begging him to give some of them to Koot El Kuloob, through whose kindness he had obtained the patronage of his lord.

Rough, superstitious, and irascible, he was not ungrateful, and so far merited the good fortune which ever after attended him.

THE STORY OF JOODAR.

"WELCOME, my brothers; I am glad to see you," was the kindly salutation of Joodar, the fisherman, to his unkind brethren, when they visited him in his poverty. They, too, were poor, even poorer than he was; for, although his patrimony had been swallowed up equally with their own in mutual litigation, he, at least, being thrifty and industrious, earned, by his daily toil, a comfortable living for himself and his mother. They, on the contrary, self-indulgent, lazy, and rapacious, had been the cause of their joint ruin by their grasping cupidity. At the decease of their father, a wealthy merchant, his property, by his direction, had been divided into four portions, one for each child, and one for their mother; but Salim and Selim, the two elder sons, who were profligate spendthrifts, had sought to appropriate the entire heritage, and to leave their mother and younger brother to shift for themselves.

Law is a hiltless sword-blade, which cuts the hand of him who wields it, even as it cleaves his opponent: its ruinous cost involved the whole family alike in penury.

Joodar, the youngest, whose great social error (not an uncommon one with the weak-minded and the benevolent) was a too high respect for the ties of blood had already, in his heart, pardoned those whose active selfishness had reduced him from comparative opulence to manual labour, and now affectionately greeted the sponging sneaks whom his foolish mother had been slily regaling at his expense. Alas for mothers! they rarely cling to the best, but seek, by an unreasoning tenderness, to compensate the more worthless of their offspring for the scorn and loathing with which the righteous regard them. I doubt whether the silly parent, although Joodar alone had burdened himself with her maintenance, did not temporarily prefer the caitiffs whose misconduct had brought her to her present straits.

And now the fisherman—for the merchant's son had betaken himself to that calling as the easiest and the quickest to be acquired—had two new dependants upon his scanty earnings, men who, on the plea of inability, tacitly refused to aid him in his daily toil. So long as he had luck, he almost gloried in the thought, that those who had been the curse of his existence were now indebted to him for their bread; but when luck had turned, and subsistence for four could only be procured upon a precarious credit, anxiety overwhelmed him. He changed his fishing-ground from spot to spot, until at last he betook himself to the deep and unfrequented lake of Karoon. Just as he arrived there, a richly-dressed traveller, a Moor to all appearance, rode up quickly on his mule, and to his surprise, addressed him by name. "Do my bidding, Joodar, son of Omar, and whatever may betide myself, nought but good can accrue to you."

"I am your servant," he answered; "tell me what I must do to please you."

"Bind my hands tightly with this silken cord; throw me into the water; watch patiently until either my hands or feet appear; if the former, cast your net quickly, and drag me out; save me, and I will provide for you for life; if the latter, be assured that I have perished. Trouble not yourself with my carcase, but take this mule and its accoutrements to Shumeyah the Jew, who will give you a hundred pieces of gold in requital."

These instructions were obeyed: in a minute the feet floated foremost to the surface, and though, contrary to his orders, the benevolent fisherman strove to recover the body, the corpse sank for ever in the dark waters. Joodar sadly drove the mule to the abode of Shumeyah: that night he had paid his debts, yet was still possessed of more than ninety pieces of gold; he intrusted them to his mother.

The next day he betook himself to the same lucky fishing-ground. Did his eyes deceive him? No: there was the same Moor, clad in the same vestments, seated on the same mule, with the same peculiar saddle-bags strapped to its sides. "Joodar, son of Omar, nought but profit can accrue to you: treat me as you did my brother yesterday; the risk is mine. Save me, and I will enrich you. Should I even perish in my glorious enterprise, a hundred pieces of gold will be paid for my mule and its furniture."

"The folly is his, not mine," thought Joodar, as he

complied with the suicidal directions of the traveller. The feet came up foremost; this time he did not even trouble himself to recover the corpse. Another purse of gold awaited him that night. The Jew sighed as he counted out the money, saying, "I knew the result beforehand; he had better have been content." Again did the fisherman intrust his gold to his weak-minded mother.

On the third day he betook himself once more to the selfsame spot. There was another Moor, whom he saw from afar off, already waiting for him. "It is a thriving business I am doing," said he to himself, "helping these heretics to drown themselves in this deep water; I doubt not the fish are fattening under their savoury diet. I suppose there will be another purse for me to-night.'

"Joodar, son of Omar," cried the traveller, "do with me as thou hast done with my two brethren."

"With pleasure," said the fisherman. "I know my trade now, and will bind your hands, toss you into the lake, and carry off your mule."

"Not so fast, friend. It may, indeed, be my fate, yet it is not my wish to die; save me, then, and thy reward shall be tenfold what thou wouldst gain by my decease; therefore should my hands appear, cast quickly thy net, and rescue me from the drowning water."

"I'll do my best," answered Joodar; and before he thrust him from the bank, he carefully inspected his net, to see that all was in readiness to cast it after him. This time the hands appeared foremost, and almost before the rising head could shout for aid, the traveller, immeshed in the rapidly thrown net, was dragged to land.

"Quick; bring me the two boxes you will find in my saddle-bags," cried the Moor, and in them he deposited two fishes, scarlet as coral, which he had brought with him from the bottom of the lake. Having secured his perilously won spoils he embraced Joodar, saying, "I owe my life to you, and will not be ungrateful. The supposed Jew is really a Moslem, and my brother. I must hurry to his house, to change my clothes; proceed thither at your leisure, and I will there not only explain all past mysteries, but recompense you also to your own satisfaction."

That afternoon the fisherman walked to the house of Shumeyah, and there found his daring acquaintance of the morning seated in quiet comfort.

"I will now reveal to you," said the Moor, "all the sad history of my family, and, if you are willing, will adopt you as my brother. Those who perished before your eyes were the sons of my father, a mighty magician, the pupil of the renowned El Abtan. He died before his master; partly, I think, from disappointment in having failed in that enterprise, the initiatory step of which I have this day accomplished. At his death, his vast wealth was equitably and amicably divided between his four sons. His inestimable book of magic alone excited the cupidity of each of us.

"'Dispute not, children of my beloved pupil,' said the aged instructor of our dear father in that art of arts. 'Ye cannot each possess the book. Let me, therefore, hold it in trust for all, and deliver it to him alone who shall acquire the treasures of Shamardal. Now these magic treasures are four:—a sword, a kohl-pot, a planisphere, and a seal-ring. Whoso shall brandish the first in anger, his adversaries will be withered as by lightning; all hidden treasures will be revealed to him whose eyelids shall be touched by the contents of the second; the whole world, and all that is passing therein, can be viewed at ease by him who shall gaze upon the third: whilst omnipotence upon earth will be the lot of him who shall acquire the fourth. The owner of that ring could take the magic scroll from any of you; therefore freely resign it to the successful competitor.'

"We felt the wisdom of his words, agreed to abide by the trial of skill (all but the ease-loving Shumeyah, who abandoned his claim), and inquired of the sage how the treasure-vault might be opened. 'Without the assent of the sons of the Red King, who have changed themselves to coral-fish, and taken refuge in the lonely lake of Kharoon, ye cannot even descry it; ye must force them to show it. But destiny has decreed that this can only occur through the latent power of Joodar, the son of Omar. None can capture them with unfettered hands; their captor must be bound by the predestined one, who must thrust him into the lake. He who fails to seize them will assuredly perish; he who captures them will perish likewise, if not saved by the net of Joodar.' Two of us have been drowned in this noble emulation; I have succeeded thus far, but the charm can only be completed by your presence.' What say you? will you travel, as my friend and adopted brother, to Fez and Mequinez? The road seems long, but, mounted as we shall be, the journey will be brief."

"I have a mother and two brethren to provide for," replied the warm-hearted son of Omar.

"A thousand pieces of gold are yours if you consent; leave that sum with them for their maintenance, and come with me: I will not prove ungrateful for your aid."

A short interview with his parent ensued, and our hero started on his travels. His patron and himself bestrode the same mule. At eventide they alighted, and the Moorish traveller, unstrapping his saddle-bags, inquired of his companion what he would like for supper. "Whatever you have provided."—"You have but to name the dish you fancy, and it will be found prepared. What say you to hot roast chickens, kabobs, rice, and honey, etc., etc.?" naming a score of dishes. To none of these did Joodar object; and after having supped heartily, his patron explained to him that this peripatetic kitchen was an enchanted one, and that no imaginable dish would be refused by its ministering spirit. "Perhaps," continued he, "you suppose, as we only started at noon, that we have not journeyed far. This is a mistake; our enchanted steed has already borne us a month's journey from the lake. Bear in mind that I have mastered the initiatory steps of magic; its grand results are yet to be achieved."

In five days, during which all their wants had been lavishly supplied from those apparently simple saddle-bags, they arrived at Fez. There they reposed for three weeks, dwelling in luxury at the superb mansion of the African magician. "It is now time," said the latter, "that we should essay the feat of opening the treasures of Shamardal."

They journeyed for some distance into the wilderness, until they arrived at the banks of a deep river. Then the magician drew forth from his saddle-bags the little boxes in which he carried the coral-fish, and muttered charms over them, at which the earth beneath quaked, and the heavens above thundered. The boxes split asunder, and two noble-looking genii, whose hands were bound behind them, like the Moorish brethren who had been precipitated into the lake of Karoon, bursting like vapour from them, floated in the air aloft. "What will you, O mortal?" they cried; "we are now your slaves, bound to you by the death you risked in mastering us."—"Open the pathway to the treasures of Shamardal; I have brought hither the predestined one who alone may venture beneath the running water. Obey, or I will scathe you with flames, as spiritual as is your essence." They bowed their willing assent, and the magician cast incense upon the fire which Joodar had been preparing. The aspect of the Moor had changed; he was no longer the man of the world, genial, persuasive, courteous, but a lordly ruler, one who could compete with intelligences as far above man as he to the soulless beasts. There was dignity and command in his every gesture; there was nobility of spirit and lofty intellect stamped upon every feature. His face, his form was transfigured; as though the glorious beings whose very opposition to his wishes had resulted from no volition of their own, but from inflexible obedience to talismans which had enthralled them for centuries, had elevated his rank in creation by their forced association with his grosser nature.

The duties of Joodar had been explained to him previously; no words of earthly import were permitted to mar the solemn chant that now issued from the lips of the magician. The words, if they might be so called, were uttered in no tongue that was known to man; they seemed to whistle, as it were, from half-closed lips; the rustling of the winds amidst foliage, the howling of gales, the plash of waves upon the shore, seemed the nearest approach to the strange medley of sounds which agitated the moaning air. As the incense floated in clouds, which assumed unearthly shapes, the water of the river was sucked up by it in a broad column, and the dry bed of the stream disclosed the gilded door of a subterranean cavern. Thrice did Joodar, who had boldly leapt into the chasm, knock loudly for admission, and then the gate flew open, and an armed spectre, rushing from it, furiously struck at him with its scimetar. He smiled as he received the painless blow, and advanced from gate to gate, assaulted in turn by arrow, spear, and mace, all equally terrifying, all equally innocuous. Yet impotent as they were, had his heart quailed he would have perished; for the fear of death, with spiritual natures (and none but such would have ventured thus far in the domain of magic), is death itself. A lion bounded upon him, two huge serpents coiled around him; he vanquished them all by his passive yet unretiring submission. The last trial was a strange one. His earlier temptations were based upon the natural terrors of an unarmed man when suddenly confronted by weapons he could not hope to withstand; he who had framed the talisman had resolved that no craven spirit should inherit his treasures. He had determined likewise that none who would yield to the delusions of prejudice should succeed to powers too exalted for the dwarfed intellect of the existing race. All the tenderness of Joodar's nature was concentrated in his filial regard for his mother. Her image rose before him as he approached the last door which intervened between himself and the mummy of the embalmed Shamardal. "Welcome, my son!" she cried. "Strip thyself!" he exclaimed,—for he had been cautioned against this phantom,—and the spectre, ever expostulating against this immodest exposure, still obeyed, until nought but the final garment concealed her nakedness from him. "Spare me this last shame, my child!" she cried; "the gate is open." And Joodar, yielding to her beseeching looks, passed onwards; but wild yells of laughter saluted him; blows were showered on him from unseen hands; and amidst the clash of doors, the thundering roar of the bursting waterspout as the river fell again into its wonted bed, he was cast, senseless and sorely bruised, before the feet of the magician. When he woke to consciousness all was still; no words of reproach met him from the Moor, although one more year of life (brief at the best) must elapse before the charm could again be broken.

During this whole twelvemonth our hero was most kindly maintained by his ambitious patron, who convinced him so effectually that the image of his mother, which had vanquished him, was a mere spectre, her embodied reflection without her consciousness, that when that vision, at the expiration of his year of expectancy, had again implored him to refrain from compelling her to expose her nudity before her son, he sternly reminded her of his beating, and forced her to disrobe. As, pleading piteously all the while, she was reluctantly loosing her innermost garment, her frame dissolved itself before his eyes; nought, now, opposed his entrance to the sepulchral chamber. From thence he removed the four enchanted treasures, taking them reverently from the embalmed corpse of the great Shamardal; and as he did so, a mighty volume of sound, like the triumphant shouts of liberated spirits, burst upon his ears. Amidst the crash of converging walls that followed the dissolution of the spell which had so long held captive the reluctant genii, a powerful current of air urged on the half-senseless adventurer to the portal of the cavern, and from thence he seemed to be wafted, without volition, to the spot where the sorcerer was still uttering his sonorous incantation. Air had been invoked to aid him; and that element, submissive to the voice of the charmer, had borne him safely to the feet of the magician.

Freely and willingly did Joodar resign the coveted spoils to his friend and patron. The only reward he solicited (when pressed to ask a recompense) was the hunger-staving saddle-bags; but a pile of gold and jewels was added by the Moor, who, moreover, lent him his wondrous mule, which, though heavily burdened, carried him to his distant home without guidance in but five days.

As he re-entered the gates of his native city, the first sight which met his eyes was that dear mother whom, despite of her tender weakness, he had always venerated. She was begging her bread. Yes, she whom he had left with nearly twelve hundred pieces of gold was now dependent on the charity of the faithful. She recognized him with a cry of delight, and the good and dutiful son, having alighted from his mule, set her beloved form upon it, and humbly escorted her on foot, to his desolate home.

"Ask me not of the money you left with me," she cried, in reply to his inquiries. "My children borrowed it from me, under the pretext of trading; we were alike weak,—I in yielding our all, they by wasting it in debauchery; now we are alike destitute." So spoke the loving mother, whose forgiving tenderness prevailed over her conviction of the baseness of her first-born.

The warm-hearted Joodar forgave them likewise, and when they presented themselves in rags before him received them with cordiality. To the astonishment of his parent he provided a sumptuous meal from his saddle-bags, and then taught her the mysterious formula by which the attendant genius was invoked.

Plenty revisited the dwelling which had become cheerless and dilapidated through long-continued poverty: repasts, such as the richest citizen might have envied, were thrice a day provided for the reunited family. The viands were served hot, yet no smoke emerged from the chimneys; enough was left each day to maintain a score of mendicants, yet neither meat, vegetables, nor farina was purchased by the occupants.

Of course the elder sons soon wheedled the secret from the silly old woman, and then felt indignant that they should be dependent upon their younger brother. "If we could only manage," said Selim, "to get hold of his enchanted saddle-bags, and his store of gold and jewels, we could take our pleasure, and revel in joys which his woman-like prudery now forbids us. Yet how can we abstract them without detection while he remains at home?" So, not content with fair apparel, the pleasures of the table, unrebuked idleness, and a comfortable house, they consulted together how they might get rid of their brother, and then fearlessly divide his property between them.

It chanced that a certain captain, a sort of kidnapping fellow, who voyaged between Cairo and the less known ports, and who, in times of old, had been a fellow-roysterer with them, was at that time sojourning in the city.

"Our brother," said they, "is a ne'er-do-well; he has almost ruined us, too, by his love of litigation. We will deliver him into your hands as a slave, provided you will engage to transport him to some distant land, from whence he can never return to disgrace us."

Whatever the rover thought, he assented to the unnatural proposition, for he was not over-particular, and slaves were worth money in the countries he traded with. He was requested to bring two of his most trustworthy followers with him, and to sup at the house of Joodar.

The brothers, on their part, apologetically narrated to their entertainer that they had ventured, from a conviction of the unfailing nature of his supplies, to invite three foreigners, who had generously befriended them in their adversity, to partake of his hospitality.

"Welcome to you, and all your friends," was the generous reply of our hero, who received his treacherous guests with confiding friendliness. That very night he was overpowered by the mariners, gagged, and carried on board the piratical craft: his mother was assured that he had voluntarily departed at the urgent summons of his Moorish friend. For he had imparted the whole story of his adventures to his weak-minded parent, who could keep no secrets from any of her children.

For more than a twelvemonth did Joodar endure the painful lot of a galley-slave; hard work and privation were his daily experience. At last the vessel, whose oars he helped to tug, was wrecked on the coast of Barbary, and he alone, of the entire crew, survived the storm. The natives were rough and churlish; it would have fared hardly with him, had not a merchant who had been trading with them, and now required a servant to accompany him to Mecca, proffered him the situation. The offer was of course accepted, and, after the ordinary incidents of travel, the weary pilgrimage was duly completed.

In that sacred city, equally to his joy and his astonishment, he encountered the Moorish magician, who, though gifted with powers which genii might have envied, reverenced the doctrines and observances which our holy Prophet has inculcated. There were none there who worshipped Allah with more fervent devotion and with more profound humility, than the exalted yet unpretentious being who could sway monarchs to his will. Lofty souls comprehend the infinite distance between the highest grade of power and intellect that can be reached by man or angels, and the illimitable omnipotence of the Supreme Divinity.

He was welcomed by the Moor with an affectionate

heartiness which was merited by the man who had honourably yielded up treasures which no mortal could have forced him to relinquish. In the privacy of his lodgings, the magician, at the request of his friend, recalled the fleeting images of all the chief events which had occurred to Joodar's family during his protracted absence. These pictures—and there is not a sound or a sight in nature which leaves not its palpable trace in the universe—told the past as clearly as a biographer could have related it. In the first vision his mother was perceived inquiring from her two elder-born as to whither her protector had departed, and the voices of the reprobates were heard asserting that their brother was of a roving disposition, and had gone away with his Moorish friend in quest of hidden treasures. The mother was next seen weeping, and the jealous brethren were heard scoffing at her tears, indignantly reproaching her "that she had never thus bewailed their own absence."

Her angry rejoinder sounded clearly, as when uttered, "You are my sons, I own; yet what but evil have I ever experienced at your hands? Joodar, on the contrary, has cherished and befriended me; I rightly, then, weep for one who is not only my child, but my benefactor." The brutal ingrates were seen beating and reviling her. In a moment this picture also became dim, and Salim and Selim were beheld quarrelling as they divided the valuables brought by their brother from Fez and Mequinez. The saddle-bags were a bone of contention; if divided they would be useless: hence, despite the suggestion of their parent, that she should retain them and use them for their mutual benefit, each of them coveted the sole possession of this inexhaustible kitchen, and tenaciously grasped it with both hands. So loudly were they disputing, that a subordinate officer of justice, who chanced to be loitering in the adjacent house, heard their angry recriminations, and apprised his superiors of the villainy that had been perpetrated.

The scene changed quickly; the brothers were now in prison, the jewels and saddle-bags in the royal treasury, and the mother living in competence from the allowance made her by government from the gold of her stolen son.

In the last few minutes these resuscitated images of the past had revealed to our hero all that was of interest to him during the eighteen months of his servitude. He took leave of the merchant who had so kindly treated him, and having duly performed all the rites that were enjoined by his religion, resolved to return to the land of his fathers. When he paid his farewell visit to the Moor, that noble-hearted man presented him with the most precious of his talismans, the mystic seal-ring of Shamardal, which controlled one of the mightiest of the genii. It was a gift worthy of the giver, one which an earthly sovereign might have begrudged the most faithful of his friends.

With a wish, he was in Cairo: so ethereal was the genius of the ring, so penetrating his essence, that words were not required to communicate the ideas of his masters. There needed but to rub the talisman, and the unexpressed desire was carried into execution. The wanderer again rejoined his mother, who, equally with himself, forgave the base ingratitude of Salim and of Selim; pity for their sufferings—since not only had they been immured in a filthy dungeon, but tortured that they might disclose the charm which swayed the saddle-bags—obliterated the memory of their offences. This harshness of the sovereign, who had, moreover, appropriated to his own use the jewels which rightly belonged to our hero, diverted his anger from the evil-doers to their rapacious judge. Hence, full of compassion, and fondly believing that solitude and misery must have changed their hearts, he bade the genius set free his imprisoned brethren and transport them to his abode. In an instant they were by his side. Squalid, half-starved, foul with vermin, they had become so wretched that they almost longed for death to relieve them from such continuous suffering. Yet this meeting with the brother whom they had sold into slavery, and he evidently so potent that the very genii obeyed him, overwhelmed them with abject terror; they would have welcomed their prison-house in preference. "What tortures we shall undergo! how horribly he will avenge himself! for who can forgive such wrongs as we have done him?" was the anguishing reflection that pierced the soul of each. Yet only for a moment: as they timidly raised their eyes, they discerned the pity that beamed from his, and heard once more his friendly salutation, "Welcome, my brothers; you shall soon forget your past sorrows in the happiness that awaits you." He raised them from the suppliant attitude into which they had instinctively cast themselves; he led them to the bath, clothed them in rich raiment, sumptuously feasted them, and treated them with consideration. But when they tried to partially excuse themselves (for they sought to recover his good opinion) by laying the blame of his abduction upon the sea-captain and their own intoxication, he interrupted them with promptness, saying, "Speak not of the matter; I know the truth; the devil tempted you, and I was treated as was Joseph: all is now forgiven. But what did the Sultan do unto you?"

"He stripped us of all, and beat us that we might reveal the invocation to the spirit of the saddle-bags, without which charm they were useless to him. We have baffled him, for we declared it was known to yourself alone."

Then Joodar rubbed his ring and willed that the entire contents of the royal treasury should be conveyed to his abode. He commanded, likewise, that a magnificent palace should be erected, right royally furnished, fitted with all appliances that might conduce to ease and comfort, and provided with an adequate number of both male and female domestics.

When the sun arose next morning, the inhabitants of Cairo were astounded at beholding the superb structure that had sprung up during the night. Thither did Joodar and his mother betake themselves to reside. His own house he abandoned to his brethren, whom he amply endowed with funds for their maintenance.

As the Sultan's treasurer, pallid with dismay, was reporting to his sovereign that all the royal wealth had disappeared, though the walls, roof, and flooring of the vault were still solid, and the massive bolts and chains had been found fastened, information was brought that Joodar had returned and taken possession of a noble-looking palace, which had been mysteriously erected during the preceding night. The jailor had been previously in attendance to excuse himself for the inexplicable escape of Salim and of Selim.

"It is plain," said the Sultan, "that Joodar is at the bottom of all this; it is he who has robbed me; arrest him without delay."

So an officer with fifty men proceeded to the abode of the presumed delinquent, and found a huge black slave reposing at his ease before the portal, who stirred not from his seat when the pompous official roughly inquired where his master could be found, but simply answered, "In the palace." Indignant at this want of respect for his authority, the irritated functionary struck at him with his mace; but, in a moment, it was wrested from his hand, and the armed attendants and their arbitrary leader driven from the spot by the incredible vigour and rapid blows of the irresistible black. In vain, obedient to the royal mandate, did the repulsed official return, with twice and then with quadruple as many men, who assailed the guardian of the palace with their swords; they were routed as before, for their weapons passed through the seeming slave even as through air; whilst the crushing blows from the earthly mace which had been torn from the hand of their leader, fell upon them quick and numerous as the blinding hailstones. What mortal could resist the ministering spirit of the ring? for he it was, who in human guise watched over the safety of his lord. Then the Sultan was wroth, and would have sent more troops against him; but his vizier, a prudent man, suggested that it was better to treat one so mighty as a friend than as an enemy.

"By your permission, sire, I will invite him to the Palace, where, far away from that terrible black, he will be more in your power." The sovereign nodded assent; and the vizier, unarmed and without an escort, calmly approached the dreaded sentinel.

"I am come from the ruler of our land," said he, bending courteously to the reposing figure, "to invite the attendance of the master of this palace at the royal banquet."

"Mortal!" replied the guardian, and this single word revealed to the vizier the nature of the invulnerable being who addressed him, "I will announce your message to my lord." Permitted, after a short delay, to enter the presence of Joodar, the minister was treated with due courtesy; but an intimation was conveyed that the sovereign must first pay his respects, as an inferior to a superior, ere the lord of spirits would deign to accept his invitation.

This arrogance was not without effect: the Sultan, accompanied by a large body of picked soldiers to display his power, rode to the palace of his haughty subject, which he found guarded by what seemed to him the most stalwart warriors of the East, but which were in reality unsubstantial creations of the genius of the ring, and, at the sight of them, felt convinced that their master must be conciliated, not coerced. The state which surrounded Joodar (a mere optical delusion) completely vanquished him; the glamour was so perfect, that he submitted with patience to the stern questioning looks of his taciturn entertainer.

"I confess," at length said the abashed monarch, after

a painful silence, "that, urged by covetousness, I have deprived your mother of some property which was intrusted to her by yourself; yet, nevertheless, my interference has saved her from utter ruin, by guarding her from those who would have stripped her of everything."

"Let there be peace between us!" answered Joodar; "I arraign not your intentions; nothing which belonged to yourself will be found missing from your treasury when next you enter it."

The monarch departed enriched by presents not unworthy of a sovereign to receive or to bestow, yet fearful for his crown, since he was conscious that henceforth he was only second in power in his own dominions. His prudent vizier perceiving his anxiety, assured him that one gifted as was Joodar would never aspire to the throne, since he already enjoyed its pleasures without its pains; finally, he advised his master, should he still dread the ambition of one who was above its temptations, to ally himself to him by the ties of blood. So the ruler of Egypt, who appreciated the ability of his minister, lived on friendly terms with his dangerous subject, and both received and returned his hospitality.

The Sultan had a charming daughter, of nubile years, who, by his orders, when Joodar, now a frequent guest at the royal abode, was feasting in private with him, and was warm with wine, passed demurely through the banquet-room.

"Is she not lovely?" said the scheming father.

"A houri!" answered Joodar.

"Who may be yours for asking," was the rejoinder:

and ere four-and-twenty hours had elapsed, our hero had become the son-in-law of his Sultan.

Time rolled on unheeded: those are the happiest, the current of whose fortunes is least ruffled by the successive tides of adversity and prosperity. The vizier virtually ruled the country, and it prospered under his skilful guidance.

After many years, a period of tranquil happiness to our hero, his doting mother and his royal father-in-law departed from life at nearly the same period. The vacated throne was offered Joodar by the people, and, little as he cared for sway, he accepted it to gratify his princely partner. He made his brothers dignitaries of the highest rank. But benefits conferred upon the innately evil only stimulate them to increased rapacity.

"How long shall our younger brother lord it over us?" said Salim to Selim. "He has no natural heirs, and we shall inherit the crown at his decease."

The same thought had entered the heart of Selim, but he had not the daring to avow it.

"He prefers you to me," continued the former; "therefore invite him to your house, and introduce this tasteless poison in his food; it slays so quickly, that death outruns suspicion."

"Agreed," said Selim, "provided you consent that I be Sultan. You shall be next in rank."

Such was the evil compact; and as Joodar, despite of past experience, would not mistrust those of his own blood, the scheme succeeded. The good King ate, and was gathered to his fathers: even while he was yet expiring, both brothers simultaneously snatched at the talisman, but Salim, who had advisedly sat next the hand which wore it, grasped it first, and bade the genius slay his fellow-criminal. So the elder brother, by this double crime, became the monarch of Egypt; and the people murmured, yet obeyed him.

Then he determined to consolidate his power by wedding the widow of his murdered predecessor, and she perforce consented; but he survived not his wedding night, for the same virulent poison which had carried off his brother was administered to himself by the avenger of her lord. That none hereafter might abuse the god-like power of the talisman, the Princess crushed the stone to atoms with a hammer, and scattered to the winds its pounded dust. As to the saddle-bags, she immediately destroyed them. Magic pleased her not; an enchanter could smile at the frowns of royalty; and though she cared no longer for rule, her feelings and her blood were alike regal. After this she retired into private life, leaving the succession to the throne to be settled by the priests and nobles.

And this is all that history has told us of the uneventful reign of Joodar.

ABOO SEER AND ABOO KEER;

OR,

THE TWO CRAFTSMEN.

IN the whole city of Alexandria you would scarcely have found two men less likely to become friends than Aboo Seer the barber and Aboo Keer the dyer. The former was truthful, just, and benevolent; the latter false, roguish, and intensely selfish. Yet propinquity does wonders; and so dull was the district, and so slack their trade, that, being next-door neighbours, they would while away their idle hours in friendly gossip. They were both masters of their respective callings; and so skilful was the dyer, that want of principle alone prevented him from succeeding in business. He would always ask an advance from the party who might bring him goods, and forthwith expend it in dainty food and luscious drink; then he would sell the articles intrusted to him, and live on the proceeds, excusing himself day by day for not having finished his job, by some specious lie, as, "Unexpected guests arrived, and the duties of hospitality compelled me to refrain from work;" and again, "My wife was confined, and of course it became impossible to devote proper attention to your order;" until at last, when the indignant customer demanded back his goods, done or undone, the liar, with unabashed effrontery, would cajole his victim in this fashion: "I must own the truth, then, though I am ashamed to relate what has occurred; I had succeeded admirably with your cloth (the tint was clear and brilliant), and when I hung it out to dry I anticipated your praise. From that moment I have never seen it; some sneaking thief—and we live in a bad quarter for rogues—must have purloined it. I am too poor to replace it; I throw myself upon your mercy." The majority of those he thus fleeced put up with his rascality, either from indolence, good-nature, or consciousness of the impossibility of making him refund what he no longer possessed; occasionally he was roughly abused, but he cared little for words. His character eventually, however, became so notorious that none would employ him except perfect strangers; his poverty became so extreme that he was almost destitute. At this juncture a customer (a rough one as he turned out) presented himself, and was served as usual; but he would not be put off with words, for when he found himself cheated he applied for redress to the magistrate, by whose order, when nothing was found in the dyer's shop to compensate the complainant, the door of the rogue's dwelling was nailed up and sealed in the presence of witnesses. Then Aboo Keer betook himself for comfort to his gossip's house, and bewailed the hardness of the times in general, and his recent misadventure in particular.

"Men of our ability," he continued, "might gain a little fortune in other lands, where competition is less excessive; besides, wandering is pleasant work: it enlarges the mind to view the habits and customs of other nations. I've made up my mind to leave this accursed city. Why not journey along with me? you can scarcely fare worse than at present; you will possibly prosper beyond your expectations."

With such words he persuaded his easy neighbour to accompany him, seeking his companionship not from any peculiar regard for him, for he was utterly incapable of affection for man or beast, but because he felt assured that the few pieces of money his friend still possessed would thus be expended in providing food for both alike. When the shrewd dyer had so far succeeded, he suggested that, as they were like brothers, they should make a solemn agreement, a covenant which, fair and equitable between the truthful and honest, would inevitably profit the perfidious, should one like Aboo Keer prove a party to its terms. It was to this effect: that whichever of them should obtain remunerative employment, that individual should maintain the other whilst out of work. It was stipulated further by these adventurers that whatsoever surplus should accrue beyond their joint expenses should be put aside, and equally divided on their return to their native land. For thither, despite their recent depreciation of it, they wished to return, since our natural home is where our thoughts can most truly be expounded by our tongues, and our ineradicable tastes and habits can most easily be satisfied.

Now the thought of emigration had long lain dormant in their minds; so when they poured forth to each other the well-digested result of many crude cogitations, their words were few, but deductive. Their skill, they argued, would be best appreciated where civilization had not taught others to compete with them; the further from Alexandria the less likely was it that the people should be civilized; *ergo*, it was desirable that they should journey to a far-off country. A large ship was to sail next morning; so they resolved to pack up their poor clothing, and make their needful preparations for departure that very evening. Aboo Seer sold his furniture for what it would fetch, and paid the passage-money for both himself and his companion, as the dyer had long ago parted with everything saleable; even the mattress he slept on was a borrowed one.

Their stock of sea-provisions was very limited, for little remained of the proceeds of the sale after their fares had been paid; but Aboo Seer trusted to the unfailing goodness of Providence, and Aboo Keer to his own tried sharpness, should hunger compel him to exert himself for food.

Good luck befriended them. It chanced that amidst the throng of passengers not a single individual was competent to act as barber; perceiving which, Aboo Seer, having thrown a towel over his shoulder, took his station upon deck, holding his razor, basin, and other tonsorial apparatus conspicuously before him. It was not long before some one addressed him, and having desired him to perform his functions on his behalf, gave him in requital (as he preferred food to money) a small cake of bread and some cheese. These he freely bestowed upon his worthless comrade, who greedily devoured them, lounging upon his bed; then, returning to his occupation, he reaped so plentiful a harvest of customers, that ere night his sea-stock was enlarged by no less than thirty little loaves, besides cheese, olives, and fish-relish. The captain, moreover, engaged his services, and in place of salary promised to provide supper each evening for himself and companion. At dusk he went to the cabin in high spirits to communicate his good tidings, to stow away his provisions, and to summon his associate to partake of the good things that were smoking upon the captain's table. Aboo Keer was fast asleep, for eating and sleeping were the chief delights of his animal existence.

"Wake up, friend," cried the joyous barber, "and see and hear of the bounty of Heaven."

The lazy glutton's eyes had scarcely opened, when he clutched at the food, and would have conveyed it to his mouth, had not his hand been arrested by his more thoughtful visitor.

"Not to-night, man, not to-night; we are going to sup at the captain's expense; let us leave these viands for another occasion."

"I have been sea-sick, and feel too weak to rise; suffer me to take a little food, for emptiness is exhausting; and go you, who are strong and hearty, and feast with the captain."

So the tender-hearted barber acquiescing, sat down, and recounted all the details of his good-luck, and merrily watched the self-designated invalid, as he cut off vast hunches of bread, and covering them thriftlessly with the relishes, and scarcely masticating them, bolted them hastily with staring eyes, as though fearful that the food over which he was snorting would be snatched from him ere he gulped it down. Yet the worthy barber was amused, for he was a humorist, not a philosopher, and discerned not the greedy selfishness of the action, but only its comicality. Smiling goodnaturedly at the voracity of the dyer, Aboo Seer departed on his visit to the captain, to whom he excused the absence of his companion on the score of sea-sickness.

"It won't harm him; he will be the better for it afterwards; but he sha'n't go without his supper," was the friendly rejoinder of the mariner, who set apart a large dish of meat, enough for half-a-dozen, and bade his guest to carry it off when their meal was over to his sick partner.

Despite of his hurry, and his earlier commencement of supper, the glutton was still gormandizing, though more slowly and half drowsily, when the barber returned; the moment, however, he descried the savoury food piled generously upon the well-filled dish, he clutched at it, recommencing his meal with renewed energy, and ceased not while a morsel was left remaining.

The temperate Aboo Seer was astounded at such a feat; but as day by day the same doings again and again recurred, his wonder fell off, and he implicitly confided in the assertion of his helpless associate, "that the necessities of his constitution required a sustenance that would be productive of evil to others less exigently organized." For Aboo Keer was a grandiloquent philosopher, who preferred thought to action, words to deeds; whilst Aboo Seer was a working-man, and, like most of his class, bowed down to specious reasoning and loftiness of expression.

The voyage at length came to an end, and the confederates were landed on a shore adjacent to a populous city. By this time the dyer, bloated from inaction, and more indolent than ever, had become so accustomed to rely on the exertions of his thrifty and industrious partner, that he gave himself up to absolute inertness. In the caravanserai where they lodged (their little room was scantily furnished from the savings of the barber) he would pass his whole time in feeding and in sleeping; the hardly-earned gains of the working partner being almost wholly expended in maintaining in idleness this helpless invalid, who assured his fatigued benefactor "that he was temporarily incapacitated for work, from the persistent dizziness that the motion of the vessel had originally communicated." His apology sufficed for this benevolent man, who, against his better judgment, both pitied and believed him.

After a month or so, sickness overtook the barber, who no longer brought home either money or provisions; for fever had seized upon him, and sucked up his vitals until he was prostrate and insensible. Then first did Aboo Keer arouse himself; for though labour was odious, fasting was still more detestable. His first action was to rifle the clothes of his inanimate friend; his next to quit the dwelling with the miserable proceeds of his ungrateful theft. His comrade would probably starve: well, "It was his fate."

After this reflection Aboo Keer betook himself to the

market-place, and then wandered about the principal streets of the city. It abounded in magnificent structures; the inhabitants were happy-looking and well-clad, the shops were elegant and well-plenished; but the uniformity of tints, the incessant white and blue that pervaded the garments of all but the extremely opulent, produced an unpleasant monotony of aspect. He divined, as it were, the gain that was about to accrue to him, and resolved to ascertain the cause of this distasteful uniformity. So when he arrived at the shop of a dyer, where every garment exhibited was of an unvarying blue he drew, forth a kerchief, and inquired the cost of its being re-dipped.

"Twenty pieces of silver," was the answer.

"Why, in my native land we think it enough to pay two for such a trifle."

"Keep it until you go back, then," was the curt rejoinder.

"Well, if these are the usual charges of the country, I must submit, but dye it red for me."

"I can't," replied the craftsman. "I know not how."

"Green, then," continued the Alexandrian, with a gathering consciousness that in this land, at least, his own superior skill would find a ready market.

"I can't; I know not how."

"Yellow, then, or lilac, or purple, or brown," he said, enumerating the various colours.

But the invariable response was "I can't; I know not how."

Then Aboo Keer revealed himself. "Know that I, too, am a dyer, and can stain clothes with all the tints I have mentioned. Being without capital, I will gladly sell my services to you, and you will profit largely by my proficiency."

"Friend," was the reply, "you know not our rules. Ours is a strict guild, and I dare not hire you. Our aim is to avoid competition, and retain the monopoly of dyeing in a few families. We are ever forty in number; the first-born son succeeds to his father; and where there is no family, then the second-born of our oldest members successively fills up the vacant place. As to colours, we confine ourselves to blue, for indigo is abundant with us; and as to strangers, we allow none of them to work with us, either as journeymen or masters."

This trade-illiberality was so unexpected that it was not until the Alexandrian had gone the round of forty masters, and heard from all of them the same unchanging tale, that he could believe in the possibility of so unwise an enactment. When once aroused,—and it took much to urge him to shake off his besetting indolence,—he was a man of action; hence he ventured upon the happy audacity of complaining to the ruler of the city of the conduct of the guild towards him.

"O King," he said, "your subjects are only garbed in white and blue, because of the ignorance of the dyers in this city. Now I, who know the art of staining cloth with red, green, yellow, brown, and purple, in every shade and diversity of tint, have, because of my poverty, offered my services as a mere journeyman to your unskilled craftsmen. Yet these incompetents reject me, because, forsooth, I am a stranger; hence, your people must either eschew all other colours, or else pay a heavy price to the foreign merchant for the imported goods. My freely offered knowledge, then, is for the benefit of your realm." So spoke the dyer, who was ever persuasive, and the ruler assented to the justice of his logic.

"You shall be the royal dyer," he graciously responded, "and woe to him of your craft who shall dare to gainsay you. My builder shall accompany you through the city, and whatever site you may select as fitting for your business, there he shall erect premises suitable to your requirements. As to capital, whatever shall be needful for your success, I take upon myself to supply. My subjects shall not remain in ignorance, through the narrow-minded rapacity of a few sluggish traders." The King presented him, likewise, with money for his immediate necessities, and, when the building had been erected in accordance with the plans of Aboo Keer, furnished him with further sums for the purchase of drugs and utensils.

There was not a handsomer shop in the whole of that beautiful city, and when cloths of every known hue were tastily suspended in flowing folds from its walls, none attracted a greater concourse of admiring spectators. They gazed with delight upon his handiwork, and all who could afford it cheerfully paid high prices to the proprietor for executing their orders. To dress in blue and white, as of old, was regarded as a mark of poverty, or senility; hence the rage for the new colours (especially with the women) became so excessive, that gold flowed into his coffers in an incessant stream. The master dyers, who had rejected him as a servant, seeing their trade leaving them, now respectfully applied to him, offering to be his assistants; but he harshly reminded them of the past, reproached them for their exclusive monopoly, and triumphantly alluded to their approaching destitution.

Let us return now to the pallet of Aboo Seer, the door of whose chamber had been left closed by his rascally associate. For three days he had lingered, untended and unfed, upon his squalid couch, for none knew that he was sick. On the fourth, the superintendent of the khan, who had missed the two foreign lodgers, suspecting that they might possibly have levanted to avoid payment of their rent, listened at the door, and heard the groans of the helpless sufferer, who had only returned to consciousness to find himself robbed and deserted. The key was still in the lock outside, so the prying official, having turned it, entered, and there lay the prostrate, yet no longer speechless, barber, who, surmising all that had occurred whilst he himself had been unconscious, eagerly inquired after his partner.

"I have not seen him for three days; I thought both he and you had departed," was the answer.

"It is he, then, who has robbed me; but search again, I pray you, my garments (for I am very feeble), lest peradventure he may have left me some little coin, that I might not die from starvation."

The superintendent complied with his request, but found nothing left. "Pity for others is want of pity for oneself," had been the unexpressed dogma of the philosophical thief. Then the sick man wept, and bewailed his evil fortune.

The charitable intruder, indignant at the cruel baseness of the pampered runaway, consoled the barber, saying, "Cheer up, you shall not starve. I will myself provide for you until your strength returns. As for the villain who has wronged you, Heaven will sooner or later avenge you." He at once fetched him some nourishing broth, and ceased not to nurse him until he was thoroughly recovered; but, so violent had been the fever, that weeks elapsed before his strength permitted him to leave the chamber. As he quitted it to seek work, he fervently expressed his gratitude to his benefactor, promising to requite him for his goodness should it ever be in his power to do so; "but Allah alone," he continued, "will, I fear, requite you, for I am a luckless being."

"And to Him only do I look for my reward; it was to please Him that I have shown compassion," was the pious rejoinder.

A handsome shop, richly adorned by broad strips of vividly coloured cloth, before which an admiring throng of idlers was congregated, soon attracted the attention of the itinerant barber. In its furthest interior, ensconced between downy cushions, stirring not, but with a lordly air giving orders to his bustling assistants, reposed the proprietor, richly clad and swollen with pride at his unhoped-for consideration. As he turned his face towards the entrance he was recognized by the poor barber, whose heart was elated by the sight of his partner's prosperity, as his long-lost associate.

"Doubtlessly," he reflected, "from the sudden stress and worry of too much business he has forgotten my very existence; perchance he thought me dead when he stripped me; at least he will now welcome and relieve me, since I always treated him with frank liberality." So he advanced confidently; but when the eye of Aboo Keer at first sighted him, it blinked with dismay; his visage became sallow, and his lips quivered, for he feared his late companion had come to denounce him, or at the least, to demand a maintenance at his hands. Then his impudence returned, and a seeming wrath lighted up his bloated countenance, as, pointing with his finger to the humble-looking stranger, he roared forth to his many slaves, "Beat him well and cast him forth from my shop;" and then, addressing his scared partner, continued, "You scoundrel! how often have I warned you never to darken the entrance of my dwelling. Will you never leave off your pilfering? Dare to come again, and I will give you up to justice." The blows of the attendants as they ejected him prevented the possibility of a reply to this false accusation. Whilst Aboo Seer was being ignominiously expelled, Aboo Keer was condescendingly explaining to the lookers-on that the ragged wretch, whom he had so leniently punished, was the impudent knave who had often before robbed his shop, and whom, when detected, he had so often spared through regard for his abject poverty. So the crowd without, which had heard what the master had related, only jeered and reviled the poor sufferer, as, writhing from the blows and protesting his innocence, he meekly threaded his way through it and sneaked back, humiliated, to his old quarters.

This beating proved a fortunate event to the hitherto unlucky fellow. After the first smart had subsided, he determined to remove the dull pains that remained by recourse to the soothing influence of the bath. So he inquired everywhere for the public baths.

"Baths? what are baths?" was the general answer. He explained their comfort, sanitary value, and social use. But his auditors replied, "When we wish to bathe, and it *is* good to feel clean and invigorated, we go down to the seashore, and there strip ourselves publicly. Even the King himself has no better resource."

Then the thoughtful barber asked the character of the sovereign, and found that all praised him for his enlightened patronage of art and science. "Whosoever discovers or introduces a good thing among us, him he delights to honour. Skilled industry and valour, he is wont to say, are the wealth and vigour of a nation." At these tidings, Aboo Seer, when likewise assured that the monarch was gracious and affable, mustered up courage to approach the throne, and despite of his manifest poverty, was courteously permitted an audience that he might explain the nature of the novelty he would introduce. And when clearly, though not eloquently, he had described the advantage of public baths, and declared his competence to undertake the superintendence of their erection and future management, he was honourably entertained, provided with money for his immediate maintenance, and furnished with all the means and appliances for their construction. And soon there arose in the midst of this fine city one of the most magnificent baths in the world,—an edifice so beautiful to behold that crowds would assemble to view it during its progress. When its interior had to be decorated, so pleased was the King's architect with the novel structure he had raised under the suggestive guidance of the barber, that he lavished upon it all the treasures of his art, finishing it in a style pre-eminently rich and attractive. A magnificent fountain plashed soothingly in the centre of the vast circular-shaped area where the bath was formed, and stately columns of the rarest marbles, with richly-gilded bases and capitals, supported the lofty dome which lighted and ventilated the building. The fame of its beauty was spread throughout the country, and the longing of the inhabitants for its opening to the public became universal. Then, when all was completed and the fittings and furniture were in due order, Aboo Seer announced the intelligence to the King; and having obtained from him ten handsome young men as attendants upon the bathers, taught them the art of rubbing with the bag and other necessary offices. The voice of the crier next invited the citizens to a public inspection of the interior, and the water was heated and the fountain played; and the stream of hot and cold fluids were set in motion, whilst Aboo Seer clearly explained to the shoals which flocked thither, the purifying nature of a bath, its salubrity and its luxury.

On the fourth day his royal patron honoured the building by his presence; he and the higher members of his Court. The King, having undressed, entered; and Aboo Seer rubbed him with the bag, and removed long strips of impure skin from his person, and displayed them to him; then, after the tank had been perfumed by mingling rose-water with its contents, the noble visitor descended into it, and was delighted when he emerged to feel the exquisite smoothness and softness of his flesh, and, after a gentle shampooing, to experience the supple elasticity of his limbs.

"The sensation," cried the gratified monarch, "is worth a thousand pieces of gold; henceforth let that be your charge for admission."

"Not so, O gracious monarch; for how could the poor afford it? Its use is needful for health and cleanliness; therefore, by your permission, let every one pay in proportion to his means, that your whole people may be benefited by your goodness to strangers."

The escort of nobles all followed the example of their lord, and all were alike enthusiastic in their encomiums; each—for none would acknowledge that his means were inferior—presented the bath-keeper with a hundred pieces of gold, and the King bestowed upon him a thousand. Next day all the city tried to enter; and soon bathing became a necessity for all who had once essayed it. Gold and silver flowed to Aboo Seer from every hand, and his wealth and importance became superior to even the condition of the dyer. He forgot not in his prosperity the goodness of the superintendent of the khan, who, through his favour at Court, was promoted to an office of higher emolument.

Among the many who frequented his establishment was the commander of that convict ship which was employed when the execution of heinous offenders was designed to be impressive from its severity. The mode of death was singular, and peculiar to that country. The criminal was stripped, thrust into a large sack, which was subsequently filled up with freshly-calcined lime, and then lowered gradually from the deck of the vessel to the depths below, so that he experienced simultaneously the double torture of burning and of drowning. As the captain had the superintendence of this cruel mode of death, he was accustomed to be slighted and shunned by the community; but when he sought to bathe, Aboo Seer treated him with courtesy, considering that no man was degraded by carrying out the legitimate sentences of the judicature. The official, however, felt grateful to the bath-keeper for his conduct, and remembered it in his heart.

Aboo Keer longed, like others, to recreate himself with the delights of the bath, but his mind misgave him as to the manner of his reception, for he was conscious that the man whom he had wronged and insulted was the owner of it. But as his desire for it could not be repressed, he arrayed himself in his best attire, armed himself with the sword of impudence, and cordially saluted his old acquaintance, saying,—

"I have at last found my friend. Why did he not visit me before this? I have long been opulent, and would not have forgotten the terms of our bargain."

"What! did you not strike and revile me," cried the aggrieved barber, "when I *did* appear before you in my sore distress?"

Then the dyer looked very sad, and exclaimed, "Surely it was not you whom I turned out from my shop. If so I swear by the holy Prophet, and by all that is sacred in our religion, that I did not recognize you (my eyes, you know, were always weak), but fancied you the thief who had daily purloined my goods. Oh surely, surely it was not my benefactor, my friend, whom I so evilly entreated. You can never forgive me; no, rather, I can never forgive myself."

And so deplorable became his aspect, so pitiable were his sobs, that the anger of Aboo Seer melted away before the vehemence of that remorse; and he tenderly sought to alleviate the deep distress of his quondam companion.

"Attribute not my wrongs," he cried, "to your own cruel hands, for my sufferings were pre-ordained, and you but the blameless and unconscious instrument of the will of Heaven. Besides, I ascribe all my good fortune to the bruises of your stick; so let all be forgotten and forgiven."

Then the cunning actor suffered himself to be calmed, and entered the bath, and was waited upon personally by the master of the establishment, and enjoyed greatly the unwonted refreshment; and after he was dressed sherbet and delicate viands were served up before him. For all this no payment was permitted by the hospitable bath-keeper, who refused his money, saying, "All things are in common between friends."

Nevertheless Aboo Keer, who judged of others by his own revengeful disposition, meditated how he might ruin his host; for he thought, "If I cause not speedily his own destruction, he will avail himself of his high favour with the King to punish me; for he cannot really forgive the injuries I have done him."

So before he quitted the building he threw out a suggestion to Aboo Seer, which met with his approval. "Your bath would be perfect," he observed, "had you not forgotten the depilatory. From respect to your patron you should offer it to him before all others."

Now the depilatory is a mixture of lime and orpiment, which removes the stray and superfluous hairs from the body.

After bidding farewell with much unction, the suspicious ingrate hastened to the palace, and obtained an immediate interview on the plea of urgency.

"Great King," he said as he approached him, "your goodness to me shall be requited. I now sacrifice my friend to my benefactor. A traitorous plot has been devised against you, and, alas! my own fellow-countryman has engaged to be your assassin. We had both been slaves to the King of the Christians, and I was emancipated because of my skill as a dyer: I taught his people the art as my ransom-money. But I left Aboo Seer and his family in captivity, and greatly was I surprised when I this day recognized him in the proprietor of the public baths. 'How have you escaped?' I inquired. 'I escaped not at all,' he replied; 'but I have sworn to slay the great enemy of the Christian monarch (mentioning your name, O King) as the price of my ransom, and my wife and family have been left as hostages.' Then I asked, how was it possible for one so powerless to put so mighty a sovereign to death, and yet avoid the vengeance of his bereaved people? 'Nothing easier—he will slay himself. I shall offer him a poisonous substance, pretending it is beneficial to remove the stray hairs from his body; and when he has applied it, the arsenic it contains will be absorbed into his system. He will become bald, his throat will become sore, and his stomach be burnt into holes. But all this will be gradual; he trusts to me, and I shall advise his continually rubbing himself with the depilatory as the sole remedy for his organic disorder.' When I reminded him of your Majesty's goodness to him, and the baseness of this premeditated crime, he had but one answer:—'I must think of my wife and my children, who will be freed on my return.' . . . There has been a momentary struggle between fidelity to my friend and gratitude to my adopted Sovereign: the latter feeling has prevailed, and I come here to denounce my countryman, but to save my King."

The anger of the monarch was kindled against Aboo Seer; the traitor and the assassin are ever hateful, and the recollection of past favours intensified the indignation of the royal patron. Yet, before any proceedings were taken against him—for such baseness seemed almost inconceivable—the King visited the bath, and was offered the depilatory, the smell of which was so fetid that he doubted not the poisonous nature of its composition; moreover, his physician detected the arsenic, which was the base of the orpiment. Then orders were issued for the arrest and execution of the detected criminal, who being condemned to suffer the death by torture, was handed over to the custody of the dreaded individual who commanded the fatal ship.

At midday, on the morrow, the King stood at his balcony, over the rippling waters of the harbour, to see his sentence carried into effect. The fatal boat was moored in front of the palace, and a heavy sack, big enough to hold a man without compressing his limbs, was slung by a rope from the sides of it.

"Shall I lower it, O King?" said the sea-captain; and the ruler raised his hand to give the signal of death, and in doing so jerked from his finger the royal signet. The sack and the signet were buried in the ocean at the same instant, and the terror of the doomed criminal could scarcely have surpassed the agony of his judge, as the jewelled ring flashed for a mōment in the sunshine ere it sank beneath the waves. For this ring was the ensign of his power; royalty and the possession of the mystic emblem of it were synonymous; should its loss be divulged, the fidelity of the troops could no longer be depended on.

The King quitted the balcony with a slow step and saddened countenance; his courtiers, who knew not what had happened, loudly whispered—"See how he grieves to inflict pain even upon the traitor who would have poisoned him."

Aboo Seer was not dead. The fatal sack had been filled, but only with lime; for the sea-captain had remembered the courtesy of the bath-keeper; and when the latter was in his custody, and had solemnly protested his innocence, saying, "Rub me with the depilatory, and see whether it will destroy my life," he resolved to conceal him until the experiment should prove or disprove the accusation. So when the ship, in the early part of the day, skirted a little islet which lay not far off from the royal balcony, he connived at the temporary escape of his prisoner by swimming, bidding him fish in his absence to provide himself with food; for the uninhabited islet belonged to the captain, and there were nets hung out to dry upon its shore.

Now the red stone of the royal signet had in its rapid descent been taken for living food by a stupid fish, who directly he had swallowed the ring swam towards the islet where Aboo Seer was at work, and, as destiny willed it, was captured by his net. Being hungry, he cut it open to broil it, and was surprised at beholding that sacred emblem of royalty, upon which the life and fortunes of the King were popularly supposed to depend. Even though condemned without a hearing, he had not forgotten the previous kindness of his patron, and he longed for, and on the return of the captain he obtained, an opportunity of restoring it to its owner.

In the disguise of a sailor he presented himself before the monarch, and holding aloft the mystic ring, displayed it before his eyes.

"How can I reward you for the recovery of my talisman?" cried the overjoyed monarch, as he replaced it on his finger.

"By pardoning him who has befriended me, and granting to myself an impartial trial; for I am the bath-keeper who was falsely accused of treason."

"No traitor would have returned this gem; you are acquitted. The captain who has saved me from bloodguiltiness shall be promoted; and your accuser, the dyer, shall be questioned."

Then Aboo Seer related his whole history, and brought forward the late superintendent of the khan, and the slaves who had beaten him, as testimonies of the baseness of the dyer.

"Yet I pray you to forgive him," said the good man, "for I harbour no resentment against him."

"You, as a citizen, may pardon him; I, as a judge, cannot," was the stern reply; and on the morrow the waves of the ocean rolled above the corpse of the tortured dyer.

From that day no evil fortune ever betided Aboo Seer. He himself was happy, and ever sought to impart a like happiness to all around him.

XAILOUN THE SILLY.

A STURDY, credulous, good-natured fool was young Xailoun, nicknamed by his friends, and known by his neighbours, as Xailoun the Silly. Left with a small patrimony, which was gradually dwindling from his utter incompetence to manage it, his relatives persuaded him to marry, and induced a sensible woman, who could appreciate his goodness of heart, although she could not help despising his feebleness of mind, to accept him as her husband. His features were plain, yet not repulsive; he was gentle in his manners; his countenance was devoid of expression, his conversation trivial, but his disposition was excellent. So far from hurting anything, his weakness seemed to proceed from an excess of goodness: he could be persuaded to any act of folly, for he was a simpleton; yet not even coercion would have led him to crime, for he had an instinctive rectitude of principle. He was so hopelessly imbecile, that his wife, Oitba, after many a vain attempt, by caresses, remonstrances, and even by scolding, to induce him to work, for he was strong and healthy, as a final resource took to beating him, a penalty which he endured with equanimity, as the natural consequence of so foolish a delusion as marriage. Labour, in his estimation, was a needless exhaustion of strength: eating, sleeping, and day-dreaming, the chief, if not the sole, ends of existence. "Heaven wishes us to be happy," he argued; "that which is pleasurable to one man is not so to another: *ergo*, as labour is your happiness, it is your duty to work; as repose is my happiness, it is my duty to abstain from toil." He could reason plausibly enough, only his quaint conclusions were invariably deceptive. Perhaps his especial weakness was a sympathetic attachment to a species of lizard, which he called his cousin, a bright-eyed little creature, who, like himself, loved basking in the sun in stolid reverie. This harmless reptile has a peculiar jerk of the head, which the simpleton construed into a gesture of assent when he addressed it in his argumentative soliloquies. As the animal never contradicted him, he naturally preferred his respectful style of conversation to the contemptuous scoffing of his human associates.

When his fortunes sank to a low ebb, it became necessary to part with one of his asses. So Xailoun led it by a halter, stalking on before, and theorizing on matters wholly irrelevant to the sale. A rogue, who knew his softness both of heart and head, slily displaced the halter from the brute, put it on his own neck, and left his comrade to dispose of the stolen animal. He himself trudged on steadily for a while, until his companion was out of sight. Then fervently ejaculating, "Thanks to thee, O Prophet! for my restoration to the shape of man," he disturbed the reverie of the simple peasant by an abrupt halt. "Halloo! what has become of my ass, and who are you?" was the not insensible address of the simpleton. "Your own ass, your faithful, hard-working donkey: thanks to the Prophet, I have had a kind master, too good for my deservings. I was a bad son, and in my wickedness beat my poor old mother; for this impiety I was changed into a quadruped. But I have repented my evil doings; my sin has been expiated, and I have become a man again." "Go in peace, friend," said Xailoun; "it is rather hard I should lose by your conversion, but of course I can't sell you." So the sharper departed, and not having any better occupation, our hero journeyed on to the fair at which he had proposed to have sold his donkey: to his surprise, he there beheld his own ass exposed for sale by the rogue's companion. "Oh! you incorrigible wretch," said the worthy simpleton, apostrophizing his old servant; "you had barely an hour to run home and beat your mother, yet you must needs go and do it." On his returning home without money, Oitba's cudgel read him a lecture on credulity, though he vainly assured her that if the Prophet could transform a man into an ass for beating a woman, he might transform a woman into an ass for beating a man.

Upon the whole, however, he improved under the discipline of the stick, which he had not the energy to resist; and as "Change, or I will beat you to a mummy," was the habitual exordium of his wife as she drove him to labour, he connected the idea of change with labour. He resolved to be changed.

He had grown meagre from want of food. So when he

noticed how plump and jolly-looking were the attendants at a baker's shop, he thought, if he could only look like them, his wife would not recognize him, and he should avoid being beaten. He proffered his services, and for some time worked steadily, and carried home his earnings to his family. Still he could not help perceiving that he was recognized as Xailoun; and as the idea of change (connected with beating) had been indelibly impressed upon him, and a chance blow occasionally followed an act of silliness, he determined for the future to be a different man. "I am to be beaten," he argued, "if I be not changed; and if I would be changed I must be no longer Xailoun."

He now quitted the baker in despair, and asked employment at an eating-house, where the servants looked so red and bloated, that he thought, if he could only resemble them, his identity would be lost. Day by day he would stare at his limbs to see how he was progressing, and this at length attracted the attention of the keeper of the rooms. "Are you admiring yourself?" said he. "No, I am only watching how my transformation is going on." "Oh! you want to be changed," quoth he. "Changed? yes, that's what I have come for." "You shall be my scullion then: you will be turned from white to black."

So the simpleton scoured the dirty pots, and not being expert returned home sooty from head to foot. His reception there was not cordial: his filthy condition was not a source of commiseration for him, but of thwacking. "What have I done to deserve this?" said the poor idiot. "You must change your mode of life; you must become a different creature," was the reply.

A pastrycook's shop was the next resource, and the docility and willingness of the young man obtained him constant employment. But the ass which ground the flour having died, the master, who comprehended the weak nature of Xailoun, gravely proposed to him to take its place. "If I do, I ought to have its dress," was his answer. So his whim was indulged, and he was harnessed with the blinkers, and other paraphernalia of a donkey.

The fatigue was so excessive, the giddiness from continually trotting round and round so maddening, that no sooner was he liberated from the yoke, than he started off, harness and all, and fled homewards at the top of his speed, to the boisterous delight of the urchins of the neighbourhood. So utterly pitiable did he look, that his stern monitress went supperless to bed, without administering an exhortatory castigation.

A new phase of the same idea now possessed him. "Heaven alone can change me; and how can my prayers be heard in this noisy city? I'll pray in the country, and as loud as I can." Accordingly he walked out into the suburbs until he arrived at a garden, where, being inordinately fond of fruit, and having a dim conception that he should be as much changed by feeding upon it as his lean ass, which he had not recognized after a few weeks' good pasture, had been, he asked employment from the owner. Being a strong, honest-looking fellow, he was hired at small wages, but with full permission to indulge his appetite. His mental weakness, however, was so perceptible, that his master, when in a dilemma, took advantage of it. One of the oxen having become temporarily incapacitated for work, he was persuaded to take its place, and was vastly delighted when the harness was put on him over his clothes. This was a change indeed! The toil, however, being severe, and the driver not too sparing of the lash, the poor wretch, the moment he was unyoked, fled for his life, harness and all, towards the city. It was dusk ere he reached it, and the gates being closed, he was compelled to take refuge for the night in a cemetery outside the walls. Some early grave-diggers espied him next morning, and beholding this uncouth figure reposing on the ground, shrank away in terror, exclaiming, "It is a ghoul, which feeds on the carcases of the dead."

Xailoun started up and fled, pursued at a distance by the grave-diggers, who, waxing bolder as they were joined by the rabble, flung their shovels at him, vociferating, "Down with the ghoul!" The village curs yelping at his heels followed closely upon his tracks; but so uncouth was his figure, so incomprehensible to them in its grotesque habiliments, that their courage failed them; they kept at a safe distance.

The poor idiot naturally sought the shelter of his own house. He was beaten back from it by his violent spouse, who could not recognize her good-looking helpmate in so strange a guise. He was changed indeed!

Captured, unharnessed, found to be human, and identified as the fool of the village, he was delivered to his wife, who at length regretted the sternness of her tutelary discipline; she endeavoured, though vainly, to impress upon his obtuse intellect that the change she had urged upon him was a moral, and not a physical metamorphosis. Poor Xailoun could only comprehend that he had not succeeded, and attributed his failure to the difficulty the Deity must have experienced in hearing his prayers in such close vicinity to a crowded and vociferous city. So he resolved this time to pray further off, and have the field clear for his own individual eloquence.

There are waste lands, desolate sites of former civilization, around most Eastern cities. To one of these spots, teeming with the ruins of ancient edifices, and shunned alike by the well-to-do, from some rumour of its being frequented by robbers, and by the poor from its being the supposed haunt of evil spirits, Xailoun betook himself, for he argued that no obstreperous rival in piety would out-pray him in that haunted city of the dead.

On a pile of stones there darted to and fro a bright-eyed lizard, one of that jerking species whose responsive noddings were regarded by the simpleton as affirmative replies to his confidential communications. He sought, as usual, for a quiet gossip with "his cousin," but the lizard sheltered himself beneath the stones, and declined the colloquy. Indignant at this discourtesy, Xailoun resolved to unearth him, and vigorously tumbled aside the heavy carved blocks in his efforts to force an interview upon his contemptuous cousin.

After a quarter of an hour's violent exertion, a square of black marble, with a ring attached to it, attracted his attention.

"Ha! ha! I have found your house at last!" he exclaimed, as he wrenched up the slab and perceived a flight of stairs; "I'm not to be baffled, I'll pay you a visit and inspect your premises." At the bottom of the vault, for such it was, he noticed several urns, the contents of which he dimly descried by the glimmer of light that streamed from the opening he had made. Having dipped his hand into one of these and brought out a handful of gold (a metal which in his poor way of living he had never come across), he imagined that it was a peculiar kind of dry food which the provident lizard had stored away for future consumption; so holding it out in his hand, he cried, in a petulant tone, "Hark you, my cousin! if you won't come and speak to me, I'll walk off with your winter provender and give it to my ass." No reply being vouchsafed, Xailoun carried his threat into execution.

When he showed Oitba the lizard's food, he was welcomed and caressed; at her bidding he carried off two panniers-full of gold, and then stopped up the orifice he had made. Being a prudent woman, she made no display of her newly-acquired wealth: necessary comforts, and a new suit of clothes for her husband were her chief expenditure.

She no longer cared for his labouring for hire, but dispatched him upon sundry errands. He could recollect one or two commissions at a time, but all beyond these were either wholly blotted from his memory, or so transmuted that he would bring back articles whose names were indeed somewhat similar, but whose natures were wholly opposite.

He had been desired one day to purchase meat, rice, and peas; the two former commissions were duly performed; the third was, of course, forgotten. "Go back," said his wife, "and keep on repeating the word aloud lest you should forget it." So Xailoun mumbled to himself, as he walked along, "Only peas, only peas." An itinerant dealer in jewellery was exhibiting his wares in the market-place, crying "Pearls! precious pearls!" The simpleton who, like most of his station, was very inquisitive, dipped his hand into the jewel-box, and, holding up the string of pearls, gazed with lack-lustre eyes upon them; then, fearful of forgetting his errand, he repeated aloud his formula, "Peas, only peas."

At this stigma upon his wares (which were not of the first quality), the wrath of the pedlar was kindled; snatching the string from the witless talker, he gave him a sound buffet for an unintentional witticism which had provoked a peal of laughter from the bystanders.

"Why did you strike me? What ought I to have said?" cried the poor innocent, rubbing his bruised face, and connecting the incident with the only party who was accustomed to strike him; the dealer, however, regardless of his question, stalked onwards, still vociferating, "Pearls! precious pearls!"

"I suppose, then, pearls are what my wife meant me to purchase," thought Xailoun; so he wended on his way imitating his late antagonist, as he cried, "Pearls! precious pearls!" Another cuff betided him as he was thrust aside by a busy trader, who thought he was mocking his own calling.

"What ought I to have said, then?" cried the humble penitent.

"Nonsense!" replied the trader, as he passed on his way.

So Xailoun walked on repeating, "Nonsense!"

Now it chanced that the corpse of a popular magistrate was being carried to the grave, amidst the loud encomiums of a throng of admiring acquaintances. The simpleton's "Nonsense" was too apt a response to their exaggerated praises of the deceased not to provoke their indignation. Confused by the storm of abuse which greeted his involuntary sarcasm, he humbly inquired what he ought to have said? As the procession swept onwards, a faithful slave, who loved the dead one well, quietly murmured, "May Paradise receive him!" So he took this ejaculation as a reply to his question; for by this time the idiot had become utterly oblivious of the original message, and contented to adopt any suggested substitute. Hence he walked on, sighing like the mourner, and lugubriously repeating, "May Paradise receive him!" until he met a cart which contained the carcase of an ass. He stared stupidly at it, but did not allow its presence to disturb the repetition he had been enjoined. "May Paradise receive him!" he cried; at which words the bystanders, who attributed his speech to a deliberate mockery of religion, so mercilessly assailed him with stones, that he took to his heels, and found a temporary refuge in the house of his mother-in-law.

After this adventure, Oitba hardly liked to trust him on an errand. Compelled one day to quit home for an hour or two, Oitba ordered her silly spouse to rock the baby, and feed the sitting hen, tasks so easy, that even *his* poor wit could scarcely fail to accomplish them. The fowl soon began to scratch itself, a feat which excited the benevolent attention of our hero. "When my head itches, my wife combs it," he reflected; so he resolved to save it trouble, and as the comb was not at hand, he scratched its poll with a nail. Not being expert, and the bird far from patient, he unluckily thrust the nail into its brain, and felt astonished at its passive endurance of his rough handling. Just as he began to comprehend the loss of his hen, and was distracted when he thought of the cudgelling he was likely to endure, the baby commenced squalling, and the eggs began to chill. "Oh, dear! what shall I do now?" was his querulous complaint; "I must nurse the child like his mother to stop its squalling, and I must keep the eggs warm, or there will be no chickens." With a puzzled expression he exposed his breast, and tried to give the babe suck, while he carefully balanced himself, as he squatted over the nest. At this juncture his wife returned.

"Let me in," was her brief demand.

"I can't, I am brooding and suckling," was his curt rejoinder.

Xailoun's position was not an easy one, and the baby evinced by the loudness of its cries that it disapproved of a male substitute for the maternal breast.

Its cries excited the irritability of the mother, who, dashing the door open, immediately noticed the unfortunate hen, the victim of Xailoun's experimental beneficence.

"Who killed my hen?" she screamed.

"She died in combing," was the apologetic response.

"And her eggs, you fool!"

"I am hatching them myself."

At these words her wrath boiled over; the blow she

gave him disturbed his balance, and he fell squash upon the eggs, daubing his nether garments all over with the yellow yolks. He bolted from the house to avoid the anticipated beating, and bore philosophically the ironical cheers and pointing digits of the mocking lads, who insinuated an even worse catastrophe than had befallen him.

"I know I am a fool, and must be changed," was his sad comment upon this and many a like incident; "I must force Heaven by the urgency of my prayers to alter me." So he cogitated for a while, and his prayers not having been answered either in the bustling city or the quiet suburbs, he arrived at a remarkable yet not illogical conclusion. "Heaven don't hear me, because I am so far off: the believer is told to turn in a certain direction when he prays, of course to face Heaven; now, if I always walk in that direction I must get to Heaven at last."

Congratulating himself upon a power of reasoning he had scarcely thought inherent in him (for he was a modest man), he duly placed himself in the prescribed position, and turning neither to the right nor to the left, marched straight onwards, regaining his track when compelled by insurmountable obstacles to deviate from his devout course, by a most elaborate compensatory system of lateral progression. His path at length led him into a forest, the trees of which induced a painful amount of calculation, since to one without a compass it was by no means easy to preserve to a nicety a prescribed route. So rigidly, however, did he abide by his rule, that even when he beheld a suspicious group of men, who were in fact robbers dividing their spoil, directly in front of him, he unhesitatingly, and to their astonishment (so solemn did he look), advanced towards them; and being in ill-luck, just arrived among them as a military force sent to pursue the thieves overtook the band, and captured the captain and sundry of his companions. Of course Xailoun, who only stared at what was going on, was pounced upon by a soldier, who would probably have run away had any resistance been attempted. Once more then he failed in his efforts to become transformed by dint of prayer.

Fellow-sufferers are usually communicative; so when the captain of the gang cursed his ill-luck, in both losing his perilously-won booty and his wild liberty at the same moment, Xailoun in his turn lamented his lost chance of reaching heaven, and being there transmuted into something so utterly different that his wife would not recognize him.

"As to heaven," said the ruffian, "I can't indeed help you to find it: for, as I never hoped to steal anything from there, I never troubled myself to find its position; but as to transforming you, I can so change you that the Prophet himself would not recognize you. I should be a mere numskull if I knew not how to disguise myself!"

Of course the witless one availed himself of such enviable skill, and the upshot was, that the dark-looking robber (who was naturally pale) became the fair-complexioned Xailoun, and the simpleton (who, like most fools, was gifted with imitative powers) stalked about with savage dignity as the swarthy brigand. This was effected by some walnut-juice, and a complete change of clothes.

The next morning all were adjudged to die; but as the

condemned unanimously deposed that the idiot had accidentally thrust himself among them, and had never shared in their misdeeds, the supposed innocent (that is to say, the cunning captain,) was set at large. As to our hero, he at first aped to perfection the swaggering bravado of a reckless villain; but when, to his bewilderment, led forth to execution, reassumed his wonted silliness of manner. Oitba saved him from a change that would have been final. She had heard of a simpleton having been captured with the thieves, and rightly divined that it was her husband; had scrutinized the luckless villains as they were led forth to die, and despite the swarthy hue, blackened eyebrows and beard of her deluded spouse, felt half convinced of his identity. His farewell address to his cousin, the lizard, whom he reproached for his blitheness when he was about to lose so near a relative, caused her immediate interference on his behalf; and once pointed out by her, there were hosts of witnesses who could testify to his well-known attributes. He was temporarily reprieved, and led before the Commander of the Faithful.

His prospect of death, the after-judgment, his previous heavenward journey, produced such a bewildering medley of ideas in the brain of the poor wretch, that, fancying he recognized in the gorgeously-apparelled Caliph the ruler of Heaven, he flung himself on his knees before him, crying at the pitch of his voice, "Change me, O Lord! change me so that my very wife may not know me." The oddity of the salutation convulsed the whole court with laughter, and the good-humoured sovereign carried on the joke by promising to accede to his request.

Conducted to an apartment he was refreshed with food in which an opiate had been mingled, and, during the stupefaction which ensued, his rustic dress was removed and replaced by flowing garments of spotless white; wings of snowy plumage were affixed to his shoulders, and, being naturally good-looking, he made a passable angel or ministering spirit. Large looking-glasses, objects he had never yet beheld, reflected his person, and, being of a loving nature, and fancying himself in a world of spirits, he turned in all directions striving to embrace the images of himself. After vainly endeavouring to kiss his reflection, and chilling his nose in the attempt, he thus philosophized: "I know why their noses are so cold; they live above, and the higher one climbs the colder it is."

This deduction delighted the Caliph, who had amused himself by watching his proceedings: he was soon tired of him, however, and left him to his domestics, who, in their turn, diverted themselves by converting the angel into a frightful Afrit. While he was asleep they stripped him, covered him with raw goat-skins, put horns on his head, and a horrible mask with eyeholes of flame-coloured glass on his face, so that every object appeared enveloped in an atmosphere of fire; then waking him roughly, they roared with laughter when they beheld his horrified antics as he again gazed upon his reflection. Screaming with terror, he burst like a maniac through the circle around him, rushed to where he had last seen the Caliph, and, lighting upon him, prostrated himself before him, crying, "O Lord, change me back to Xailoun."

"Calm thyself, poor wretch, and sleep," was the reply;

"waking, thenceforth and for ever thou wilt be Xailoun the Silly."

Oitba presented herself at the public audience of the next morning; she bore two purses of gold in her hand. "My husband, O Caliph, is a born fool, but good at heart. I have brought with me our little fortune to compensate any injury he may cause the State; release him, I pray you, and let it be understood henceforth, that he is not responsible for actions which want of intellect, not want of principle, may lead him to perpetrate."

The Caliph, who preferred to increase rather than diminish the little store that was offered him, made some trifling present, which, being magnified by rumour, became so large a sum that Oitba ventured on the strength of it to enlarge her expenses in accordance with the treasure her husband had discovered. The stick was for ever laid aside, and the united pair passed their lives amidst every comfort, for the next few visits of Xailoun to his contemptuous cousin's secret hoard, so increased their resources, that all necessity for self-denial ceased to be required. A slave was purchased by Oitba for the special purpose of controlling her husband's folly, and his "Oitba forbids it," served as a salutary check to the absurd vagaries in which he would otherwise have indulged. So he enjoyed his strangely acquired wealth in peace, and as age advanced proved less demonstrative in his peculiarities. He became too well satisfied with the lot of Xailoun to seek another change.

JAMASP, AND THE QUEEN OF THE SERPENTS.

"HE is a stupid lout, and will never come to good. Handsome fools think themselves above work, but young Jamasp must either toil or starve. His stuck-up mother has, to my knowledge, now parted with every coin and nearly every trinket, from her absurd notion of cramming knowledge into that dolt's head. So much the better for me. Times are hard, and we must all look out for ourselves."

So spake the hard-working, hard-dealing, mother of certain wood-cutters, whose circumstances were more flourishing than their reputation. Without the least unfriendly feeling towards her neighbour (the feeble-minded relict of one of the most famous sages of the East), the wood-dealer had watched her once envied play-fellow's gradual decline in fortune with placid complacency. In childhood there had been little difference in social position between the two females; but a Hindoo philosopher, in his scornful disregard of all worldly notions, had deliberately preferred the prettier but weaker-minded of the two, to a more nobly-born wife, believing in his simplicity that an ignorant and dowerless maiden would cherish and venerate him, whereas, should he wed her superiors, they would neglect him in their love of display and luxurious indolence. Whether right or wrong in his estimate of the higher class, the sage erred greatly as to the anticipated humility of his peasant-bride: however much he might be reverenced abroad, in his own house he was slighted and sneered at, because his gains and income were not commensurate with the baseless expectations of her who had pardoned his pedantry for the sake of his property.

Not long after his marriage he had died, not worn out by his studies,—for he had been so abstemious that the in-action of his body had not proved injurious to his health,—but in the prime of his life, a victim to that Indian scourge, the cholera. Either nature or his skill in medicine had enabled him at the time to battle successfully against the attack, so that he recovered, to all appearance, and again resumed his wonted pursuits; but he felt that the pestilence, though forcibly ejected, had, during its brief mastery, withered his vital organs, and that his shattered constitution did not retain sufficient vitality to resist the ordinary wear and tear of life. Had it not been for his expected paternity, he would not have been reluctant to die, for after his marriage he had become melancholy and misanthropical, declaimed against the possibility and even the rightfulness of being happy, and often repeated the world-old adage, that "all is vanity and vexation of spirit."

His last act, like most of his usual doings, was more philosophical than wise. Instead of selling to some younger enthusiast or ardent tyro in science those precious manuscripts, for the acquisition of which he had devoted all which the frugality of his father had bequeathed him, he cast them with his own hands far into the ocean, and smiled sadly as he saw them sink into its abysses. It might be he was unwilling that other sages should profit by their perusal and rival his far-spread fame; yet, possibly, he had noticed that the ignorant and thoughtless practically enjoy life more than the learned, and splenetically immolated the seductive causes of his wasted existence. Previous to their destruction, however, he sedulously condensed the concentrated essence of all his knowledge, and inscribed it upon five slips of papyrus, which latter having inclosed in a simple casket of cedar, he intrusted to his wife as the sole yet all-sufficient heritage of their unborn babe. Then, having conscientiously discharged what he deemed his duty, he betook himself to his bed, and, with scarcely a sigh, tranquilly resigned his harmless if useless existence.

So quickly after his decease did Jamasp, for so was the posthumous child of the sage designated, come into the world, that the soul of the gentle father might almost be supposed to have passed into the body of the tender babe. In its features were shadowed forth all the pure-minded simplicity and noble benevolence of the self-denying parent; as it grew up there was an exalted spirituality in the aspect of the child which forcibly reminded one of the unspoken yearning of its sire (who, remember, was a Hindoo and a heathen) to be absorbed in the Divinity; but there the resemblance ceased: the boy showed no trace of ancestral intellect; the lad, as he grew in stature, became strong, active, and handsome. The vigour of his body, the weakness of his mind seemed alike to have been inherited from his peasant mother.

About a score of years had elapsed from the decease of the Indian sage to the opening of our tale, during which period his impoverished widow had parted with every saleable article that the frugality of her husband had accumulated. Of course she now lamented him, and reproached herself with her neglectful depreciation of his merits. But this is too common an occurrence to deserve mention. What is more to the purpose, she resolved to impart her worldly troubles to her quondam playmate and present neighbour, the now thriving woodseller, a shrewd, notable woman, whom, at her sudden rise in life, she had at first contemptuously looked down upon, and subsequently treated with condescending familiarity, proffering her unasked advice with the authority of one who had achieved distinction by her own unaided merits. Times had changed; the gently dictatorial adviser had now recourse for counsel to the humble trader, not from any great confidence in its efficacy, but from that craving for sympathy which so strongly influences the female mind. Moreover, like most weak-minded persons, she had a tolerable idea as to what her conduct ought to be, yet had not the moral courage to carry out her notions without the sanctioning approval of her gossips.

It is pleasant to the ignoble and little-minded to utter bitter truths with impunity, to those who were once their superiors in station or in fortunes; it is likewise agreeable to the same widely-diffused class to actually profit by the misfortunes of their friends. This the trader managed to effect; for having first brusquely pointed out the utter incapacity of Jamasp to earn his living as a trader without capital, and indicated his brawny frame as a special evidence that Providence had designed him for severe manual toil, she finally offered that her sons should instruct him in the not very difficult art of wood-cutting, and should teach him to thread the intricacies of the forest, selecting the likeliest spots, provided that the widow could manage to buy him an axe, an ass, and suitable panniers, and that the young man would agree to sell her the product of his labours at one-half of the price she vended the wood at. The bargain was accepted; the last trinket was parted with to purchase the required articles; and the greedy trader, having at last succeeded in persuading her uncouth sons to permit the young man to work in their company, commented upon the transaction as in our first paragraph.

Their compliance with her wishes was far from a ready one; for the gain would be their mother's, not their own; and there is a trade jealousy of interlopers even among the rudest mechanics. They had secrets of their own, too, to hide; assuredly their clothing, habits, and style of living were far more expensive than could have been honestly derived from their scanty earnings; for the now thriving woodseller was not too liberal a paymaster, even to her own children.

However, they sullenly assented, and Jamasp, now permitted to accompany them to the hill-country, proved so active, vigorous, and industrious, that in a short time his earnings, ill-remunerated as he was, actually exceeded their own, and he and his mother were enabled to live in comparative comfort. His comrades soon found that his inaptness for book-learning was not the result of mental incapacity, but merely the revolt of his intellect against the forcing process, by which the widow had essayed to drive wisdom into his hard-worked brain. She had positively benumbed his mental faculties, which were at least of the average capacity, by the very intensity of her endeavours to fill him with wisdom. She doted upon her child, her only one, the youthful image of his lost father, (whom, now that his idiosyncrasies could no longer clash with her own whims and prejudices, she profoundly loved, firmly believing, moreover, that she had always done so,) and stubbornly resolved to make her boy as wise, and consequently as good (for so she argued), as his lamented sire.

Of course she had his horoscope drawn by the best astrologer in the neighbourhood, who prognosticated all happiness to him, if he could only get over the terrible crisis which an awful conjunction of planets threatened him with on his attaining to manhood.

"His would be no common career," said the oracle; "his success or failure in life no long and arduous struggle for mere competence, but a desperate contest with fortune, to be quickly terminated, whether its result should be good or evil."

"But *how* will it end?" inquired the impatient widow, interrupting the sapient soothsayer.

"All things are not revealed to us," he replied; "Providence, in its mercy, hides much future sorrow from us, lest we should grieve too much beforehand at the inevitable."

"Yet tell me, I implore you," she continued, "whether, and by what means, his deadly peril may be averted?"

"Wisdom alone can avert a threatened evil," was the sententious reply of the retreating professional, who having received his fee, was by no means anxious to prolong the interview.

So the widow, who interpreted this apophthegm literally, and conceived that her offspring might by intense and continual study arrive at such a pitch of wisdom as to baffle adverse fate in the terrible ordeal he was destined to encounter, resolved that no pains or cost should be spared, on her part, to arm her darling against this fearful prognostication. Poor boy! he was so incessantly afflicted with endless lessons (more particularly in theology, a very common yet not very fascinating study for children), that nothing but the vigour of his maternal constitution, and the dwindling means of his surviving parent, saved his body from premature decay. As it was, the cramming system exhibited its usual effect upon the precocious; his expression eventually assumed such a fixed aspect of puzzled stolidity, that the more skilled artisans refused to instruct him in their trades, asserting that he had not wit enough to master the difficulties of their craft.

So the poor widow lamented, and would have despaired of the future of her boy, had not the astrologer whom she had consulted and believed, so egregiously erred in one or two of his predictions—"the effect of a slight miscalculation," he apologetically asserted, "where his remuneration had not been sufficient to ensure his adequate attention," that the fond mother took courage, and wisely resolved to leave all to Providence. Had she arrived at this conclusion earlier, it would have been better for Jamasp:

late as it was, his brain had time for repose, and he was now rather a fool by past reputation than in sober reality.

His new occupation forced him to employ his latent powers of observation and of judgment; for fitting trees grew not in every spot, and he was conscious, that if once lost amidst the ravines of the stupendous mountains, from whose soaring peaks he reaped his perilous profits (felling many a pine that slanted over a fathomless abyss), he must indubitably perish from hunger or wild beasts. Hence he busied himself in learning all that nature and the practical experience of his rough companions could teach him; so that ere long he had become an expert wood-ranger, with a hardy and healthy body, and a mind which having lain fallow for an adequate period, and then become invigorated by moderate and judicious exercise, had now finally asserted its natural energies.

His rude mates, who daily witnessed his feats of skill and daring, no longer despised him; and as sooner or later he must perforce detect their illegal proceedings, resolved to make him a participator in them. So one day, when all had been driven by a violent storm to take shelter in the same cavern, they offered him a share in their secret enterprises, which they assured him were far more profitable than their ostensible drudgery.

"We are not," they said, "banditti. We never plunder our neighbours; but if knavish merchants *will* cross our wild frontiers, to take the bread from hard-working craftsmen by selling their foreign goods cheaper than they can be made in our native land, why, they deserve to lose both lives and merchandise. Not that we ever kill anybody; only we so manage that a stray mule or camel should occasionally drop its burden, or fall over a precipice."

Jamasp was one of those simple-minded men who can neither perceive the difference (so far as regards the moral principle) between robbing a fellow-countryman, and plundering a stranger, nor comprehend the essential distinction between depriving a man of his own by fraud, or taking it from him by force. So not being experienced in the world, he did not content himself with declining their well-meant offer, but roundly rebuked them for their roguery.

This indignant and, according to their notions, ungrateful reception of a proposal which had been offered with rough good-humour as a boon and a compliment, irritated the three brothers, who felt themselves aggrieved and insulted by the blunt plainness of the epithets he had applied to their marauding. But they nursed their wrath in silence, and only evidenced it by refraining from further converse with their squeamish monitor.

The mouldering ashes of a fire (which had been lighted when first they took shelter), by whose friendly blaze they had dried their saturated garments and cooked their homely food, now diffused a grateful warmth. The three unwitting robbers crouched over it, for the air was chilly in those elevated regions; but our hero repelled by their gloomy taciturnity, and discerning that in their present mood his company was no longer agreeable to them, retired further into the recesses of the cave, and throwing himself upon the dry sand, in one of the innermost nooks, listlessly scooped up the soil that lay beneath his hand, as he moodily pondered upon the revelations of that morning. He was scarcely conscious of his occupation, until his thoughts were aroused from their dreamy reverie by a slight blow experienced by his fingers, as they struck against an upright ring of brass firmly soldered to a convex plate of metal. He started to his feet, and tugged vainly at the ring: then in the spirit of good fellowship, hoping, moreover, that his unselfish frankness would dispel any angry feeling which might rankle in the hearts of his companions, he briefly communicated his discovery to them; and they, elated by his tidings, eagerly assisted him in clearing away the mass of sand which had buried the shield-like lid of a capacious cistern. Was it only a well—or was it a treasure-chamber? Neither: the ponderous cover being hurriedly torn up, its removal disclosed to their expectant eyes a vast reservoir of virgin honey.

Even when roughly estimated at one-half its market price, such being the probable reduction at which alone the pious dealers would have purchased it in bulk, the value of the enormous store of honey, and of its huge copper covering, would be a little fortune to the four peasants. So, exulting in the anticipated profits of their short day's work, they returned without delay (for the storm had now subsided) to their several homes; and having provided themselves with jars, buckets, and other appliances for removing and storing up the savoury liquid, they started next morning for the scene of their labours, with every ass, mule, or horse they could hire or borrow. So vast was the hoard of luscious food, so distant was the cave from the town they dwelt in, that, although they worked strenuously and unremittingly, they could not quite empty the pit in one day. As from the first they had agreed to keep the discovery secret, even from their nearest relatives, until, at least, the honey had been sold and the proceeds shared, the widow had no inkling of the good fortune which had betided her son.

Next morning, almost before the sun had risen, the party again visited the nearly exhausted reservoir; but the hearts of the three brethren were evilly disposed towards their more scrupulous mate. Suspicion had already been engendered by the unqualified refusal of Jamasp to join in their depredations; now fear and covetousness supervening, urged them still further in the path of crime.

"I suppose," whispered the youngest, who had contrived that the widow's son should head the little caravan, whilst he and his kinsmen brought up the rear, "that our gentleman comrade will claim one-half of our honey because he chanced to find it, and threaten to expose our patriotic amusements"—and he smiled grimly as he termed them so,—"to the authorities, if we don't submit to his extortion."

"Nobody would miss him. He has no friends but his mother and *ourselves*," replied the second, glancing furtively at the louring faces of his brothers, and encouraged by their relentless physiognomy; "tigers are numerous in these parts."

"No violence!" said the eldest approvingly. "Never shed blood unnecessarily. The pit is very deep, and quite perpendicular."

So they managed that Jamasp should be last in the emptied cistern, and then sneaking away without even indulging in a farewell taunt, conscientiously quitted the cavern without slaying him, and returned to their distant home, where they sold their acquisitions to such advantage that straightway they became small capitalists and thriving traders. Success made them moral men (at least in seeming), for they soon found that the daily gains of cheating and extortion tacitly submitted to by society, and regarded as incidental to their calling, were not only safer, but far more profitable than occasional brigandage. As for the bereaved widow, she wept for the loss of her foredoomed son, who dying by the fangs of a savage beast (for so had it been reported) in his early manhood, had thus fulfilled the prophecy of the astrologer.

Let us now return to the deserted victim.

What shouts he raised for rescue, what mingled prayers and reproaches he uttered, what almost superhuman yet futile efforts he made to scale the smooth and upright walls of his prison-house, may rather be imagined than depicted. He had been let down by a rope, which still dangled from the brink. In vain he seized it; it was loose, and fell inwards as he pulled it; he formed a loop at its extremity, and violently cast it in all directions, hoping that it might possibly catch some jutting projection of the rock which would support his weight: the cord was too short, however, to reach the rugged sides of the cavern. Convinced, after many efforts at climbing, of the hopelessness of struggling further against fate, for the polished sides of the stone reservoir afforded him no foothold, he finally prostrated himself in prayer, resigning himself to the will of the Almighty. From this posture he was aroused by the sensation of something crawling upon his hand; he shuddered as he beheld a large black venomous scorpion, and instinctively jerked it from his person, and trampled it to death. This incident saved his life; it caused him to reflect. How could the insect have crawled upon him? Had it fallen from above, the sound of its descent (so still was all around him) would have attracted his attention. There must be some other mode of entrance, or the creature could not so noiselessly have crept upon him unawares.

Then, once more having gazed anxiously above, beneath, and around him, he perceived, on a level with his shoulder, a narrow orifice, from which the scorpion had evidently emerged. There might be more within. Well, what mattered it? There was a possibility of escape. Death in any shape was preferable to the otherwise inevitable agony of slow starvation. He thrust, then, his knife into the dark chink, and to his joy found that the seemingly solid rock crumbled beneath its blade; then he introduced his hand, and tore out a large piece of cement, and soon light poured in freely from the rapidly enlarged cavity. By strenuous exertions he made the opening sufficiently large to enter, and then having stood upon the little mound of rubbish which he had scooped out, and thus raised himself to a fitting level, he leaped as it were into the hole, and after a brief yet painful contest with the falling earth, found himself in safety on the other side.

The prospect now before him was scarcely reassuring: it seemed to threaten the same doom which he had so lately exulted in having avoided; only his prison was more capacious. It was midday, and the light which streamed down perpendicularly from above showed him that he was standing in a narrow gully, between two abruptly precipitous walls of rock. The mountain, by some volcanic agency, had been rift asunder; and the almost touching cliffs seemed to heighten in the distance. Still there was hope, for some devious torrent might have forced a rude yet practicable passage to the summit.

The youth then advanced rapidly along the smooth and sandy pathway, which, sloping downwards for many a mile, still presented the same monotonous aspect. Far up he could faintly descry gleaming veins of virgin gold meandering in profusion along the white crystalline rock, which, though stained here and there with rusty deposits from minute rills, was everywhere solid as adamant. As he gazed for an instant upon the intense azure of the sky above, and the boundless sheet of snowy quartz which stretched as far as his eye could reach, the latent poetry of his soul was roused; he became conscious of the mingled awfulness and beauty of the scene before him; he comprehended the stern mercilessness of smiling Nature.

Then, as he still advanced, the character of the strata changed. The path became soft and pasty, the walls more grey and opaque; no longer shining, they only gleamed faintly as the now slanting sun-light was reflected from them. Here and there cropped out rich green masses, which sparkled more brightly than the mica-slate in which they were imbedded. One of these, washed from its matrix by the storms of centuries, lay on the hitherto untrodden path. Instinctively attracted by its glitter and bright hue, Jamasp almost unconsciously stooped down and picked up the fallen mineral: it was a group of emeralds, whose clustered cubes, though perceptibly flawed by their fall, would have adorned a prince's diadem. The acquisition of this prize quickened his love of life, and acted as a stimulus to his flagging strength. Life seems much more precious, because more enjoyable, in the rich than in the poor; and now Jamasp had that in his possession which would ensure him competence, if not wealth. So, though weary and somewhat hungry, he manfully trudged on with reanimated spirit.

Would the mountain range go on for ever, or would he at length behold the walls diminishing in altitude, until a plain appeared? Eventually it must be so, he argued, but when? Would his strength hold out until food and freedom could be obtained, or were his bones destined to rot upon the now oozy soil? For although no sound of falling waters disturbed the solemn silence, and no mould or clay was visible overhead (daylight was fast fading); the pathway grew more and more muddy, and his feet occasionally plashed in slimy pools as he wearily staggered onwards. The water grew deeper at every step. It was already up to his knees; should he advance? There was little choice. Behind was certain destruction, in front the possibility of tracing from whence the waters had descended, and perchance of ascending in their channel. Again the stream grew wider and deeper, the bottom more and more slippery. His progress became slower. The liquid had nearly reached his lips; he quaffed it, felt refreshed, and betook himself to swimming. No longer did he gaze upon the menacing walls of his prison; he stubbornly breasted the opposing stream. Soon, however, he became faint with weariness, and his ineffective strokes became more and more feeble.

What warm and spicy breath is that which fans his cheek? Has he unconsciously passed the icy gates of death, and entered Paradise? His aching limbs told him how vain was that imagination, but his awakened eyes told him likewise that he was rescued from immediate peril. In the lethargy of despair he had arrived, without seeing it beforehand, at a sudden gap in the hill from which a low-based, crater-shaped mountain lake, when surcharged with rain, poured its surplus water into the rift he had been traversing. A ledge, not a foot from the level of the stream, ran continuously round the lake, and to this haven of shelter from a watery death did Jamasp cling, and with a last effort threw his exhausted frame upon its hard surface. What blissful ease was the voluntary torpidity which followed! But darkness was approaching; so, after a brief rest, he again roused himself to fresh struggles for his existence.

Not more than a mile from where he had entered the hollow circuit, he perceived, at an oblique angle from the ledge, a clean smooth road, that gradually wound upwards; following which he found himself upon a broad platform, which, jutting forth high above the lake, exhibited at one glance its entire dimensions. The panorama around was very beautiful, and unexpected as it was lovely. Rich masses of vegetation, contrary to the usual habits of nature, surrounded the waveless surface, clinging vines—at least, they seemed so in the gloomy obscurity of the evening—trailed on every rock.

The wearied adventurer, leaving the smooth plateau, clambered towards the grapes; he had nearly plucked a large and tempting bunch, when he recoiled in horror from the slough of a gigantic boa, and a loud and angry hissing from an adjacent brake drove him shuddering from the spot. He knew all now. The jewels, the snake, even the dark spots, which had seemed to flit like far-off birds across the narrow strip of sky above the mountain-rift, were now comprehensible to him. He was in, or near, the celebrated valley of jewels, which no man had dared to enter from terror of its serpent guardians!

Quickly retracing his steps, he retreated to the central platform, and having noticed a ring of seat-like elevations, with a raised rocky couch pre-eminently conspicuous in the middle, flung himself recklessly upon it, and, worn out with incessant fatigue, soon became oblivious of all things. Fear itself had yielded to overpowering weariness.

It was broad daylight when he awoke, and the warm sun was pouring its bright beams upon the landscape, disclosing a sight so startling, that his appalled senses almost relapsed into the lethargy from which they had just been freed. Far as his eye could reach, the ground in the distance undulated with moving snakes; yet none molested him, none menaced him, none approached him. Reposing in vast coils upon the circle of seats of which his own rocky couch was the centre, lay extended in calm majesty a score or so of mighty Pythons, serpents of such magnitude, that the boas which he had encountered in his forest rambles seemed but earthworms in comparison. No hissing sound was audible, but the rustling of the gliding reptiles, as they marshalled themselves between the raised seats, was like the wind whispering to the autumn leaves. The dense mass of deadly creatures hemmed him in on every side, but none ventured to intrude within the apparently charmed circle.

There is a calmness of despair that enables us to notice objects which, were our terror less intense, were our hope of life more assured, would probably escape our cognizance. The knolls, which in the gloom of the evening he had regarded as mere turf-covered rocks, now flashed brilliantly in the sunshine from the uncut crystals of a thousand gems; their very groundwork was composed of tree-like masses of native gold. His own couch was a solid pile of diamonds and of emeralds.

For a while (to him it seemed an age, yet it was only a few minutes) the hideous array glared at him with lurid eyes, yet refrained from assaulting him. Then a colossal boa, with slow and stately march, glided through their yielding ranks, bearing upon his broad back a monstrous pearl shell (the gift of some tributary sea-snake) on which reposed, in calm dignity, the loveliest of painted serpents. Its scales of pure and silvery white reflected prismatic colours, as the sunbeams danced upon them; its long and gracefully tapering body was crowned by the diminutive head of a lovely maiden, whose lofty brow was surmounted by a coronet of priceless rubies, the symbol of her rank. In dulcet tones she thus addressed the unconscious invader of her territory, the unwitting usurper of her throne:—

"None shall hurt thee here, bold intruder though thou art; for I am Queen of the Serpents. Thou hast sought sanctuary in the very temple of our power, and I will not violate the sacred law of hospitality. Bear witness, all my people, that I receive this wanderer as my guest, and harm him not if you value your existence."

At this kind speech, evidently comprehensible to her mute subjects, Jamasp vacated the royal seat, and prostrated himself in humble gratitude. The Queen bade her attendants to provide him with a repast of freshly-plucked fruits, and even condescended to partake along with him of the grapes, pomegranates, bananas, pistachios, etc., which were brought them. After which, having dismissed her martial retinue, she courteously inquired of the wanderer his past history, and being gratified by its recital, vouchsafed in her turn to amuse him with an adventure of her own.

THE TOMB OF SOLOMON.

"Potent though I am," said she, "and surrounded by warriors whose weapons are more fatal than any forged by man; ruler though I am, not alone of the reptiles, but of the beasts of the earth and the fishes of the sea,—for should they oppose me, my subjects would slay them with their poison-fangs,—I have felt the bitterness of captivity: I have been at the mercy of a child of Adam. It happened thuswise:—

"A young Indian prince, Belukia by name, having descried in the treasure-chamber of his deceased father a small cabinet supported on a column of Egyptian marble, opened it from curiosity, and found its sole contents to be a casket of carved ebony, which enclosed a roll of papyrus. Being of a studious temperament, he carefully perused the manuscript, and soon felt strangely interested in its contents. It was a theological treatise in direct opposition to that creed in which he had been educated, and had been written for the sole use of priests and rulers: to all others it was forbidden. It demonstrated the unity of the Deity worshipped under a hundred names by the unspiritual masses, who, indeed, adored his several attributes as distinct individualities. It prophesied, too, the early coming of a heavenly Being, who should subdue all men by his goodness, and purge their souls from earthly passions.

"Had not his heart been pure and noble, these heretical doctrines (for they were such to his nation) would have been scornfully rejected and despised. To him, however, they proved so acceptable, so enthralling, that he made a solemn vow to seek for the godlike being who was to purify mankind, even should he wander to the most distant regions of the earth.

"Full of zeal, enamoured with doctrines which alone fulfilled his inner consciousness of what was right, he resigned the administration of his kingdom to the sage and trusty vizier of his late father, and having bidden farewell to his surviving parent, started for Jerusalem; for it was there, so far as he could gather from the hazy prophecy, that the pre-ordained One would be heard of, or beheld.

"The journey was long and perilous; many moons

waned ere he reached the land he sought; and there, all being contented with their own superstitions, none either knew of or cared for (though all expected) the long-prophesied emanation of Divinity. Chance, however, threw him in the way of Offan, a sage who had vainly devoted his life to the pursuit of the more abstruse sciences. The daring spirit of that student would have rendered him worthy to contest the mastery of the universe with those mysterious beings who are the pre-ordained guardians of the course of nature; but his soul, though courageous, was grovelling; he craved supernatural power, not for the glorious privilege it confers of redressing the wrongs of fortune towards others, but solely for the acquisition of sensual enjoyment for himself. He listened with a smile to the artless narrative of the simple prince, who, for a visionary project, from which no gain could accrue to himself individually, had abandoned the delights of ease, pleasure, and almost absolute power, for the many privations of lengthened travel; and gleaned from his conversation the one all-important fact, that I, the Queen of the Serpents, who alone knew the hidden virtues of all plants, held empire in the regions that bordered upon his own, and often, indeed, approached the very frontiers.

"'I will for once be frank,' said Offan: 'our interests do not clash, and companionship will prove agreeable to both of us. *My* objects once attained, and I own they are illimitable knowledge and power, I promise to devote all my then boundless resources to trace out the mysterious being you yearn for; and rest assured, that if he be now upon the earth, I shall enforce his presence. For my books have taught me the precise spot where Solomon, lord of man and spirits, the ring upon whose finger confers universal dominion upon its wearer, still reposes in unburied majesty, lifelike yet inanimate. So remote from the ordinary route of commerce is the islet to which he was borne, that no ship has ever visited it, even accidentally; such sunken rocks and coral reefs surround it, that no vessel could approach its shores without destruction. There is but one way to succeed; our feet must be anointed with the juice of a marvellous plant known only to the Queen of the Serpents, which will enable us to tread upon the waters as upon dry ground. This secret, and even the exact situation of the fatal islet, I have long known, but until this day I knew not the abode of the Snake Queen. Let us, then, hasten to capture her, and permit her to ransom herself cheaply by finding us the herb we are seeking.'

"The Belooch Prince readily assented, and in due time both adventurers arrived in my dominions. They were bold, yet wary; and the more noble of the two knew well the weaknesses of my race, and my own familiar haunts.

"Milk, being usually unattainable, proves an irresistible attraction to us, and a very small bowl of it tempted me to the mouth of the cave within which the daring couple had secreted themselves. I lapped it eagerly, and then tried, and almost equally liked, the contents of a larger bowl which lay beside it, full to the brim with a sweet and very potent wine. This beverage so intoxicated me, that I lay benumbed and innocuous before my captors, who having watched my proceedings from their asylum, took advantage of my helplessness, placed me in a cage, and waited anxiously for my recovery.

"'Fear not,' said the Prince courteously, when I had at length shaken off the poisonous lethargy; 'we will not harm you: all we require is that you will point out to us the water-repelling plant which will enable our feet to tread the ocean waves without sinking beneath them. Merely indicate that to us, and immediate freedom shall reward your compliance. Forgive my unavoidable roughness, and let there be peace between us.'

"Although naturally indignant at my capture, I assented to these terms, and was soon liberated; for the herb, however uncommon it may be elsewhere, is indigenous to this country, and by no means scarce.

"My subjects, and the fish and fowl, who submissively act as my spies and emissaries, have furnished me with the sequel to my own misadventure. Offan, and the Prince, having expressed the juice of a few plants, and enshrined the liquid in a golden phial, proceeded to the sea-coast, and there, having anointed their feet, traversed the waste of waters until they arrived at the islet of Solomon.

"The land, if it might be so called, was a mere gigantic rock, lashed by perpetual waves and utterly destitute of vegetation. It yielded nothing that would induce the adventurous mariner, who should by any possible contingency have safely crossed the foaming line of breakers which girded it, to linger for a moment; it produced nothing that could sustain life in the unhappy wretch whose tempest-tossed vessel might have been shattered upon the guardian reef. The wisest of mankind had evidently selected it as the most inaccessible spot upon earth, the safest repository for his treasures, the most impregnable ot mausoleums, a sepulchre more secure than the solid pyramids of Egypt.

" After aiding each other in a painful ascent of the rugged cliffs, the resolute travellers at length scrambled to the summit, which they found perforated in all directions by precisely similar caverns, whose sinuous windings would have wearied the patience of any casual explorer. The long studies of the sage here enabled him to overcome the extreme difficulty of resolving which to enter; had chance decided his footsteps, weeks might have elapsed ere the sepulchre of the King could have been discovered, and death by famine would have been the inevitable lot of the searchers for his tomb. Offan, however, did not hesitate for a moment. Observing in the far interior of one of them a faint glimmer of light succeeding to the darkness in which all the hollows alike were enveloped, he impetuously led the way, and, blindly rushing through the murky portion of the cavern, after a brief space of time beheld a sight that fully recompensed him for all the previous hardships he had endured. Royally apparelled and seated upon a throne of flashing diamonds, from whose collective light-secreting powers proceeded the pale lamp-like illumination that rendered the whole scene dimly visible, a majestic form of more than ordinary stature, whose stern features bore the impress of command, seemed, from afar, instinct with life and power. But the orbits were devoid of eyes; there only had the flesh-preserving skill of the mummy-artist failed to preserve the semblance of vitality. The wondrous ring, blazing, with innate light, upon the bent emaciated finger, which seemed retentive of authority even after death, Offan would have torn, without reverence, from the stiffened hand; but ere he could touch the corpse, there glided suddenly from beneath the throne a spectral snake, the guardian genius of the deceased monarch, which, interposing its threatening form between the living and the dead, by the suddenness of its contiguity caused the sacrilegious adventurer to instinctively recoil.

"'Back, daring mortals!' for by this time the Prince had overtaken his companion; 'fate has not destined either of you to wield the sceptre of Solomon. The allotted time has not yet come when I shall be free; and, until then, I must needs immolate all who shall resist my warning. Retire at once. I have no pleasure in slaying, no love for the dead; but I am doomed to watch over the carcase of him whom in life I feared and hated.'

"Thus spoke the once rebellious genius, who had struggled of old for that liberty which was still withheld from him as an enduring punishment for his stubborn opposition.

"The Belooch Prince submissively retired; for the scorching fire now issuing from the jaws of the monster, which swelled each moment into vaster proportions, and the angry glitter of its baleful eyes convinced him of the inutility of a contest with a superhuman adversary. Not so did Orfan; muttering an impotent charm, he leaped boldly forward, in the vain hope of clutching the ring before he should be overpowered by its vigilant guardian: once in his own hand, dissevered from the corpse, and he would become lord of spirits and master of life. What cared he for a momentary scorching? it could be cured in a like moment by the virtues of the ring. But so instantaneously searching was the lightning-like flame which gushed from the throat of his snake-shaped foe, that all power of movement ceased within him; the flesh fumed as it were from his calcined bones, and he withered in a moment to a shapeless mass.

"Alas! for the ambitious voluptuary. But Belukia, after much suffering, returned to the kingdom of his fathers, baffled, indeed, in his immediate project (a wild yet noble one), but improved by an experience of life's troubles. Henceforth he could sympathize with the unfortunate and the adventurous; too frequently they are identical."

The Snake Queen paused, and having indicated a neighbouring grotto as the residence of her guest, and appointed for him a guard of honour which should attend to his requirements, retired to her subterranean palace. There was no lack of refreshing fruits and luscious honey: the lake furnished him with beverage, his attendants were assiduous, and his dwelling-place (the climate being perfection) far from disagreeable. The Queen, moreover, was a pleasant gossip, and the days of Jamasp sped happily and quickly.

But trouble was at hand. She loved him, and ere long boldly avowed she had spared him for his beauty, that he might be the partner of her throne. "Else had he, the unwitting intruder upon her dominions, shared the fate of all other mortals who had ventured into her fastnesses.

Belukia and his comrade had alone escaped with impunity."

There is some occult horror of the reptile world implanted in the breast of man; and though the human head of the Snake Queen was exquisitely beautiful, and her voice loving, soft, and gentle, the idea of passing his existence with so unnatural a bride was inexpressibly repulsive to our hero. However, lest he should be thought ungrateful, he concealed his disgust, and, as he could not escape from his dangerous hostess, urgently pressed the Queen for permission to revisit his native town previous to their nuptials, that he might relieve the anxiety of his widowed mother, and provide for her necessities by the sale of his emeralds. Yielding a reluctant assent to his importunities, for thoroughly enamoured she could refuse him nothing, he was furnished with a guide, and after a few days' journey found himself once more near the scenes of his boyhood.

Before he left he was taught by his fond gaoler a low whistling sound like the whispering of a wanton zephyr, which, when uttered in the honey-cave, would summon her to his side, to guard him from any of her irritable subjects whom he might inadvertently tread on when returning to the borders of the mountain-lake. During his sojourn in the land of the serpents, he had daily immersed himself in the limpid waters of that stream; and the ardent Queen having noticed how much he delighted in this health-giving purification, to expedite his coming back to her, made him swear never to bathe again until his return to her dominions. He took the oath willingly and promptly, for he preferred an eternal abstinence from the pleasures of the bath to sharing the couch of the woman-headed snake.

"Keep your plighted word, dear one," she had cried on parting, when, having coiled herself gently around him, she had kissed him with her lovely but icy lips; "I feel a presentiment that my very life will depend upon your truthfulness."

And so they parted; she gliding back to her now desolate palace (for what was sovereignty to her without *his* gladdening presence?), soon to keep an unremitting watch around the honey-cave; he stepping briskly and blithely on his homeward route, rejoicing to quit for ever one for whom he felt simultaneously a conflicting gratitude and aversion.

Jamasp was received by his mother as one risen from the dead. She fainted in his arms, and when recovered from her trance wept and laughed alternately, with uncontrollable emotion. When she had become more composed he narrated his strange adventures; and she, woman-like, after hearing of the base treachery of the woodcutters, hastened to upbraid them for their villainy, and threatened to publicly accuse them of their past misdeeds. They were now flourishing traders, with reputations that could not bear aspersion; so propitiating her immediate wrath by a timely gift of money, they dismissed her for the night, and took counsel together as to how best they might avoid exposure. Next morning they sought the poor abode of their late comrade, and having freely bestowed upon him one half of their wealth (which successful commerce would soon replace), asked and obtained his silence and his pardon.

Then Jamasp, having sold his emeralds for a large sum of money, became a rich merchant, and was no longer esteemed a fool, but a clever fellow. His sense and prosperity were universally attributed to his having perused the brief compendium of all philosophy, which had been bequeathed him as his sole inheritance; but in truth, when the casket had been opened, the precious papyri contained only moral apophthegms, enouncing the vanity of all corporeal pleasures, and suggesting an eternal contemplation of the perfection of the Divinity, with the hope of being eventually absorbed in His essence, as the height of human felicity. Jamasp was too young, too capable of earthly enjoyment, to accept with docility this supreme philosophy.

His friends, for he had now many, questioned him as to the cause of his long absence, and his strange repugnance to bathe along with them. He frankly told them all, except, of course, his abandonment in the pit, and the treasures he had perceived in the valley of jewels. They, on their part, joked him about his serpent bride, and laughed at his scrupulous observance of an oath which had been unfairly exacted as the price of his freedom. But they could not induce him to violate it, despite of his own great longing for a salutary gratification. One day, however, the proprietor of a bath, who was his personal acquaintance, having asked him to enter the building for a friendly chat, invited him to accept of a bath as a token of his regard, but was answered as usual by the story of his enforced vow. The customers, not a few of whom were his daily associates, were in a merry mood;

so flocking round him, and laughing all the while, they stripped off his clothing with friendly violence, and mirthfully plunged him into the warm fluid. "Henceforth," they exclaimed, "your oath is valueless; having once entered the bath, you may without fresh perjury again and again refresh yourself with its healthful pleasures."

Now the chief vizier of the King chanced to be bathing, and felt much interested in the narrative he had heard. When Jamasp then, purified in his person, despite of his own conscientious resistance, had dressed himself, he was straightway conducted by the orders of that minister into the presence of his Sovereign, that he might amuse him likewise by a repetition of his adventures.

The royal palace lay at some considerable distance from the little town, and on his arrival there a delicious repast was prepared for him, and a dress of honour bestowed upon him, ere he was ushered into the presence of the ruler of his land. The subjects of Gusardan (for so was the monarch named) never beheld their Sovereign, who secluded himself from all the world; for he was a leper.

Reclined upon a sofa, and muffled from head to foot with a long flesh-coloured veil, the King listened, at first with an amused air, and then with excited agitation, to the marvellous story of the quondam woodcutter. At its close, tossing from him the light covering which had concealed his features, he suddenly revealed to our hero the snow-white scurfy flesh, here and there eaten into cancerous holes, which he had so long sedulously guarded from the gaze of his courtiers.

"See the horrible state to which I am reduced," he

cried with overwhelming emotion, "and save your Sovereign; bring hither the Queen of the Serpents—she alone can cure me."

For his physician had assured him that the sole remedy for his otherwise incurable complaint was the stewed flesh of the Snake Queen, a panacea which until that moment he saw no possibility of procuring. He concealed, however, from Jamasp his designs upon the life of the half-human reptile, for the friendly feeling of our hero towards the being who had spared him (whatever might have been her motive) was too apparent to escape his anxious observation.

Yet the widow's son mistrusted even whilst he pitied the poor King, and vainly sought to excuse himself from the task assigned him. He did not even like to play the part of Belukia, and force from his captured patroness the secret of that remedy which would restore the suffering monarch to the enjoyment of health. Sooth to say, he was ashamed to meet the loving snake, and resisting all offers of wealth and station as the price of his compliance, urged his violated vow, and the possibility of her vengeance as an adequate reason for his reluctance to encounter her.

Then the enfeebled King silently desponded, and again veiled himself; but the vizier, who alone besides was present, thus in angry tones addressed the unwilling offender: "Refuse to obey, and you quit not this palace alive: never shall you reveal the pitiable plight of our sovereign to your fellow-citizens; else will they despise and revolt against their lord. Take now your choice. I pledge my word that no evil shall happen to your benefactress (as you foolishly term her) should she accede to our wishes; I vow, on the other hand, that unimaginable tortures, to escape which death itself would seem a boon, shall otherwise wrest from you your secret mode (for all else is known to us) of invoking her presence."

Who could resist such menaces? Yet it was not until the torturers had essayed their foul skill upon his anguished frame that he yielded a sullen compliance to the will of the pitiless vizier, who had been calmly watching his writhings with an assured and triumphant smile of irony.

Heavily ironed, and guarded with stern vigilance by ruthless soldiers, he was taken to the remote cave, and there forced to utter the far-sounding sibilation which would entice the hapless Queen to her captivity. Poor loving wretch! she was close at hand, longingly waiting for the expected sound. Scarcely had it passed his lips, when she glided through the crevice in the old reservoir, and found herself, not in the embrace of her beloved youth, but in the muscular arms of a brawny forester, who, clasping her suddenly by the neck, forced her into the cage that had been prepared for her reception. The manacles upon the hands of Jamasp, his woe-begone aspect, the tears which gushed from his eyes when he beheld her so roughly handled, told her, without words, how unwilling had been his participation in her capture.

"I forgive you my early death, Jamasp," she cried. "I know the reason of my capture, and the disease of the King. It is my life they are seeking; but perhaps you knew it not, else you could scarcely have betrayed one whose sole error was in loving too well a child of Adam."

Then did Jamasp solemnly protest his ignorance of their

intended cruelty, and declared what tortures he had endured ere he had consented to be a party to her capture.

"Carry me, then, dear Jamasp, yourself, and I will whisper in your ears whilst you bear me on your head, what you must do in this sad contingency."

He was permitted to carry the encaged snake, and returned, still encircled by menacing guards, to the palace of his sovereign. There, by the orders of the overjoyed monarch, he was at once liberated, richly appareled, and promised his choice of all the dignities in the kingdom. Now the vizier heard the promise, and quaked for his own office; for all men, he thought, must envy him his power.

On the road, the Snake Queen had sadly, yet with calm resignation, told the man she loved the doom which was awaiting her.

"They will bid you sever my body into three pieces, and stew it upon the fire, as a savoury dish for the sick monarch. I *must* perish, for surrounded as we are escape is hopeless; but let not my blood be shed by you: refuse boldly; the King will side with you."

"I will die rather," replied the penitent Jamasp.

"You shall not die," rejoined the captive, "but live and prosper, if you will carefully follow my advice. The vizier will order you to watch beside my seething flesh until the scum shall float upon the surface of the broth, then to pour forth a cupful of the liquor and reserve it for yourself; again to wait until the boiling recommences, and pour forth a second cup for him. Act not thus; but let our common enemy swallow the first cup, and then drink the second yourself. The first juice is deadly; the second brain-clearing, and the bestower of all wisdom."

So our hero followed her advice, boldly refusing to perform the office of an executioner; and as the cook refused to slay a semi-human being, the impatient vizier himself smote off the lovely head, and hewed asunder the crystalline body with his remorseless scimetar. At that moment an imperative summons for his immediate appearance arrived from the King; so, leaving strict orders as to the broth, precisely as had been foretold by the victim, he abruptly quitted the spacious kitchen.

When, at length, he returned, the first cup was presented to him by the obsequious Jamasp, who assured him that he had not ventured to sip his own from deference to his superior rank. With a baleful smile, for he had resolved that a possible rival, and assuredly a contumacious adversary, should perish, he fixed his cruel eyes upon the youth, who loathingly gulped down the not unpalatable liquid; then triumphantly he swallowed his own portion, and fell shrieking with inconceivable agony upon the ground. His flesh swelled, blackened, and rotted from his bones; his carcase stank with so horrible a fœtor, that it was dragged away with a hook and rope, and cast unburied upon slackened lime, for no man ventured to touch it for fear of contagion.

But Jamasp, who, mistrusting his own fate, fled swiftly from the scene of horror, only at first felt increased powers of observation and quickened judgment from his undesired draught; from that time, however, all knowledge became easy of acquirement by him.

The leper-king ate of the stewed flesh of her who had been slain to cure him; and he, too, was punished; for the flesh became burning fire within him, and the fever that consumed him raged to wild delirium, and a thousand times in his three days of torture did he experience the anguish of that violent death which had been inflicted, by his orders, upon his unoffending victim. Then, at last, thanks to the cooling drinks they gave him, he burst into a profuse sweat, the hideous chasms which the leprosy had hollowed in his body gradually filled with healthy flesh; his outer skin peeled off, and the inner showed itself soft and rosy as in a new-born babe.

Months elapsed ere vigour was restored to his debilitated frame, and as by that time the fame of the wisdom of the sage's son was spread abroad, the grateful monarch promoted him to the post of his defunct minister. But seldom thenceforth did a smile irradiate the sad countenance of Jamasp, for remorse preyed upon him for betraying her, who, even in death, had cared for his happiness.

MAAROOF THE TREASURE-SEEKER.*

I DOUBT whether in all Cairo there was a more miserable being than Maaroof. It was not merely that he was a poor man, so poor, indeed, that he knew not in the morning whether he should gain wherewithal to purchase food for the evening, but that he was cursed with an affliction, the poignancy of which none but those who have themselves experienced it can duly estimate. He had wedded a shrew,—one, moreover, who was self-willed, violent, and full of fancies.

He had not always occupied the humble position in which he now moved, for his father had been a wealthy merchant, and the blood of kings flowed in the veins of his mother. But in his youth he had beheld a sight, the remembrance of which haunted him for ever after, and dispelled all purposes of steady industry. He had seen the City of Brass; he had gazed upon the countless trea-

* Including the 'City of Brass,' part of the 'Seven Viziers,' part of 'Ibrahim and Jemeeleh,' etc.

sures that were stored in its mansions, yet had not been permitted to remove a single jewel.

It happened thuswise. On his first journey with merchandise, he had encountered the cavalcade of a certain Emir, Moosa by name, who had been dispatched by his lord, El Melik, who ruled at Damascus, to procure him some of those brazen urns which fame has handed down to us as the prisons of rebellious genii. The tradition ran that, when they were unsealed, a spiral column of smoke would eddy forth, which assumed for an instant only the image of a towering giant, whilst, "Pardon, O Prophet!" thundered forth from the rapidly dissolving form. To behold so wonderful a sight was longed for by El Melik, and as some travellers had assured the monarch that these urns were frequently fished up by a negro race, worthy and hospitable islanders, who dwelt in the Southern Main, he had resolved to procure and inspect them. Accordingly, he had sent the Emir with a large retinue in that direction; and as Maaroof was journeying by a like route, he joined, by permission, the princely traveller.

After some days' riding they lost their road, and wandering further and further from the track of caravans, found themselves at the base of a mighty range of mountains,—precipice upon precipice soaring upwards until the summit of the highest was lost in the clouds of heaven. All around looked barren and cheerless; for the earth seemed scorched up, and was split into vast clefts by the action of subterranean fires, and not a blade of glass or a pool of water was visible as far as the eye could reach. Suddenly a blast of wind, howling from the adjacent gulf, scattered the dense mist that had obscured the sun, and the rays of that luminary, reflected from thirty towers of gilded brass which were perched upon the loftiest of the mountains, almost blinded the eyes by their painful brilliance. Once in a century only had such a sight been permitted to mortals, for in that elevated region of constant mist, the clouds rarely displayed the far-famed City of Brass; and so perilous was the road to it, so far removed from the ordinary routes, that no man living could boast that he had entered it. Yet the whole company knew of its existence, had heard tell how hundreds of years ago this mighty city, whose broad-based walls were eighty cubits high, had been ruled over by a queen, during whose reign the surrounding land had been so desolated by ceaseless famine, that everything that had life within its nostrils had perished.

The Emir Moosa, who, like his sovereign, was greedy of strange sights, determined not to lose so rare a chance of inspecting this renowned city; and as the weather continued bright, and the labour of his many attendants enabled him to bridge over the awful chasms that intervened between the adjacent heights, he at length, after long and painful climbing, reached the ridge round which the brazen towers were symmetrically disposed. Not a keyhole was visible in the metallic gates: the walls were too lofty to scale, and the disappointed Emir with his weary escort having ridden round the vast circuit of the fortifications in the fruitless hope of espying some other mode of entry, prepared to depart. But Maaroof, who noticed on the principal gate the bas-relief of a horseman pointing with his finger to some antique and half-obliterated letters graven on the walls, lingered to decipher the following inscription :—

"Let him who would enter,
Turn the pin in my centre."

He read, shouted, grasped a boss which he perceived jutting out from the sculptured belt of the warlike effigy, and violently wrenched it round: then with a terrific din the metallic gates dashed open, as it were, of their own accord, and all the company entered the city of the dead. The buildings seemed perfect as on the day of their erection; gold and jewels were found mixed with carious bones; but the merchandise had rotted and the furniture had decayed. The handsomest of the buildings had evidently been a palace or temple, and from its grandeur and superb architecture attracted their special curiosity. They strayed through its courts and chambers until they arrived before a door of cedar-wood, inlaid with ebony and ivory; having passed through which, they were startled by the sight of three individuals, life-like but motionless. Upon a couch, a perfect mine of carbuncles and emeralds, at the summit of a high dais, reposed a lovely woman, guarded on either side by a huge black slave, one armed with a sword, the other with a bar of steel. A tablet of gold lay on the ground before them; on this was written, "If you value life, touch not the queen: let her be an eternal testimony to the skill and opulence of this lost nation. All that is without this chamber she gives to her visitors." So exquisitely preserved were the handsome features of the principal figure of this natural group, that it was difficult to believe that she no longer breathed: her two guardians, though cleverly sculptured, were mere images of wood. The dress of the female was entirely composed of pearls; a golden crown with a border of large rubies spanned her brow; a necklace of diamonds, as large as pigeons' eggs, hung loosely round her neck.

The Emir gazed with awe upon the sight, and bade his people respect the last wishes of departed royalty, close again the palace, shut the brazen gate, and as their provisions threatened to fail them, to instantly depart from the city on the quest for the mystic urns. To refrain from treasures such as their eyes now gazed on was more than they could bear: a daring mutineer ran up the steps of the dais, and tried to snatch the crown from the inanimate figure of the starved queen; scarcely had he touched her body than he became lifeless as herself. The sword and bar had descended simultaneously upon him, moved by some hidden machinery that connected the automatons with the lifelike corpse. When the weapons had achieved their destined work, they returned with a jerk to their threatening position. None dared move the body, and the mutiny was quelled: the Emir and his escort retrod the perilous pathway they had formed, and after much privation reached again the main road from which they had diverged, and, it is said, succeeded without further difficulty in the object of their mission.

But as to Maaroof, from that hour he never rested; the unguarded treasures he had feasted his eyes on so surpassed the slower profits of trade, that he relinquished thenceforth all idea of merchandise. His ideas became too princely for his station; he looked down upon the thousand comforts which were at his beck: unlimited wealth, the representative of every enjoyment, the assuager even of sorrow and suffering might be acquired in a week by daring and good fortune. Was he to be blamed, if with the buoyant hopes of youth and its too sanguine spirit of enterprise, he risked his all upon efforts which proved his ruin?

He had left the Emir Moosa at the nearest town (yet it was far away, for the curse of sterility still lingered upon the adjacent lands) to the city of the dead, and from thence he headed expedition after expedition to recover the treasures he had perforce abandoned. He would have gone alone, for he felt conscious how irresistible was the temptation of despoiling the capitalist who had defrayed the cost; but it was imperatively requisite to carry large stores of provisions; and the awful precipices which had been surmounted, the frightful chasms which had been passed by him, when escorted under the most favourable circumstances by experienced and disciplined warriors, convinced him of the necessity of being accompanied by a large body of daring mechanics. Labour, low as the individual cost may seem (especially to him who receives the wage of it), is the most costly of expenditure; and as exploration after exploration failed, from the black brooding clouds which concealed the site of the lost city, the hopes and the resources of our hero diminished in like proportion. Fortune seemed his enemy; for when he had become so reduced that he could only form a partnership with one or two adventurers who still trusted to his glowing accounts of the treasure-city, the clouds would burst asunder and disclose the pathway he had traversed in happier days. Yet he could never trace it to the brazen towers; either the abysses had grown more profound than ever, or the needful wood to cross them had been miscalculated. It was hard enough for the famishing explorers to transport their fodder and provisions, without any superfluous burden being carried on their mules. At last, after many a baffled enterprise, he became penniless.

In love he had been equally unlucky. Before he had started upon his mercantile journey he had become a married man. Who would not have envied him, had they beheld his wife? It was a love-match, the fruits of a romantic incident in his young career; and the risks he had encountered in gaining his bride should have rendered her ever loving, and obedient to his gentle sway. But the same passions which had favoured his suit proved adverse to him in his fallen estate. He had beheld the portrait of a lovely woman in a book that he had purchased, and so life-like did it seem, so fascinating in its weird beauty, that he could not obliterate the image from his thoughts.

"Tell me, I beg you," said he to the dealer, "from whence you obtained this miniature; is it the work of fancy, or was it copied from a living female?"

"Sandalanee can inform you, for from him I purchased it," was the answer; "he lives in the quarter El Karkh."

Thither hurried the impetuous youth, for desire is fanned in youth by the mere breath of imagination, and destiny so far favoured him that he became intimate with the painter. In a friendly gossip the purchased sketch was exhibited, and the name of the original demanded.

"She is a distant connection of my own," said Sandalanee; "one whom I would gladly wed, did my rank permit it: she is the daughter of the Governor of Suez, and so averse to marriage that I, with more than competence, and in art second to none, have failed to win her. Her name is Jemeeleh."

Our hero did not inquire whether the years of the amative painter were or were not twice as numerous as those of the beauty; he obtained her address, and sallied forth in quest of her, despite of her rumoured reputation as an incorrigible vixen. She dwelt on a little islet in the bend of the great river, a spot which belonged to her father, and from which all males were rigorously excluded. There was one exception—a deformed gardener, who from an elevated seat watched all who might approach; and by good luck, as Maaroof in his ignorance then esteemed it, his own humpbacked tailor chanced to be the brother of the guardian. By the introduction of the former and the connivance of the latter, he was enabled to gaze upon the charms of the lovely maiden in her solitary retreat, to profit by the passionate longings of her wanton temperament, and to bear her off as his willing prize from her wealthy parent. He had carried off his mistress in a vessel manned and equipped by the treacherous Sandalanee, been drugged and thrown ashore by his crew, who had borne the helpless girl to their unscrupulous employer; had, after a narrow escape from death, rescued his bride from the clutches of her would-be ravisher, and eventually conducted her in all honour to his own home, where he legally espoused her. Surely mutual peril, mutual endurance should have endeared them to each other.

To provide her with all those elegances to which she had been accustomed, was the stimulus which urged

Maaroof to his chimerical pursuit of the hidden treasure. He was not luxurious in personal expenditure, and never repined at the painful privations which he suffered in the wild mountainous region that encircled the City of Brass. Perhaps Jemeeleh might have pardoned his frequent absences (though I doubt it, so warm were her passions), because they were inspired, or at least influenced, by his tenderness for herself; but penury, and its attendant slights and denials, proved unbearable to a woman whose every wish had hitherto been gratified. Among her intimates was an old woman, one of the thousand pious hypocrites who enter the harem under the pretext of sanctity. She was neither more nor less than a procuress, who, for a bribe from some wealthy *roué*, would further his intrigues with willing wantons. After the third or fourth visit of Maaroof to the scene of his fascination, he descried, on his return home, a costly veil, one which he had neither given himself, nor had his wife previously possessed, hidden, as it were, beneath the seat she had been occupying. It was the gift of a rich young merchant, who had been fully repaid (at least he so considered) for his liberality. Jemeeleh, at that time inexperienced in deceit, could not account for its possession, and blushed and equivocated when interrogated respecting it. Distrust and coldness ensued; and as Maaroof was assuredly the handsomest man she knew, and one whom she would have preferred to any other admirer, could he have always gratified her caprices and her passions, the mischievous crone was consulted as to the mode by which the suspicions of the husband could be effectually removed, and his ardour resuscitated.

"Had the veil any peculiar mark by which it could be identified?" inquired the crafty adviser.

"My husband noticed it was burnt at the edge," said the abandoned wife.

"Leave all to me, then," was the response; "he shall soon apologize for his shrewd suspicions."

When Maaroof, the next morning, was passing the shop of the amorous merchant, a previously rehearsed scene was played to deceive him. The young profligate was reviling, and roughly handling an aged female, who bore this treatment with humble equanimity, owning she had merited it by her delinquency.

"Why are you ill-treating the poor old creature?" inquired the tender-hearted Maaroof.

"I trusted her with a costly veil to repair for me," was the answer; "it had a slight hole burnt in it, and she engaged to restore it to my slave-girl, perfect as ever, in two days. Now she pretends to have left it in some harem, but knows not where; I suspect the loss was intentional."

"Indeed, I lost it," said the cunning crone. "I am very poor, and obtain alms from the charitable inmates of so many harems, that I know not at this moment where precisely I did leave it; but to-morrow I make my rounds, and shall easily recognize it by its scorched edge."

"Permit her to depart," said the deluded treasure-seeker. "I will be responsible; it was accidentally left in my own dwelling."

So Maaroof asked pardon of Jemeeleh for his suspicions, and after a little scolding it was graciously accorded.

Success gives confidence; so the next time she was

caught transgressing, she extricated herself by her own unaided cunning. Being very greedy for presents, she had encouraged the addresses of two lovers at the same time. One was a dependant of the higher in rank, and as the latter had made his appearance while the former was closeted with her, she had hidden the inferior in a secret chamber. Scarcely had she coyly received the advances of the wealthier visitor, than intimation was brought of the return of Maaroof. Her husband became witness to a scene improvised by herself, and skilfully seconded by the surprised admirer. As Maaroof entered the house he beheld a man in a towering passion reviling his wife, and menacing her with a drawn sword. At his approach Jemeeleh cast herself into his arms for protection, and the actor took advantage of his embarrassing entanglement to escape from the house.

"What caused this scene?" cried the deluded husband, after she had recovered from a well-simulated fit of hysterics.

"I was sitting on the terrace-roof of our house," she answered, "when a young man, flying in terror from an armed opponent, rushed across the barrier wall, and flinging himself at my feet, implored me to save him from an unmerited death by concealing him in my dwelling. I had barely time to hide him beneath the trap-door of our chamber, when the ruffian who fled at your presence followed his victim, and demanded him at my hands. I denied his presence, for I could not abandon a suppliant to slaughter before my eyes; hence your opportune return has perhaps saved even myself from the unreasoning violence of his rage. I have sacrificed the proprieties, but I have saved the life of a fellow-creature."

"You have done well," said Maaroof, "we will assuage the terror of the imprisoned one."

So with his own kind hands he set free the younger of the two profligates, and saw that the coast was clear before he dismissed him from his abode. That man never again polluted the sanctity of his home; but Jemeeleh gloried in her cunning, and no longer repressed her lusts or her rapacity.

Maaroof soon learnt enough from his neighbours to be mentally convinced of the wrong that was done him by his wife; yet could never convict her in the fact. His frequent absence had given her every opportunity for intrigue; but he had now become so impoverished, that he could barely maintain himself and Jemeeleh by the pittance he received, from day to day, for his own manual labour. Yes, he who had ridden at the head of fifty horsemen, glorying in the prospect of unlimited wealth, and rejoicing in the beauty of his newly won bride, now disheartened, and without a single piece of gold in his possession, longed above all things to be rid of a wife who at once betrayed and insulted him. For her temper, naturally sharp and overbearing, had not improved under adversity, and she hated and despised the man whose love had reduced her to poverty. As he no longer quitted the city, she had no opportunity for indulging herself in gay garments and delicate living at the expense of her lovers, and indignant reminiscences of past enjoyments made her eloquently vituperative. She was a tall and masculine woman; her husband slender, and enfeebled by self-denial—for the best of all the food was devoured by Jemeeleh—scraps only appeased the appetite of the earner of the viands. That which was at first proffered from affection was soon taken as a right, and the quondam treasure-hunter was scolded, ay, and sometimes smitten as a rebellious slave, when his purse could not fulfil the demands made upon it by the beautiful virago.

When his last coin had disappeared, and he had not the wherewithal to purchase even bread, a fancy for some honey sprang up in the mind of the long-indulged Jemeeleh. After inveighing against her spouse for having reduced her to a position in which even honey was a rare luxury (he bore all this patiently, for there was some truth in the accusation), she imperiously demanded that he should procure her some that very day. He humbly assured her that he was utterly without the means of buying it; for the scanty surplus of each day's earnings had been invariably expended in propitiating the temper of the shrew by gratifying her appetite.

"Steal it if you can't buy it!" she exclaimed, shaking her slipper at him; "only bring home the honey, or you shall rue it."

In this emergency, for he dreaded above all things an angry altercation with the woman who had once been dear to him, he betook himself to a small provision-store, where occasionally he obtained credit.

"I don't keep bees' honey," said the plausible tradesman, "but you can have cane-honey, which is cheaper, and goes further."

Though Maaroof was aware that cane-honey was only a specious trade name for common treacle, he accepted the proposed substitute; he dared not, indeed, dispute the matter with the only shopkeeper who would supply him upon trust. He apologetically handed the coarse relish to his exigent spouse, saying, "It is only cane-honey, but I could procure nothing better upon credit."

"Wretch!" cried the disappointed gourmand, "would you put me off with trash like this? Do you call *this* honey?" And she flung the treacle in his face; and not content with that insult, for it had plastered but one side of it, she struck him so violently on the unsoiled cheek that she knocked out one of his teeth. Then passion overcame the long submissive husband, and he returned the blow, yet rather to deter her from further violence than to punish her as she deserved. Screaming for help like one aggrieved, she seized her husband's beard, and tore at it with all her might. Verily Maaroof had not the better in this domestic conflict.

When her neighbours entered the room, they saw how matters stood, and reprimanded the virago for her outrageous conduct. She, however, not satisfied with her revenge, for it was the first time her partner had ventured to resist her temper, summoned him before the Cadi of the district for beating her, and pretended that he had broken her arm and injured her chest. The witnesses, however, proved the contrary; so the case was dismissed. Again she applied to another magistrate, with like success, and eventually appealed to the supreme tribunal.

As the acquitted defendant had, each time, been forced

to disburse the customary fees of office, the prospect of further litigation involved the necessity of either parting with his tools, so that he could no longer obtain a living, or of an immediate flight from Cairo. He preferred the latter expedient, and led a wandering life of constant hardship, rambling further and further from Egypt, until he arrived at the most distant region of the earth. As travel-stained and footsore, he passed at dusk through a handsome suburb of the capital of Sind, he was accosted by an angry group of four individuals, whose previously loud voices had been hushed at his approach.

"We have just agreed," said the deputed speaker, "to avoid litigation, and abide by the decision of the first stranger who will consent to act as umpire. The judge's fee shall not be wanting."

"What, then, is the subject of your dispute?" inquired the willing arbitrator.

"Four foreigners, partners in some mercantile transaction, left their joint stock of loose cash in my charge. Within a week, one of them reclaimed it, gave me a discharge, and, being a rogue, bolted with the money, thus swindling his three partners of their respective shares. They now claim three-fourths of the deposit at my hands."

"Yes," interrupted one of the merchants, "for we stipulated that it should only be returned upon the joint application of all of us."

"The case, then, is simple," said the traveller; "the money cannot be refunded until the absconded partner shall join in demanding it."

The three foreigners bowed to his decision, and as their

departure from the country had been solely delayed from this unsettled dispute, at once quitted the city. Their departure proved advantageous to Maaroof in the sequel.

Our hero was invited by the man who had gained by his verdict to enter his stately mansion, and after having washed himself, found his shabby clothes replaced by robes as handsome as those which adorned his host.

"Surely we have met before," said Maaroof, when, after a savoury repast, they were left alone by the attendants. "I have gazed upon you, and the memory of past frolics shared together comes vividly before me. Are you not Ali, the son of our druggist, Ahmad?"

His entertainer, whose antecedents were not wholly favourable, winced at the question, and at first equivocated; but, as the conviction of the guest as to his identity could not be shaken, he changed his tactics, and, assuming an air of jovial frankness, laughingly observed:—

"So you recognize me. I would not acknowledge my name until I had tested your acquaintance with our native town. I am, indeed, Ali, the scamp of our district, who so often led you into mischief, and whom all the wiseacres prophesied would come to ruin. Don't you remember what fun we had together as boys: how we worried the Christians by running off with the books from their churches?"

And they roared with laughter as they pictured to themselves the enraged priests, who, panting, perspiring, and loudly threatening the vengeance of Heaven upon their sacrilege, had, after a long and fruitless chase, picked up the muddy volumes from a foul kennel.

"Nevertheless, when I see the style in which you are living, I can hardly realize the fact of your being my old playfellow," said the guest, after their merry reminiscences. "What capital did you possess when you arrived in these parts?"

"A very small one, I can assure you; but luck and talent soon enabled me to enlarge my operations. I will tell you my history, and then give you some good advice, to guide your conduct with the arrogant natives."

THE KING OF THE BEGGARS.

"It's all fair in business, I know, to outwit each other; but it's very annoying to get the worst of a bargain. I had heard before I started for this country that sandal-wood was so highly valued here, that the profits of the dealers who imported it were almost incredible. Hence, I invested my little all in that profitable commodity, and having indicated my cargo to the officer of the port, was permitted to disembark. I had been warned that the inhabitants were knavish and overreaching, yet as I had never yet been worsted by sharpers, who, thinking all but themselves fools, are easily gulled by fair words (and I can romance with any man in this lying city), I paid little heed to the caution which had been suggested. I had scarcely stepped on shore, when a respectable-looking citizen, who had ascertained what I had imported at the custom-house, and prepared accordingly, inquired what merchandise I had brought with me; and upon my replying truly, and stating I had been told that sweet-scented wood was much used in this country, smilingly assented, but added, 'Yet for what vile purposes! See for yourself, and duly estimate the value of the information you have received.' He entered a caravanserai, and there I beheld a mule-driver cooking his food over a fire of the wood I had held so precious. I was so disconcerted that I almost wept from vexation, and felt cheered when the sharper, for such he was, offered me in exchange for my cargo a big measure full of any commodity (jewels alone excepted) I might prefer; for I calculated that if I asked for gold I should not lose much, if at all, by my venture. Consequently, I accepted the offer, but would not name my preference on that day; for there are some drugs more precious than gold itself. He had scarcely left me, when I was pounced upon by another sharper, a one-eyed man, who, accusing me of having put out his eye, demanded the right of plucking out one of mine, if I would not pay him the value of that he had lost. The decision of this affair I likewise put off until the morrow; and as my shoe had burst, left it to be mended at the stall of a cobbler. I merely promised him, in lieu of a stipulated sum, to gratify him when I returned for it.

"'Done!' he cried, with a sardonic chuckle that roused my suspicions. 'You heard the agreement, my friends.' And some sinister-looking fellows, who had gradually surrounded the stall, grinning at each other, cordially assented.

"In the course of the same day I strolled into a refreshment-room, where I joined a merry party who were playing at a game of forfeits, expecting that the penalty, if I lost (and I was bound to perform the behest of the winner), would be one of those absurdities which are usual concomitants of that childish game. When I proved unsuccessful, they bade me drink up the sea, unless I would forfeit all that I had about me.

" 'By this time to-morrow,' I said, 'I shall have received the price of my cargo, and will then settle the affair with you.' So I was permitted by the hopeful sharpers (for they too belonged to that fraternity) to leave the room without being hustled.

"Before night I had found, to my vexation, that I had not only been swindled about the wood, but had likewise got into three awkward dilemmas. I had thought myself a clever fellow: I need scarcely dilate upon my humiliation. My despondency was noticed by a mendicant whom I had relieved on my first landing. He observed the gloom upon my visage, and rightly conjectured what had happened.

" 'Ah! master,' said he, 'our knaves have proved too keen for you; but take my advice, and you may perhaps turn the tables upon them. Go to our king; I don't mean the king of the rich, but the sheikh of us beggars; he is blind as a bat, but the eyes of his intellect are so piercing that no man has ever yet outwitted him. If any one can save you, it is he; he gets us out of all our scrapes, and his fee is but trifling.' I adopted his suggestion, rewarded him as my guide for leading me to the palace (it was a dirty vault) of the lauded potentate, and, after a preliminary offering, revealed my difficulties for his solution. Having pondered for a while, he thus answered me:

" 'As to the purchaser of your cargo, you would lose, should he fill the measure with gold, for every pound of sandal-wood is here worth ten pieces of that metal. Bid him, then, fill it with living fleas, half of which precisely must be females.

" 'As to the false accuser, assert that your own eye is larger and hence better than his, and demand that both should pluck out an eye to weigh against each other; the one-eyed will refuse, for else he would become perfectly blind.

" 'As to the cobbler, who would refuse to be gratified by any gift less than all your property, address him thus: "The king has just defeated his adversaries; are you not gratified?" He must say yes, or he would be punished as a traitor.

" 'As to the forfeit, say boldly, "I am ready to drink up the sea, but you must bring it me in bulk, for I am neither bound to walk to the shore nor to gulp its brine in driblets." You will thus circumvent all these rogues and save your money.'

"I acted by his counsel, and was not only extricated from my predicament, but received a considerable sum from the purchaser of the sandal-wood to let him off his bargain. Eventually I gained so large a profit by my investment, that I obtained credit everywhere; and now, thanks to that and my own natural swagger, I am considered the first merchant in the country.

" So much for my experience. Now for my advice. This is a commercial country, and wealth is esteemed above all things. He who is poor is despised; he whose friends are poor shares in the obloquy. None will recognise the vagrant of this morning in the well-clad merchant of to-morrow. The great secret of success here is to obtain credit; seem rich, and you soon become so, for fast and marvellous are the profits of trade. I will provide you in the morning with a purse of gold, which you must treat as dross, and introduce you to my set, as a friend and foreign correspondent, the chief merchant of Cairo. Your merchandise, you understand, is in transit: at the worst, your ship can be wrecked without loss to yourself, and our integrity will be unimpeached."

"I like not such crooked ways," said Maaroof. "I had better own at once I have lost my all, and crave employment."

"Yes, and shame *me*," replied his host. "If you were as well versed in fables as I am, you would think differently. Perhaps you never heard the saying of the young lion?"

"I know not what you mean."

"I'll tell you, then; the fable is but brief. A young lion, who had never seen a man, astonished at beholding the beasts of the forest in commotion, inquired the cause of their consternation, 'We are flying from the son of Adam,' they cried, without pausing in their flight. 'What terrific monster can that be? thought the royal beast. I will at least take a look at him ere I follow the example of the forest-dwellers.' A meagre and aged carpenter, who stooped beneath the weight of the planks he bore upon his shoulders, emerged from the trees. The lion scornfully advanced towards him: 'Son of Adam, what do you purpose here?'

"'To build myself a house, by your permission, O King of the plains,' was the humble answer.

"'Build on,' said the flattered beast, 'but if I like it, I shall take it for myself.'

"A big box, with a very strong lock and hinges, was soon constructed, and the lid left open. His majesty stept in to see whether it was large enough for him, and the man slamming down the lid, locked in the lion. '*Cunning is better than strength*,' cried the caged beast; 'and so have I, too, found it.'"

Long adversity weakens good principles; so Maaroof yielded to the counsel of Ali, and, on the morrow, in accordance with it, answered each inquiry of the merchants as to whether such and such an article was included in his cargo, by the preconcerted reply, "I have plenty of it." And as this was affirmed of every commodity, and as the contents of the purse were lavished with careless profusion, and chiefly in alms, his reputation for incalculable wealth became established. When, therefore, on the day after, he shook his empty purse at an importunate mendicant, saying, "I would give you alms were I as well known here as elsewhere, for I could then borrow the purse of my neighbour," one of the merchants, anxious to oblige so wealthy an individual, proffered the loan of his, which he at first refused, saying, "I cannot pay until my ship comes over," but when pressed, accepted with courteous thanks. And from time to time, as his lavish expenditure required it, he obtained, unasked, a like favour from other merchants. At length, as no merchandise made its appearance, suspicion was aroused, and loans were no longer proffered. Then addressing Ali when in the company of the very individuals to whom he had been introduced by him as a vast capitalist, he said, with a grand air, "Ali, lend me your purse;" and the cunning man was compelled to do so, for how could he refuse to trust the great merchant of whose acquaintance he had boasted? When they were alone, however, he demanded it back, but the adventurer had profited by the teaching of his playmate, who had originally suggested the answer, and replied, "Wait until my ship comes over."

"Nonsense!" growled Ali. "You know you have nothing."

"Yes; I have plenty of it," said his apt pupil.

In the heyday of his reputation for opulence, the King of that country, who, like his subjects, worshipped wealth, conceived the idea of wedding his daughter to him; for thus, he thought, he should induce the millionaire to settle in his city, and in the event of his decease keep all his riches in his own family. But, as he had no son, his chief minister had determined to marry her himself, and succeed to the throne when it should be vacated by his decease. Hence he insinuated that Maaroof was no merchant, but a mere pretender; upon which the monarch, who prided himself upon his acuteness, hit upon an expedient to detect his ignorance. He exhibited before him a pearl, for which he had paid a thousand pieces (a large price in the estimation of the monarch), and asked his opinion of its value.

"Rubbish! unworthy of your majesty; worth merely a thousand pieces," was the contemptuous verdict of the adventurer, as he broke the pearl and threw away the fragments.

"Have you better in your stock?" asked the astounded despot.

"A sackful! Wait until my ship comes over and select for yourself."

Then the King, thinking to profit by the generosity of so wealthy a son-in-law, offered him his daughter, and was surprised when Maaroof declined the honour until the arrival of his merchandise.

"For how shall I otherwise defray the expenses of the festival in a style worthy of your daughter and my own established name?"

This opposition increased the longing of the monarch to effect the alliance. He intrusted the Egyptian with the keys of his treasury, bidding him expend from it without stint until the arrival of his long-expected vessel.

So Maaroof wedded the Princess, and spared not the riches of the King upon the joyful occasion. And after the ceremony, a lucrative office of trust and dignity was bestowed upon him, and he lived upon his own resources. He proved a tender and loving husband to the King's daughter, and won her heart entirely. Yet, as time went on and no merchandise arrived, the monarch began to doubt his veracity, and at the suggestion of his ambitious minister (who would have hated any son-in-law of his master, however virtuous) bade his daughter cajole her husband into telling her the truth. "I will torture him to death," said the indignant parent, "if he has imposed upon our credulity."

"My beloved," said the Princess at nightfall, as she fondly caressed her husband, "I fear for thee. All men say thou hast deceived my father; and as the truth must be revealed at last, it is better to be prepared for the event. Let us take counsel together, that I may save thee, for thou knowest thou art an impostor, and didst become so for love of me. Was it not so, darling?" And she wound her arms around him and kissed him. By this affectionate guile he was brought to confess, and he unfolded his past history to her, neither concealing the straits he had been reduced to, nor the degrading cause of his flight from Cairo.

"Listen, my own," said the Princess at the conclusion of his adventures. "I love thee more than ever for thy frankness, and this reliance upon me. Know that I was bidden by my father and his minister to coax thee into confession, that they might slay thee for thy deceit; but here all men are deceitful; and thou art not worse, but only more successful, than the rest. The depth of my affection for thee was not sounded: they thought I should loathe and despise thee as a swindler." Now arise at once; take with thee my gold and jewels, which are worth, if I err not, fifty thousand pieces; mount our swiftest courser, and fly to some spot where my father has no sway; there trade as a merchant, send me thy address, and I will forward thee all I can amass, to increase thy capital. I will ever be faithful to thee, and should I survive my father, thou shalt share my throne."

He passionately embraced her, crying, "If separated in this life, we shall be united in the day of resurrection;" and reluctant to leave so noble-hearted a woman, would have dallied had she not forced him to depart. Clad as a royal messenger, he passed unobstructed through the city gates, and urging his swift courser to its utmost speed, galloped ere daylight beyond pursuit.

The next morning the king sent for his daughter, to question her. Indignation flashed from her blazing eyes as she forestalled his inquiries.

"That wretch of a vizier had nearly diverted the affection of my husband from me. Just as I was about proving him, an eunuch brought him a letter, which I sportively snatched from his hands, and read aloud. It ran as follows:—'Pirates attacked us with fireballs, and burnt goods to the value of some thousand pieces of gold; but we mastered them, and now await their trial and condemnation. This retards our arrival.' 'Let the rascals keep their heads,' cried my husband, 'they deserve, indeed, to lose them, but my credit must not be imperilled by so paltry an affair; had I not been the son-in-law of the king, it would have been ruined for ever by this ridiculous delay.' And he mounted his horse, and rode off to bring on his merchandise by land."

Thus she delayed for a time—I say not that she acted rightly, but was it not pardonable in a loving wife?—the pursuit of her husband.

Maaroof rode onwards until his wearied steed could no longer bear him. Then he dismounted, and asked hospitality from a husbandman.

"I have not the means of entertaining you at hand," said the peasant; "but I will start at once for the nearest village, and purchase the best I can."

In his absènce the sudden guest busied himself in ploughing the ground, a work his host had desisted from in order to fulfil the duties of hospitality. His ploughshare soon stopped, its progress being arrested by some unyielding obstacle. The ground was new, or rather it was the site of an ancient city, and had not been tilled for centuries. Maaroof urged on the oxen; they strained, but could not proceed; he then examined the cause of the stoppage of his team, and beheld a strong ring of metal, which was firmly attached to a large slab of marble. He raised the stone with difficulty, and was rewarded by the discovery of a deep vault, wherein tall vases promised him all the delights of a treasure-chamber. He descended the flight of steps which led to it, and ascertained to a certainty that each vase was filled to the brim with gold and precious stones. His first intention was to remove all these, his next to investigate still further the contents of the vault. At the further end, enshrined in a casket of crystal, he descried a seal-ring, the stone of which was engraved with sprawling characters which resembled the tracks of flies upon a wall. He could not read the ciphers, although he was not unlearned; so in the vague hope of some mysterious power to be engendered by their touch, he placed it on his left hand, and rubbed the hieroglyphic characters with the inner part of his right-hand fingers. Darkness enveloped all things, and from the brooding mist there issued a voice, saying,—

"Now and ever at thy service, O lord of the talisman. Wilt thou that I destroy a town, or re-build a deserted city? All things are alike to the impassible slave of the enchanted ring."

"Who art thou, then," said the fugitive, "and wherefore art thou servant to this ring?"

"Even as gold to the children of earth is the symbol of past labour, so is the talisman to the children of air the symbol of expended intellect. He whose exalted soul mastered the spirits of the elements, left us thralls to his ring, even as you mortals are thralls to the legacy of gold. I am your slave. What further information can you seek?"

Courage reanimated the heart of Maaroof. He had experienced many vicissitudes. He had risen from a mechanic to be son-in-law to a mighty monarch. He had ruled men; to rule genii was perchance easier. So his plans were matured at their very conception, and he issued his orders to the impalpable presence as though addressing one of the servants of his palace.

"Raise all these treasures to the surface of the ground, and bring hither a goodly company of attendants and of mules, that I may transport these riches to the spot I have fled from."

"To hear is to obey," was the humble rejoinder of the potent spirit, and in scarcely the interval of the lightning flash and the loud bellowing thunder, the plain was filled with a vast train of beasts of burden, and a still larger concourse of lusty drivers and armed Memlooks. The dress of all betokened the opulence of their owner, and such a *cortége* as that of Maaroof, the merchant prince, had never yet entered the gates of Sind.

The genius of the ring preceded the caravan in the guise of a messenger, and his letter invited the monarch to send an escort for the protection of riches whose amount had never been reckoned. This courier arrived so opportunely that the vizier, who had just been asserting that the departure of the Egyptian was a mere evasion of justice, was confounded; the Princess, who half fancied that the acknowledged poverty of her bridegroom was but to test her love, felt puzzled; and the cunning Ali, who believed all men were alike deceivers, felt convinced that a scheme had been concocted to hide the folly of deluded royalty.

When Maaroof became possessed of this vast wealth, he liberally recompensed the hospitable peasant, and repaid twofold all to whom he was indebted. His charming bride saluted his return with rapture, exclaiming,—

"I suspect thou wert testing my affection for thee when thou didst pretend to be poor."

But he replied evasively, "I have assayed thy soul, and found it virgin gold; I am rich, I own, beyond the dreams of avarice."

His jewels and other valuables were deposited in the King's treasury, and despite of excessive prodigality seemed never to diminish; for they were continually renewed by the genius of the ring.

Now the old king would not leave well alone, but consulted with his vizier how he might discover the source of the mysterious wealth of his liberal son-in-law.

"Wine openeth the heart of man," was the apophthegm by which the minister suggested to his lord the course of action he would have advised.

The people of that land were accustomed to the use of wine; but our hero, the follower of the true Prophet, knew not its very smell. So when invited to drink it by the crafty colleagues who palmed it off upon him as grape-sherbet, he innocently quaffed the intoxicating juice. In the confiding trustfulness engendered by that subtle fluid he acknowledged he was indebted to his ring for the acquisition of his illimitable wealth, and at the request of his boon-companions gratified them by a sight of the hieroglyphical characters engraved thereon.

"Permit us," said the King, "to study these ciphers at our ease, by withdrawing it from your finger."

So the confiding son-in-law would have passed it to the father of his beloved; but the vizier clutched it from him.

"Will the genius," said he, "equally obey the commands of any who may rub this talisman? I would fain see this marvel."

"I suppose so," said Maaroof; "you can try."

The vizier rubbed the ring, and its servant obeyed the summons.

"What would you?" said he; "shall I devastate this land, or shall I quadruple its produce? All things are alike to me the impassible."

"Away with this impostor," said the unforgiving minister, who had never forgotten that the stranger had baffled his matrimonial project, "to the most desolate spot upon earth; there let him perish from exposure and starvation."

The words had scarcely passed his venomous lips when the Egyptian found himself within sight of the City of Brass. He was stretched on the barren plateau of an isolated ridge, which no mortal being could descend from without mechanical appliances. The lofty walls of the long-lost race rose grandly before him; the well-remembered towers gleamed brightly in the rays of the setting sun. How often had he longed, ay prayed, to view again the spot he had quitted so reluctantly; his aspirations were accomplished—he was there, to die of hunger within bow-shot of the city. There were none to soothe his dying moments; he was alone in the midst of a vast solitude.

Yet not for long. The great belt of low black clouds which shut in the doomed city from the outer world, was suddenly riven asunder as by lightning. A living form crouched by his side; another flash as the spirit departed, and all was darkness. No sounds of insect life disturbed the silence of the night; there was not food enough in that vast wilderness to sustain the life of a solitary fly.

The deep sobs of the invisible object at his feet evinced that it belonged to humanity, so Maaroof inquired of his fellow-victim his name and country.

"Within an hour I was lord of Sind; now, like you, I am a living corpse. My son,—for I know from my own cruel sentence you are the husband of my child,—I never meant to hurt you: my fatal curiosity has involved us both in ruin. You had scarcely vanished, and the voice of the awful being still deafened my hearing when I bethought me of the ring, meaning to recall you; for you had ever treated me as king and father. My vizier was playing with it, eyeing me as a cat would a helpless mouse; he was timing, as it were, the speed of his winged messenger, and I quailed beneath his look of sneering triumph. 'Perhaps you imagine,' at length he said, 'I shall deposit the talisman in your own royal hands.' 'It was intended for my inspection,' I meekly remarked, for I felt I was in his power, but dreamed not he could harbour malice towards me. 'I was not good enough to be son-in-law to the king,' he continued; 'henceforth *I* am the King. You preferred that beggarly upstart to him who saved you from the cares of rule. Dotard! go and console him.' And again was I conscious of the ineffable presence of the pitiless spirit; again did his chilling formula thunder in my ears: and scarcely had my minister pronounced upon me the doom of exile and starvation than my legs seemed to fail me, and I found myself prostrate on this hard and rugged soil. Accursed be the ingrate! I raised him from a slave to a noble, because of his cleverness."

"This is no time for unforgiving wrath; unless, my father, a miracle should intervene, we must die within three days. Pardon me for my past deception, even as I have pardoned you for my early death."

They wept together, and prayed fervently.

Next morning the active minister summoned all the troops, and convened a council of the head officials. He scattered gold in handfuls among the soldiers, he promised promotion to the officers, he presented rich dresses and costly jewels to the nobles and civic dignitaries.

"Our lord has departed from us," said he, "and I have punished with death that impostor, his son-in-law. The throne is vacant: I purpose to wed the Princess, and to ascend it. Is there any one here present who has a better claim? If so, let him step forward and gainsay me."

Again was largesse showered among the troops, who

shouted with enthusiastic joy. None ventured, therefore, to oppose the usurper, who was consequently hailed as Sovereign, and assumed despotic authority. His first act was to apprise the daughter of the late king of his inexorable resolve to wed her that very day, or, failing her assent, to pass the night with her, however repugnant to her wishes. In vain did the holy priests (who at her private intercession ventured to address the tyrant) represent that it was contrary to religion to espouse a widow ere the days of her retirement had expired: the tyrant only mocked them, saying, "What is religion to me? I have the power of a god;" and he showed his magic ring, and warned them of its pitiless servant. So they left his court in sadness, saying to one another, "We have a devil to rule over us; our influence has departed." And the report of his supernatural might was spread abroad; no man thenceforth dared to oppose him, but all loathed, even the very army which was carousing at his expense, the avowed sorcerer.

Now the Princess, like most women, was full of guile; she felt conscious that no escape was possible from the possessor of the terrible talisman; so she resolved to throw the murderer of her father off his guard by the cordiality of her compliance with his wishes. She knew not whether her husband was still alive, but had resolved to perish rather than be faithless to him; her own weak hand should requite that forced union, should avenge the wrongs of father and of husband. She arrayed herself, then, in her most becoming garments, and when, at night, the amorous usurper entered her chamber with a shamefaced look, yet with bullying words, announcing his determination to embrace her as his wife without the tedious delay of a ceremony, she relieved him from the embarrassment which he really felt, by softly replying, "Wherefore not? I have waited very long for you. Shall I not love my own wise countryman more than the low impostor for whose wealth I was sacrificed?"

She thus cajoled him, and he was enraptured with delight at the prospect of a willing bride; so after they were alone, she sported and toyed with him, but when he threw his arm around her, she cried with blushing cheeks, "What horrible head is that I see glaring upon me from your signet-ring?"

"Probably my spirit-slave: what matters it?"

"Nay, dearest, modesty forbids that any being should witness our caresses: remove your ring for a while; all is safe; we are quite alone."

So he, desiring in that hour of bliss to gratify the woman who had charmed him by her cheerful acquiescence to his wishes, removed the ring from his finger, and put it far away from either of them. Sportively wrestling with him, as though she sought to inflame his passions by coyly repelling his too ardent advances, she contrived to suddenly, and as it were accidentally, throw him to the ground on the side furthest away from the talisman; then snatching it from the shelf on which he had laid it, she summoned its ministering spirit to her aid. In vain did the deluded lover seek to wrest it from her hand. "Petrify him!" she had cried, ere the rolling mist had assumed the outlines of humanity or the awful formula of the impassible had been pronounced; and the hands which were tearing both signet and flesh from her fingers, were arrested in their violence; and the rage, horror, and surprise which distorted his features were immutably fixed in the living statue. She would not take his life: it would have been a sorry vengeance for the contamination she had endured from his wanton touch. At her bidding both father and husband were transported, in a minute, from the land of desolation, and again clasped in her loving arms.

On the morrow, the old King, though sadly shattered by the terrible ordeal he had sustained, held his court in solemn grandeur. The statue was brought from the cellar into which it had been cast, and was tried as a living being. It could feel, but could not move. As a convicted traitor, the sword or the bowstring would have awaited the vizier; as an avowed Infidel, he was sentenced to be calcined! His master did not long survive him: that night of horrors, that day of anticipated starvation, had crushed for ever his vital powers. Maaroof, as the husband of his daughter, was the virtual lord of Sind.

Years rolled on; our hero was happy both as husband and as father. The cares of government proved light to him; the people were content; the nation was at peace. He had no occasion for his magic ring, and as it was cumbrous and ugly, he hid it in a secret repository in his bedchamber, in a spot known only to his wife and his eldest son, a precocious boy, nearly ten years old. Events were few and far between; he passed an easy life of unvarying tranquillity, a perfect contrast to the chequered career of his earlier days. An incident, at last, took place, which painfully recalled to his memory the degrading history of the past. He was wont to mingle familiarly with his subjects, and preferred sauntering alone, to the attendance of that retinue which his predecessors had judged essential to their dignity. He fancied at times that a tall, foreign-looking, ragged female, whose features were decorously concealed, was dogging his footsteps; perchance she might have some petition to present, or alms to solicit, yet had not courage to advance in the presence of others. So, after noticing her behaviour for about a week, from thoughtful good-nature, he gave her an opportunity of addressing him, by walking a little way from the busier haunts of the city. He had rightly divined her wishes. She followed him rapidly, and when alone threw back her veil, and exhibited the once beautiful face of that wanton shrew, whose vile temper and loose habits had driven him from Egypt. Years, misery, and debauchery had sadly altered her for the worse, yet it needed not her words to convince him of her identity.

"I am come," said she, in humble accents, "not to demand the rank and privileges of a wife, for I have forfeited all claim to them by my own misconduct; but to implore a mere existence from your bounty. Could you have witnessed the degradations I have sustained, the contumely I have borne in silence, and comprehend the anguish of my repentance for the ingratitude I had shown, you would pity and forgive the erring woman who was once so dear to you." She wept bitterly; and Maaroof, who had long ceased to think of her with anger, and regarded his old troubles with the same complacency as the traveller looks back upon the rough road by which he has climbed to some desired elevation, raised her from the ground upon which, in the bitterness of humiliation, she had cast herself.

He saw mentally before him, not the squalid vagrant with eager eyes and hollow cheeks, but the handsome woman whom he, himself scorched and bleeding, had borne from the burning mansion which the desperate Sandalanee had set fire to that the lovers might not survive him; he saw the fond maiden, who had nursed him night and day through the raging fever caused by the injuries sustained in her rescue; he saw the weeping girl who, for her elopement with him from the luxurious palace of her lordly father, had been cast off for ever by her indignant sire. Then the memory of the home he had been forced to abandon through the insults, the violence, the malice, the mercenary looseness of Jemeeleh flashed through his brain with equal rapidity. The contest of feelings evoked by these vivid pictures of the past was but momentary: tenderness prevailed.

"You shall not starve," he said. "I feel no anger towards you, since Heaven has avenged me. We can never more be husband and wife, but I will again provide you with all those comforts you relinquished to unite your fate to mine. But, tell me how you have traced me to this remote region?"

"Rumour had spread throughout the earth the marvellous tale of the enchanted ring, and some of the restless beings whom you guided to the treasure-city, wandering hither, had recognized their former chief in the wealthy lord of Sind. Relying on their veracity, I have begged my way from Cairo, and, thanks to the nobility of your soul, rejoice that I have so humbled myself."

A small pavilion in the grounds of the palace was given up to Jemeeleh, and an income fully adequate to maintain her as a lady was allotted to her. At first she was grateful and content, but evil was too engrained in her nature to permit her to rest in tranquillity. Forgetful that the royalty of Maaroof was derived from the Princess he had espoused, she at first hated the latter for having alienated (as she chose to consider it) her husband's affection from her, and at last began to hate her very benefactor for not making her his queen. "Had it not been for me, he would have stopped in Cairo, and drudged as a poor mechanic," she would murmur to herself; "yet he never addresses me but with cold courtesy. Ah! if I could only discover where he has hidden the source of his power, the mystic talisman, he should bitterly regret his want of gratitude."

It was probable that its hidden receptacle would be revealed to the heir of the throne; so the crafty woman sought to ingratiate herself with the lad in order to wheedle the secret from him. He did not like her. The innocent experience an innate yet undefinable repugnance to the evil-minded, whilst yet unconscious of their guilt. Nevertheless she succeeded, by slow degrees, in worming the secret from the lad; for what youth can resist the guile of a cunning woman? On his twelfth birthday he had received a small diamond-hilted scimetar, a toy, but an efficient weapon, from his father, and in thanking his parent, said, as he glanced proudly at the slender blade, "I feel some day I shall use it against your enemy."

"I have no enemies, my boy," replied the simple Maaroof; "I never yet wronged man or woman."

It was not long after that birthday, when Jemeeleh resolved to make a desperate attempt to acquire the talisman. She knew she was risking her fortunes should she be detected in her crime, but felt assured that her life at least would be spared by her gentle husband. So in the dead of night she traversed the passages that led to the King's apartment, and perceived the secret repository, just as it had been described to her by the boy. Her hand was in the drawer; she felt a large and heavy ring: it surely must be the right one; yet all was dark. She would make sure by the moonlight that was streaming in from the casement of the room she had just passed through. Yes; those were the strange ciphers which none of the possessors of the ring could ever read.

"Now *I* am the Queen, and Maaroof's master!" she cried in her triumph. It was short-lived, for ere she could rub the ring with the other hand, her head was smitten off by the trenchant blade of a tiny scimetar, and falling to the ground roused the sleeping King from his profound slumber. Sword in hand, he started from his couch, shouting for his attendants. The antechamber was filled in a minute by scores of swarthy slaves, each brandishing a weapon in one hand, and holding aloft a burning taper in the other. The instant blaze of light disclosed a startling sight to the agitated monarch. In his night-clothes, with bloody feet and scimetar, stood proudly erect his youthful heir; on the floor beside him lay the decapitated trunk of the former tyrant of his home. For the moment it was inexplicable. But the lad, pointing to the talisman still clutched tightly in the hand of the corpse, cried exultingly,—

"Take it again, my father. I felt I should slay your enemy, and I have slain your only one."

He had known Jemeeleh's envy of his mother; he had mistrusted her frequent inquiries about the ring, and when by chance he had beheld her prowling that night on some mysterious errand, he had quietly followed her, and by his well-timed blow had preserved his parents from a terrible future.

Thenceforth Maaroof lived in peace.

FINIS.

PRINTED BY J. E. TAYLOR AND CO.,
LITTLE QUEEN STREET, LINCOLN'S INN FIELDS.

www.ingramcontent.com/pod-product-compliance
Lightning Source LLC
Chambersburg PA
CBHW030909270326
41929CB00008B/621

* 9 7 8 3 7 4 4 7 5 2 8 1 7 *